OpenNI Cookbook

Learn how to write NIUI-based applications and
motion-controlled games

Soroush Falahati

[PACKT]
PUBLISHING

open source
community experience distilled

BIRMINGHAM - MUMBAI

OpenNI Cookbook

First published: July 2013

Production Reference: 1190713

Published by Packt Publishing Ltd.
Livery Place
35 Livery Street
Birmingham B3 2PB, UK.

ISBN 978-1-84951-846-8

www.packtpub.com

Cover Image by Ramin Gharouni (ramin.graphix@gmail.com)

Credits

Author
Soroush Falahati

Reviewers
Vinícius Godoy
Li Yang Ku
Liza Roumani

Acquisition Editor
Usha Iyer

Lead Technical Editor
Amey Varangaonkar

Technical Editors
Aparna Chand
Athira Laji
Dominic Pereira

Copy Editors
Insiya Morbiwala
Aditya Nair
Alfida Paiva
Laxmi Subramanian

Project Coordinator
Leena Purkait

Proofreader
Stephen Copestake

Indexer
Monica Ajmera Mehta

Graphics
Ronak Dhruv
Abhinash Sahu

Production Coordinator
Shantanu Zagade

Cover Work
Shantanu Zagade

About the Author

Soroush Falahati is a Microsoft MCPD certificated C# developer of Web and Windows applications, now preparing for a new MCSD certification from Microsoft. He started programming at the age of 13 with VB5 and then continued to VB.Net, C#, C++, C for microcontrollers, as well as scripting languages such as PHP and JavaScript.

He is currently the owner of an e-commerce company that uses web applications and smart phone apps as primary advantages over other competitors.

As a hobby, Soroush supports robotic teams by voluntarily training them on how to program microcontrollers.

I would like to thank my family, who supported me at the time of writing of this book with their patience, just as they always have been patient through the rest of my life!

Also, I want to thank PrimeSense, which gave me access to confidential material and helped me through the writing of this book. I would like to especially thank Eddie Cohen, Software Team Leader, who answered my many questions and Jeremie Kletzkine, the Director of Business Development.

About the Reviewers

Vinícius Godoy is a computer graphics university professor at PUCPR. He is also an IT manager of an Electronic Content Management (ECM) company in Brazil, called Sinax. His former experience also includes building games and applications for Positivo Informática—including building an augmented reality educational game exposed at CEBIT—and network libraries for Siemens Enterprise Communications.

In his research, he used Kinect, OpenNI, and OpenCV to recognize Brazilian sign language gestures. He is also a game development fan, having a popular website entirely dedicated to the field, called Ponto V (`http://www.pontov.com.br`). He is mainly proficient with the C++ and Java languages and his field of interest includes graphics synthesis, image processing, image recognition, design patterns, Internet, and multithreading applications.

Li Yang Ku is a Computer Vision scientist and the main author of the Serious Computer Vision Blog (`http://computervisionblog.wordpress.com`), one of the foremost Computer Vision blogs. He is also the founder of EatPaper (`http://www.eatpaper.org`), a free web tool for organizing publications visually.

He has worked as a researcher in HRL Laboratories, Malibu, California from 2011 to 2013. He did AI research on multiple humanoid robots and designed one of the vision systems for NASA's humanoid space robot, Robonaut 2, at NASA JSC, Houston. He also has broad experience on RGBD sensor applications, such as object recognition, object tracking, human activity classification, SLAM, and quadrotor navigation.

Li Yang Ku received his MS degree in CS from University of California, Los Angeles, and has a BS degree in EE from National Chiao Tung University, Taiwan. He is now pursuing a Ph.D. degree at the University of Massachusetts, Amherst.

Liza Roumani was born in Paris in 1989. After passing the French scientific Baccalaureate, she decided to move to Israel.

After one year in Jerusalem University, she joined the Technion Institute of Technology of Haifa, where she obtained a BSC degree in Electrical Engineering.

Liza Roumani is currently working at PrimeSense Company, the worldwide leader in 3D sensors technology.

www.PacktPub.com

Support files, eBooks, discount offers, and more

You might want to visit www.PacktPub.com for support files and downloads related to your book.

Did you know that Packt offers eBook versions of every book published, with PDF and ePub files available? You can upgrade to the eBook version at www.PacktPub.com and, as a print book customer, you are entitled to a discount on the eBook copy. Get in touch with us at service@packtpub.com for more details.

At www.PacktPub.com, you can also read a collection of free technical articles, sign up for a range of free newsletters, and receive exclusive discounts and offers on Packt books and eBooks.

http://PacktLib.PacktPub.com

Do you need instant solutions to your IT questions? PacktLib is Packt's online digital book library. Here, you can access, read and search across Packt's entire library of books.

Why Subscribe?

- ▶ Fully searchable across every book published by Packt
- ▶ Copy and paste, print and bookmark content
- ▶ On demand and accessible via web browser

Free Access for Packt account holders

If you have an account with Packt at www.PacktPub.com, you can use this to access PacktLib today and view nine entirely free books. Simply use your login credentials for immediate access.

Table of Contents

Preface

As a step towards interacting with users through the physical world, learn how to write NIUI-based applications or motion-controlled games.

OpenNI Cookbook is here to show you how to start developing Natural Interaction UI for your applications or games with high-level APIs while, at the same time, accessing raw data from different sensors of different devices that are supported by OpenNI using low-level APIs.

What this book covers

Chapter 1, Getting Started, will teach you how to install OpenNI along with NiTE and shows you how to prepare an environment for writing an OpenNI-based application.

Chapter 2, OpenNI and C++, explains how to start programming with OpenNI, from basic steps such as creating a project in Visual Studio to initializing and accessing different devices and sensors.

Chapter 3, Using Low-level Data, is an important chapter of this book, as we are going to cover reading and handling output of basic sensors from each device.

Chapter 4, More about Low-level Outputs, shows how you can customize the frame data right from the device itself, including mirroring and cropping.

Chapter 5, NiTE and User Tracking, will start using the Natural Interaction features of NiTE. As a first step, you will learn how to detect users on the scene and their properties.

Chapter 6, NiTE and Hands Tracking, will cover topics such as recognizing and tracking hand movements.

Chapter 7, NiTE and Skeleton Tracking, will be covering the most important features of NiTE: skeleton tracking and recognizing users' skeleton joints.

What you need for this book

You need to have Visual Studio 2010 to perform the recipes given in this book. You will also need to download OpenNI 2 and NiTE from their official websites. If you are going to use Kinect, you may need to download the Kinect SDK from Microsoft's website as well.

Who this book is for

OpenNI Cookbook is a book for both starters and professionals in NIUI, for people who want to write serious applications or games, and for people who want to experience and start working with NIUI. Even OpenNI 1 and OpenNI 1.x programmers who want to move to the new versions of OpenNI can use this book as a starting point.

This book uses C++ as its primary language; so for reading and understanding you only need to have a basic knowledge of C or C++.

Conventions

In this book, you will find a number of styles of text that distinguish between different kinds of information. Here are some examples of these styles and an explanation of their meaning.

Code words in text, database table names, folder names, filenames, file extensions, pathnames, dummy URLs, user input, and Twitter handles are shown as follows: "Also, we checked if the initializing process ended without any error by creating a variable of type `openni::Status`."

A block of code is set as follows:

```
printf("OpenNI Version is %d.%d.%d.%d",
    OpenNI::getVersion().major,
    OpenNI::getVersion().minor,
    OpenNI::getVersion().maintenance,
    OpenNI::getVersion().build);
```

New terms and **important words** are shown in bold. Words that you see on the screen, in menus or dialog boxes for example, appear in the text like this: "From the **File** menu, select **New** and then **New Project**."

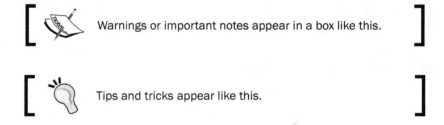

Warnings or important notes appear in a box like this.

Tips and tricks appear like this.

Reader feedback

Feedback from our readers is always welcome. Let us know what you think about this book—what you liked or may have disliked. Reader feedback is important for us to develop titles that you really get the most out of.

To send us general feedback, simply send an e-mail to feedback@packtpub.com, and mention the book title via the subject of your message.

If there is a topic that you have expertise in and you are interested in either writing or contributing to a book, see our author guide on www.packtpub.com/authors.

Customer support

Now that you are the proud owner of a Packt book, we have a number of things to help you to get the most from your purchase.

Downloading the example code

You can download the example code files for all Packt books you have purchased from your account at http://www.packtpub.com. If you purchased this book elsewhere, you can visit http://www.packtpub.com/support and register to have the files e-mailed directly to you.

Errata

Although we have taken every care to ensure the accuracy of our content, mistakes do happen. If you find a mistake in one of our books—maybe a mistake in the text or the code—we would be grateful if you would report this to us. By doing so, you can save other readers from frustration and help us improve subsequent versions of this book. If you find any errata, please report them by visiting http://www.packtpub.com/submit-errata, selecting your book, clicking on the **errata submission form** link, and entering the details of your errata. Once your errata are verified, your submission will be accepted and the errata will be uploaded on our website, or added to any list of existing errata, under the Errata section of that title. Any existing errata can be viewed by selecting your title from http://www.packtpub.com/support.

Piracy

Piracy of copyright material on the Internet is an ongoing problem across all media. At Packt, we take the protection of our copyright and licenses very seriously. If you come across any illegal copies of our works, in any form, on the Internet, please provide us with the location address or website name immediately so that we can pursue a remedy.

Please contact us at copyright@packtpub.com with a link to the suspected pirated material.

We appreciate your help in protecting our authors, and our ability to bring you valuable content.

Questions

You can contact us at questions@packtpub.com if you are having a problem with any aspect of the book, and we will do our best to address it.

1
Getting Started

The first step before writing an application or game using OpenNI is to install OpenNI itself, the drivers, and any other prerequisites. So in this chapter, we will cover this process and make everything ready for writing an app using OpenNI.

In this chapter, we will cover the following recipes:

- ▶ Downloading and installing OpenNI
- ▶ Downloading and installing NiTE
- ▶ Downloading and installing the Microsoft Kinect SDK
- ▶ Connecting Asus Xtion and PrimeSense sensors
- ▶ Connecting Microsoft Kinect

Introduction

As an introduction, it is important for you to have an idea about the technology behind the topics just mentioned and our reasons for writing this book, as well as to know about the different devices and middleware libraries that can be used with OpenNI.

Introduction to the "Introduction"

Motion detectors are part of our everyday life, from a simple alarm system to complicated military radars or an earthquake warning system, all using different methods and different sensors but for the same purpose—detecting motion in the environment.

But they were rarely used to control computers or devices until recent years. This was usually because of the high price of capable devices and the lack of powerful software and hardware for consumers, and maybe because end users did not need this technology. Fortunately, this situation changed after some of the powerful players in computer technology tried to use this idea and supported other small innovation companies in this task.

We believe that the idea of controlling computers and other devices with environment-aware input devices is going to grow in computer industries even more in the coming years. Computers can't rely any more on a keyboard and a mouse to learn about real environments. Computers are going to control more and more parts of our everyday life; each time they need to understand better our living environment. So if you are interested in being part of this change, work through this book.

In this book, we are going to show you how to start using current devices and software to write your own applications or games to interact with the real world.

In this chapter, we will introduce you to some usable technologies and devices, and then introduce some of the frameworks and middleware before speaking a little about how you can make applications or games with **Natural Interactive User Interfaces** (**NIUI**).

 This way of interacting with a computer is known as **3DUI** (**3D User Interaction** or **3D User Interfaces**), **RBI** (**Reality based interaction**), or **NI** (**Natural Interaction**). To know more, visit `http://en.wikipedia.org/wiki/3D_user_interaction` and `http://en.wikipedia.org/wiki/Natural_user_interface`.

Motion-capture devices and the technologies behind them

The keyboard and mouse are two of the most used input devices for computers; they're the way they learn from outside of the box. But the usage of these two devices is very limited and there is a real gap between the physical world and the computer's understanding of the surrounding environment.

To fill this gap, different projects were raised to reconstruct 3D environments for computers using different methods. Read more about these techniques at `http://en.wikipedia.org/wiki/Range_imaging`.

For example, **vSlam** is one such famous project designed for robotic researchers who try to do this using one or two RGB cameras. This project is an open source one and is available at `http://www.ros.org/wiki/vslam`.

However, since most of these solutions depend on the camera's movement or detection of similar patterns from two cameras, and then use Stereo triangulation algorithms for creating a 3D map of the environment, they perform a high number of calculations along with using complex algorithms. This makes them slow and their output unreliable and/or inaccurate.

There are more expensive methods to solve these problems when high accuracy is needed. Methods such as **Laser Imaging Detection and Ranging** (**LIDaR**) use one or more laser beams to scan the environment. These methods are expensive and actually not a good option for targeting end users. They are usually big in size and the mid-level models are slow at scanning a 3D environment completely. Yet, because they use ToF (Time of Flight) for calculating distances, they have very good accuracy and a very good range too. The devices that use laser beams are used mainly for scanning huge objects, buildings, surfaces, landforms (in Geology), and so on, from the ground, an airplane, or from a satellite. Read more on http://en.wikipedia.org/wiki/Lidar.

To know more about the other types of 3D scanners, visit http://en.wikipedia.org/wiki/3D_scanner.

In 2010, Microsoft released the Kinect device for Xbox 360 users to control their console and games without a controller. Kinect originally uses PrimeSense's technology and its SoC (System on Chip) to capture and analyze the depth of the environment. PrimeSense's method of scanning the environment is based on projecting a pattern of a hundred beams of infrared lasers to the environment and capturing these beams using a simple image CMOS sensor (a.k.a. **Active Pixel Sensor** or **APS**) with an infrared-passing filter in front of it. PrimeSense's SoC is then responsible for comparing the results of the captured pattern with the projected one and creates a displacement map of the captured pattern compared to the projected pattern. This displacement map is actually the same depth map that the device provides to the developers later with some minor changes. This technology is called **Structured-light 3D scanning**. Its accuracy, size, and error rate (below 70 millimeters in the worst possible case) when compared to its cost makes it a reasonable choice for a consumer-targeted device.

To know more about Kinect, visit http://en.wikipedia.org/wiki/Kinect.

PrimeSense decided to release similar devices after Kinect was released. Carmine 1.08, Carmine 1.09 (a short range version of Carmine 1.08), and Capri 1.25 (an embeddable version) are the three devices from PrimeSense. In this book, we will call them all PrimeSense sensors. A list of the available devices from PrimeSense can be viewed at http://www.primesense.com/solutions/sensor/.

Before the release of PrimeSense sensors, Asus released two sensors in 2011 named **Asus Xtion** (with only depth and IR output) and **Asus Xtion Pro Live** (with depth, color, IR, and audio output) with PrimeSense's technology and chipset, just as with Kinect, but without some features such as tilting, custom design, higher resolution, and frame rate compared to Kinect. From what PrimeSense told us, the Asus Xtion series and PrimeSense's sensors both share the same design and are almost identical.

Both of PrimeSense's sensors and the Asus Xtion series are almost twice as expensive compared to Microsoft Kinect, yet they have a more acceptable price than the other competitors (in the U.K., Microsoft Kinect is priced at $110).

Here is an illustration to help you understand how Kinect, Asus Xtion, and PrimeSense sensors work:

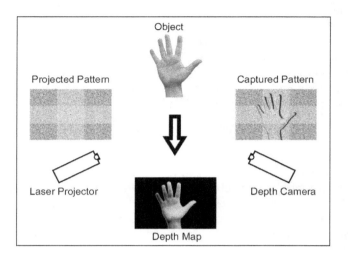

More information about this method is available on Wikipedia at http://en.wikipedia.org/wiki/Structured-light_3D_scanner.

After the release of Kinect, other devices aimed to give better and faster outputs to users and yet keep the price in an acceptable range. These devices usually use ToF to scan environments and must have better accuracy, at least in theory. SoftKinetic devices (the DepthSense series of devices) and pmd[vision]® CamBoard nano are two of the notable designs. Currently, there is no support for them in OpenNI and they are not very popular compared to Kinect, Asus Xtion, and PrimeSense's sensors. Their resolution is less than what PrimeSense-based devices can offer, but their frame rate is usually better because of a simple calculation they use to produce a depth frame. Current devices can offer from 60 to 120 frames per second ranging from 160 x 120 to 320 x 240 resolutions, whereas Kinect, Asus Xtion, and PrimeSense's sensor can give you up to 640 x 480 resolutions at 30 to 60 frames per second. Also, these devices usually cost more than PrimeSense-based devices (from 250 to $690 at the time of writing this book).

Microsoft introduced Xbox One in 2013 with a new version of Kinect, known as Kinect for Xbox One (a.k.a. Kinect 2), which uses ToF technology and custom-made CMOS for capturing both RGB and depth data along with projecting beams of laser. From what Microsoft told the media, it is completely made by Microsoft and, unlike the first version of Kinect, this time there is no third-party company involved. It is unknown if this new version of Kinect is compatible with OpenNI, but Microsoft promised a Windows SDK, which means we can expect a custom module for OpenNI from the community at least.

You can read more about ToF-based cameras and their technologies on Wikipedia at http://en.wikipedia.org/wiki/Time-of-flight_camera.

Fotonic is another manufacturing company for 3D imaginary cameras. Fotonic E series products are OpenNI-compatible TOF devices. You can check their website (http://www.fotonic.com/) for more information.

In this book, we use Asus Xtion Pro Live and Kinect, but you can use any of PrimeSense's sensors and it will give you the same result as Asus Xtion Pro without any headache. We even expect the same result with any other OpenNI-compatible device (for example, Fotonic E70 or E40).

What is OpenNI?

After having good hardware for capturing the 3D environment, it is very important to have a good interface to communicate and read data from a device. Apart from the fact that each device may have its own SDK, it is important for developers to use one interface for all of the different devices.

Unfortunately, there is no unique interface for such devices now. But OpenNI, as the default framework, and SDK, for PrimeSense-based devices (such as Kinect, PrimeSense sensors, and Asus Xtion), have the capacity to become one.

OpenNI is an organization that is responsible for its framework with the same name. Their framework (that we will call OpenNI in this book) is an open source project and is available for change by any developer. The funder of this project is PrimeSense itself. This project became very famous because of being the first framework with unofficial Kinect support when there wasn't any reliable framework. In the current version of OpenNI, Kinect is officially supported via the Microsoft SDK.

OpenNI, on one hand, gives device producers the ability to connect their devices to the framework, and on the other hand gives developers the ability to work with the same API for different devices. At the same time, other companies and individuals can develop their own middleware and expand the API of OpenNI. Having these features gives this framework the value that other competitions don't have.

As mentioned in the title of the book, we will use OpenNI as a way to know this field better and to develop our applications.

What is NiTE?

NiTE is a middleware based on the OpenNI framework and was developed by PrimeSense as an enterprise project.

NiTE gives us more information about a scene based on the information from the depth stream of a device.

We will use NiTE in this book for accessing a user's data and body tracking as well as hand tracking and gesture recognition.

NiTE is not the only middleware; there are other middleware that you can use along with OpenNI, such as the following:

▶ Hand Grab Detector from PrimeSense for recognizing hands in the closed mode: http://www.openni.org/files/grab-detector

▶ 3D Hand Tracking Library and TipTep Skeletonizer for recognizing fingers: http://www.openni.org/files/3d-hand-tracking-library and http://www.openni.org/files/tiptep-skeletonizer

▶ 3D Face Identification from the University of Southern California for face recognition: http://www.openni.org/files/3d-face-identification

And a whole lot more. A list of SDKs and middleware libraries is available at OpenNI.org (http://www.openni.org/software/?cat_slug=file-cat1).

Developing applications and games with the Natural Interactive User Interface

With the seventh generation of video game consoles, interacting with users via motion detection became popular, with the focus on improving gaming experience, starting with the Nintendo Wii controller and followed by Microsoft Kinect and Sony PlayStation Move.

But gaming isn't the only subject capable of using these new ways. There are different cases where interacting with users via natural ways is a better option than traditional ways, or at least can be used as an improvement. Just think of how you can use it in advertising panels, or how you can give product information to users. Or you can design an intelligent house that is able to identify and understand a user's orders. Just look at what some of the companies such as Samsung did with their Smart TV line of productions.

With improving the device's accuracy and usable field of view, you can expect the creation of applications for personal computers to become reasonable too, for example, moving and rotating a 3D model in 3D modeling apps, or helping in drawing apps, as well as the possibility of interacting with the Windows 8 Modern interface or other similar interfaces.

As a developer, you can think of it as a 3D touch screen, and one can do lots of work with a 3D touch screen. What it needs is a little creativity and innovation to find and create ways and ideas to use these methods to interact with users.

Yet, developing games and applications is not the only area that you can use this technology for. There are projects already underway for creating more environment-aware indoor robots and different indoor security systems as well as constructing and scanning an environment completely (such as the KinectFusion project or other similar projects). It's hard to ignore and not mention the available Motion Capture applications (for example, iPi Motion Capture™).

As you can see, there are lots of possibilities in which you can use OpenNI, NiTE, and other middleware libraries.

But in this book, we are not going to show you how to do anything specific to one of the preceding categories. Instead, we are going to cover how to use OpenNI and NiTE, and it all depends on you and how you want to use the information provided in this book.

In this chapter, we are going to introduce OpenNI and cover the process of initializing OpenNI as well as the process of accessing different devices. The next step for you in this book is reading RAW data from devices and using OpenNI to customize this data from a device. NiTE can help you to convert this data to understandable information about the current scene. This information can be used to interact with users. We are going to cover NiTE and its features in this book too.

By using this information, you will be able to create your own body-controlled game, an application with an NI interface, or even custom systems and projects with better understanding of the world and with the possibility of interacting more easily and in natural ways with users.

The main programming language with OpenNI is C, but there is a C++ wrapper with each release. This book makes conservative use of C++ for simplicity. We used a little bit of OpenGL using the GLUT library to visually show some of the information. So you may need to know C++ and have a little understanding about what OpenGL and 2D drawing are.

Currently, there are two official wrappers for OpenNI and NiTE: C++ and Java wrappers. Yet there is no official wrapper for .NET, Unity, or other languages/software.

Community-maintained wrappers, at the time of writing this book, are **NiWrapper.Net** which is an open source project supporting OpenNI and NiTE functionalities for .NET developers and ZDK for Unity3D, which is a commercial project for adding OpenNI 2 and NiTE 2 support to Unity. Of course, there are other frameworks that use OpenNI as the backend, but none of these can be fitted in the subject of this book.

OpenNI is a multiplatform framework supporting Windows (32 bit and 64 bit; the ARM edition is not yet available at the time of writing this book), Mac OS X, and Linux (32 bit, 64 bit, and ARM editions). In this book, we are going to use Windows (mainly 64 bit) for projects. But porting codes to other platforms is easily possible and it is unlikely to create serious problems for you if you decided to do this.

Downloading and installing OpenNI

The first step to use OpenNI to develop any application or game is to install the OpenNI framework on your development machine. In this recipe, we will show you how to install OpenNI; actually it is as easy as 1-2-3.

How to do it...

1. Open your browser and navigate to www.openni.org/openni-sdk. The following screen will be displayed:

2. Download the latest version of OpenNI for your platform and CPU architecture. We recommend downloading both 32-bit (x86) and 64-bit versions of OpenNI if you are using a 64-bit OS.

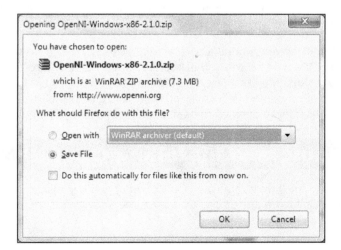

3. Open the downloaded file; it is usually a ZIP file that can be opened by different programs (including but not limited to WinZip, WinRar, 7Zip, and so on) and even Windows Explorer. Then run/open the OpenNI installer from within the zipped archive:

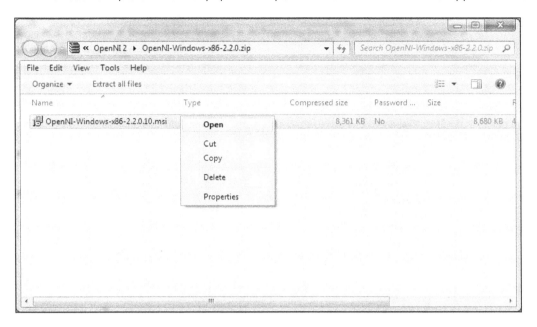

4. Click on **Install** in the installer dialog:

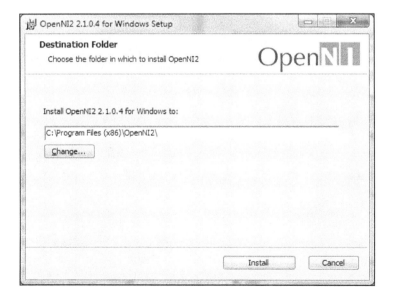

5. Wait for the installation process to complete. If any dialog appears to ask for an approval of drivers during the installation process, simply click on the **Install** button:

6. At the end of the installation, click on **Finish** and you are done.

How it works...

There is nothing special here; we downloaded and opened the archive file and then executed the installer package. Also, we accepted the installation of new drivers to the Windows catalog.

See also

▶ The *Downloading and installing NiTE* recipe

Downloading and installing NiTE

If you want to use high-level outputs and some advanced tracking and recognition features of NiTE, you need to install it as well. NiTE is a middleware based on the OpenNI framework and needs to be installed after it.

Getting ready

Before installing NiTE, you need to have OpenNI installed using the *Downloading and installing OpenNI* recipe in this chapter.

How to do it...

1. Before downloading NiTE, you need to register yourself in OpenNI.org. For doing so, please open your browser and navigate to `www.openni.org/my-profile`. Now fill all the fields and click on the **Submit** button:

2. After the registration, if everything goes fine, you'll be able to download NiTE. Open your browser and navigate to `www.openni.org/files/nite`:

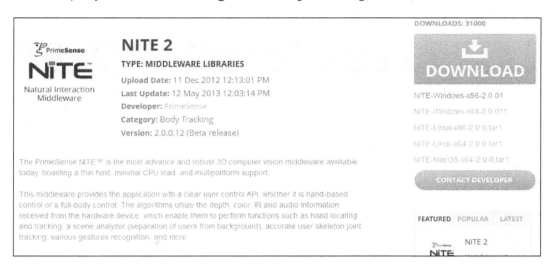

3. Download NiTE using the big **DOWNLOAD** button at the upper-right corner and then select your desired version of it:

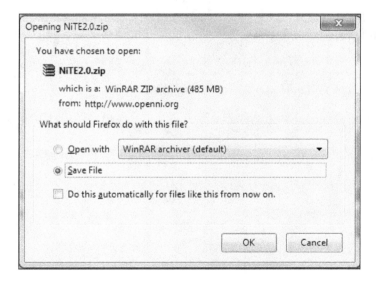

4. Open the downloaded file; it is usually a ZIP file that can be opened by different programs (including but not limited to WinZip, WinRar, 7Zip, and so on) and even Windows Explorer. Then run/open the actual installer from within the zipped archive:

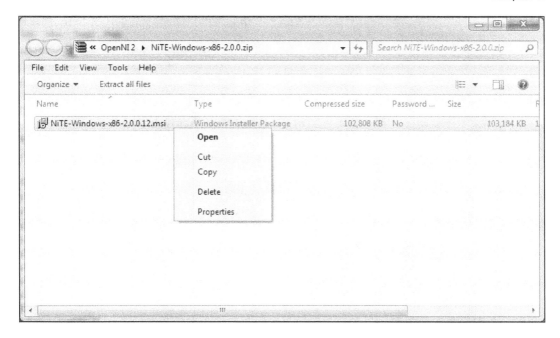

5. Read and accept the license arguments, then click on **Next** and then on **Install** in the installer dialog:

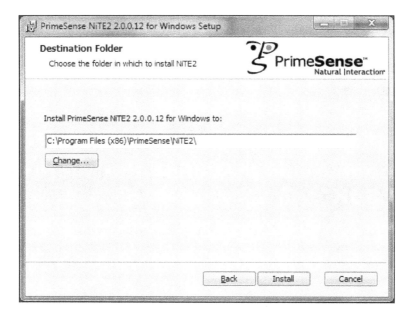

6. Wait for the installation to complete and, at the end of the installation, click on **Finish** and you are done:

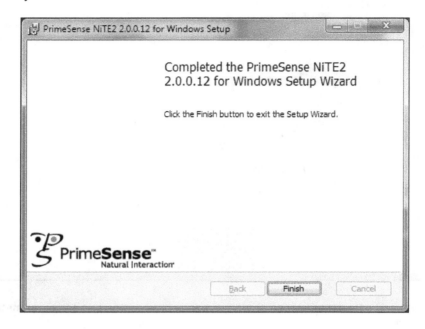

How it works...

Actually we did nothing special here either; all we did was register, download, and install NiTE for our version of the OS and CPU architecture.

See also

▶ The *Downloading and installing OpenNI* recipe

Downloading and installing the Microsoft Kinect SDK

For using Kinect on Windows 7 and Windows 8, you need to install the Microsoft Kinect SDK. This SDK lets OpenNI access Kinect for Windows and Kinect for Xbox devices.

How to do it...

1. Open your browser and navigate to `www.microsoft.com/en-us/kinectforwindows/develop/developer-downloads.aspx`:

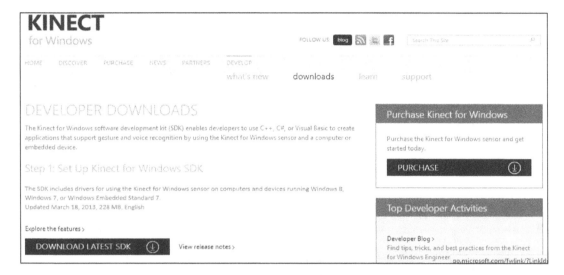

2. Download the Kinect SDK by clicking on the center-left button named **DOWNLOAD LATEST SDK**.

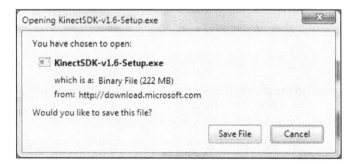

 Please note that the current version of OpenNI (OpenNI 2.2) works only with Version 1.6 and higher of Microsoft Kinect SDK. The current stable version of Kinect SDK is 1.7.

3. Open the installer package after it's downloaded, read and accept the license arguments, and click on the **Install** button.

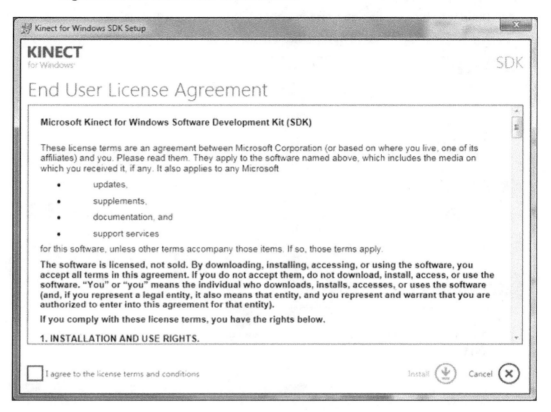

 Please note that Microsoft Kinect SDK can only be installed on Windows 7 and later.

4. Wait for the installation process to complete. At the end of the installation, click on **Close** and you are done.

How to do it...

Just as with the previous two recipes, we did nothing worth explaining except for downloading and installing the Kinect SDK, Kinect Drivers, and the Kinect Runtime.

See also

- ▶ The *Downloading and installing OpenNI* recipe
- ▶ The *Downloading and installing NiTE* recipe

Connecting Asus Xtion and PrimeSense sensors

After installing OpenNI, you need to connect your device to your PC. In this recipe, we will show you how to connect and expect Windows to recognize your device. Actually, both of these devices use only one USB port and drivers are also a part of OpenNI, so in this recipe we are not going to do anything other than connecting and waiting.

Getting ready

Before connecting your device, you need to have OpenNI installed using the *Downloading and installing OpenNI* recipe in this chapter.

How to do it...

1. Unbox your device and connect its USB cable to one of your computer's USB ports. If any message appears on the screen about the failure of recognizing your device, you can simply change the connected USB port and see if it makes any difference.

 Please note that your device may not be compatible with USB3. It is possible for PrimeSense and Asus Xtion users to update their device firmware to add support for Audio and USB3. Check out the PrimeSense website (http://www.primesense.com/updates/) for downloading the latest firmware.

2. Now, the following pop up will appear on your Windows notification bar:

3. You must wait for the installation to complete or click on it to visually see the installation steps:

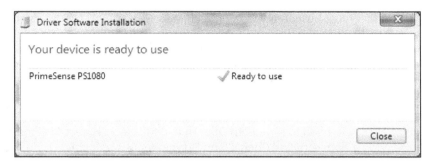

4. When **Ready to use** is displayed, it means everything is good and you have connected your device successfully.

5. You can check if it is successfully installed by going to **Device Manager**. To open **Device Manager**, right-click on the **My Computer** icon and select **Manage**, then navigate to **Device Manager** from the left-hand side tree. Then check if you have the **PrimeSense** node installed in the right-hand side panel, as shown in the following screenshot:

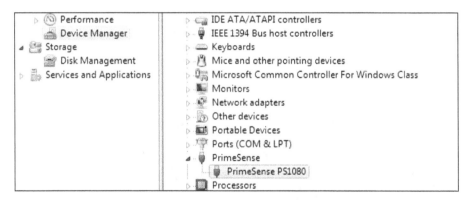

How it works...

The preceding steps are actually quite self-explanatory; we connected our device, waited for it to be recognized by Windows, and then let automatic installation finish.

See also

▸ The *Downloading and installing OpenNI* recipe

▸ The *Downloading and installing NiTE* recipe

Connecting Microsoft Kinect

If you are going to use Kinect, you need to connect this device properly to your PC. In this recipe, we are going to show you this operation. Of course, there are only a few changes between this and the previous recipe that is about the Adapter and Power Supply Kit in Kinect for the Xbox version of Kinect; everything else pretty much remains the same.

Getting ready

Before installing NiTE, you need to have both OpenNI and Microsoft Kinect SDK installed using the *Downloading and installing OpenNI* and *Downloading and installing the Microsoft Kinect SDK* recipes in this chapter.

How to do it...

1. Unbox your Kinect device and, if you are using Kinect for Xbox, connect the Kinect Sensor Power Supply Kit to the device. This kit converts the Kinect special port to a power and a USB port so that you can connect it to your PC. If you have Kinect for Windows, then your device probably has this kit built in. If you don't have this kit, you can buy it from the Microsoft Store:

   ```
   www.microsoftstore.com/store/msstore/pd/Kinect-Sensor-
   Power-Supply/productID.221244000/catID.50606600/
   parentCategoryID.50790100/categoryID.57399200/list.true
   ```

   Or you can use a short URL from `tinyurl.com` (`tinyurl.com/kinectpowerkit`):

2. Then connect its USB cable to a USB port on your computer and connect its adapter to a power plug.

Unlike other devices, Kinect is compatible with USB3 ports from the very first moment.

It is because Kinect uses an internal USB2 hub that is compatible with USB3 even when the device itself may not be. This also means connecting Kinect to a USB hub or next to any other sensor can make it unusable or undetectable.

3. Now the following pop up will appear on your Windows notification bar:

4. You must wait for the installation to complete or click on it to visually see the installation steps:

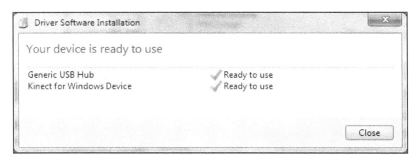

5. When **Ready to use** is displayed, it means everything is good and you have connected your device successfully.

6. You can check if it is successfully installed by going to **Device Manager**. To open **Device Manager**, right-click on the **My Computer** icon and select **Manage**, then navigate to **Device Manager** from the left-hand side tree. Then check if you have the **Microsoft Kinect** node installed in the right-hand side panel, as shown in the following screenshot:

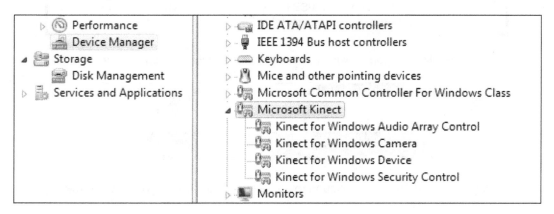

How it works...

The preceding steps are actually quite self-explanatory; we connected our device, waited for it to be recognized by Windows, and then let automatic installation finish.

See also

- ▶ The *Downloading and installing OpenNI* recipe
- ▶ The *Downloading and installing NiTE* recipe
- ▶ The *Downloading and installing the Microsoft Kinect SDK* recipe

2
OpenNI and C++

In this chapter, we will cover:

- ▶ Creating a project in Visual Studio 2010
- ▶ OpenNI class and error handling
- ▶ Enumerating a list of connected devices
- ▶ Accessing video streams (depth/IR/RGB) and configuring them
- ▶ Retrieving a list of supported video modes for depth stream
- ▶ Selecting a specific device for accessing depth stream
- ▶ Listening to the device connect and disconnect events
- ▶ Opening an already recorded file (ONI file) instead of a device

Introduction

In this chapter, we will introduce primary datatypes of the **OpenNI** and the **NiTE** along with some basic information about how to access and select a data stream. Then we will try to show you some examples of events triggered by devices such as connecting or disconnecting an OpenNI supported device from computer.

But first, let's get some background about the whole OpenNI's principle first.

The OpenNI object

OpenNI object is the starting point of everything in the framework. Using the OpenNI class we can access a list of connected devices as well as the version of OpenNI itself. Then using this information we can access a device object and read data.

This class uses the singleton pattern, which means there is only one instance of this class and all of its methods are static.

Also in OpenNI 2 we have the ability to register two callback functions by OpenNI object for capturing device connected and device disconnected events.

The device object

Device object is representing the actual physical device where each device supports a number of sensors (for example, depth, color, and IR) that can be accessed using Device object. We need to ask for access to a device before using its sensor's output. Also using this object, we can access some device-wide settings. Read more in *Chapter 4, More about Low-level Outputs*.

The VideoStream object

Using the VideoStream object we can access the output data of color, IR, and depth sensors. VideoStream in the new version of OpenNI supports event-based reading that gives us the ability to register a callback function to execute when a new frame of data becomes available.

Sharing devices between applications

Unlike OpenNI 1.x, where we could share a device between two or more applications at the same time, we can't share a sensor's output at all with OpenNI 2.x. In the new design, the first application always locks the device; not only is there no way for the second app to change settings of sensors, there is no way to even use the output of locked sensors in any way as well.

VideoStream paused state

Most of the time, a sensor will not start producing data output when initialized until the programmer asks it to start generating data using the `openni:VideoStream::start()` function. Also it is possible to stop a stream from generating data using the `openni:VideoStream::stop()` function.

Creating a project in Visual Studio 2010

In this recipe we will show you how to prepare a project in Visual Studio to start programming with OpenNI 2 and NiTE 2. Using NiTE 2 is optional but it will offer following features to you::

- ▸ The capability to track hands and recognize hand gestures
- ▸ The capability to recognize one or more users and track their movements

▶ The capability to recognize different parts of the user's body and extract his/her skeleton map and joint positions

Please note that you don't need NiTE if you want to simply work with depth/ IR or Image stream. But if you want to go one step forward and work with the middleware layer, you need to install NiTE and use it.

Without NiTE, we can only use low-level data such as the output of different physical sensors of one or more devices.

Getting ready

Download and install the free version of Visual Studio 2010 Express Edition from the following link:

```
http://www.microsoft.com/visualstudio/eng/products/visual-studio-
2010-express
```

Please note that by using **Visual Studio 2010 C++ Express** you can't compile 64-bit applications without **Windows SDK**. You can download Windows SDK from the following link:

```
http://go.microsoft.com/fwlink/?LinkID=191424
```

Also you can use Visual Studio 2012 Express for Windows Desktop, which supports C++, C#, VB.net, and compiling of both 32-bit and 64-bit applications. Visual Studio 2012 Express shares almost the same user interface as Visual Studio 2010 C++ Express and there should be no big problem when using this recipe. Use the following link for more information and download Visual Studio 2012 for Windows Desktop:

```
http://www.microsoft.com/visualstudio/eng/products/visual-studio-
express-for-windows-desktop
```

We are using **Visual Studio 2010 Ultimate Edition** but there must be no notable difference in these steps for Visual Studio 2010 C++ Express or Visual Studio 2012 for Windows Desktop.

For OpenNI 2.1 and older, you can't use Visual Studio 2012. If you have decided to use Visual Studio 2012 you must use OpenNI 2.2 alpha or later versions.

Also download and install OpenNI and, if needed, NiTE as shown in *Chapter 1, Getting Started*.

How to do it...

We are going to create a project in Visual Studio 2010 and configure our project to use OpenNI libraries and headers. First of all open Visual Studio 2010 and then follow the ensuing steps:

1. From the **File** menu, select **New**, and then **New Project**.

2. Select **Visual C++** from the left panel and **Win32 Console Application** from the right panel.

3. Enter a name in the **Name** field and click on **OK**.

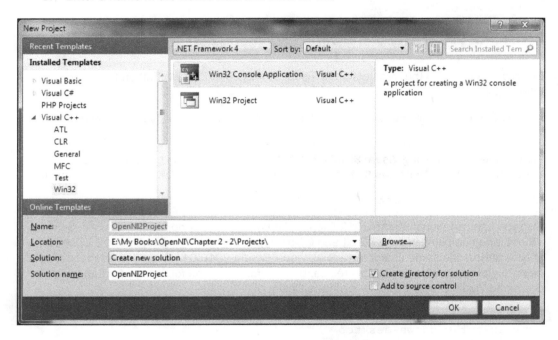

4. Wait for the project creation process and after that create a 64-bit platform type for your project by clicking on the **Build** menu and selecting **Configuration Manager**.

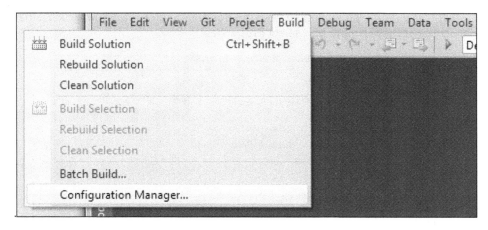

5. From the **Active solution platform** dropdown, select **New**, and in the new dialog box select **x64** from the top dropdown, **Win32** from the bottom dropdown, and click on **OK** and **Close**.

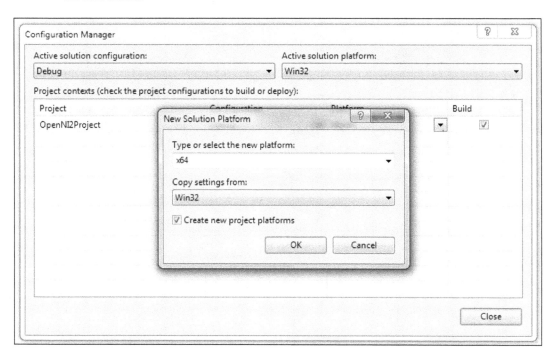

6. Right-click on the project name from the **Solution Explorer** window, which is usually located at the top right, and select **Properties**.

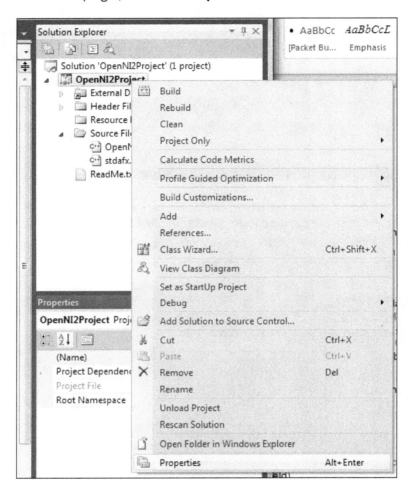

7. Select **All Configurations** from the top-right dropdown (the **Configuration** dropdown) and **Active(x64)** or **x64** from the top-right dropdown (**Platform** dropdown).

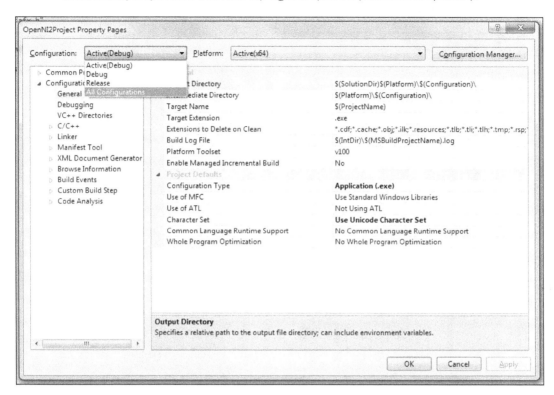

8. Locate **C/C++** and expand it.

9. Select the **General** node, edit **Additional Include Directories** (using the down arrow to the right of this field), add $ (OPENNI2_INCLUDE64), and, if you want to use NiTE in your project, enter $ (NITE2_INCLUDE64) too on a new line then click on **OK**.

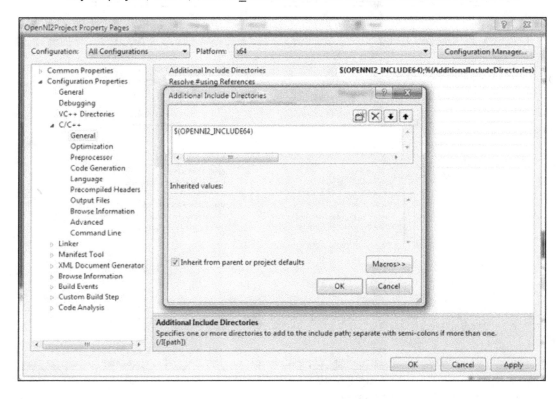

10. Locate the **Linker** section and expand it.

11. Select the **General** node, edit **Additional Library Directories**, then add $(OPENNI2_
LIB64), and, if you want to use NiTE in your project, enter $(NITE2_LIB64) too on a new line then click on **OK**.

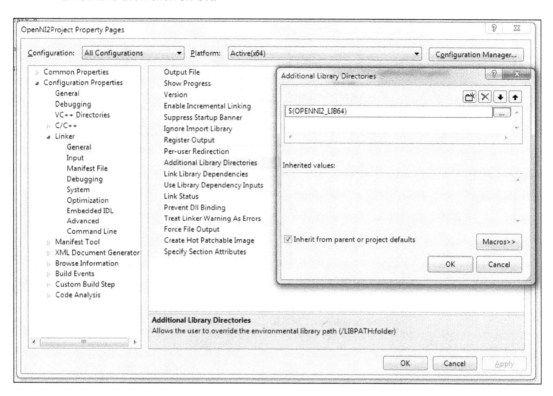

12. Select the **Input** node in the same section (**Linker**), edit **Additional Dependencies**, then add OpenNI2.lib and, if you want to use NiTE in your project, enter NiTE2.lib too on a new line then click on **OK**.

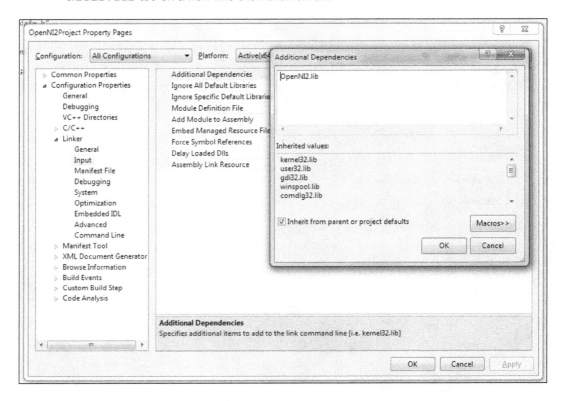

13. Navigate to **Build Events**, expand it, select the **Post-Build Event** node, edit the **Command Line** field from the right panel, and enter:

```
xcopy "%OPENNI2_REDIST64%*" "$(OutDir)" /y /s /e /i /d
```

14. And if you want to use NiTE2 in your project then enter the following line too:

```
xcopy "%NITE2_REDIST64%*" "$(OutDir)" /y /s /e /i /d
```

15. Then click on **OK** and in the parent window click on **Apply**.

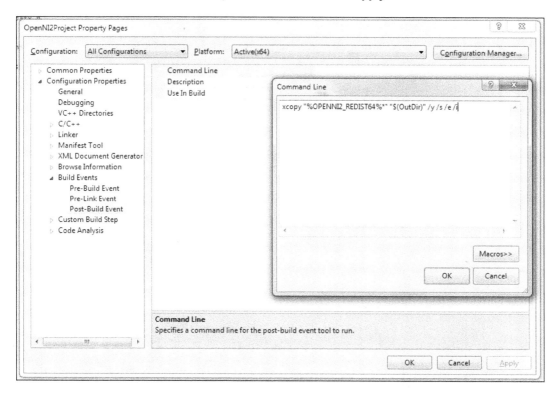

If you are using Visual Studio 2010 Express Edition and want to compile in 64-bit, you need to follow this step; otherwise, skip it:

► First make sure you have Windows SDK installed, then navigate to the **General** category from the left panel, and edit **Platform Toolset** from the right panel

► Select **Windows7.1SDK** or any other version of SDK you have installed based on your operating system and apply the settings as shown in the following screenshot:

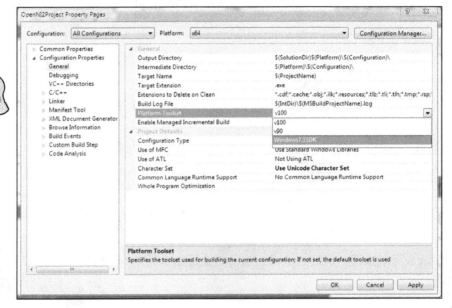

16. Now we must set the options needed for a 32-bit platform in case we want to compile a 32-bit binary too (or if we only want to compile 32-bit binary). Select **All Configurations** from the top-right dropdown (the **Configuration** dropdown) and **Win32** from the top-right dropdown (the **Platform** dropdown).

We will ignore the image of each part from now because settings are much like earlier steps with small changes.

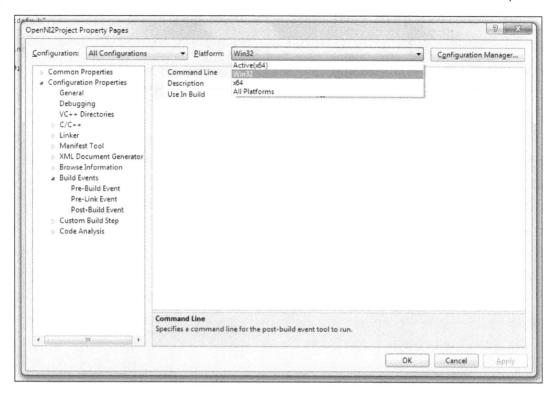

17. Locate the **C/C++** section and expand it.

18. Select the **General** node, edit **Additional Include Directories** (using the down arrow on right of this field), then add $(OPENNI2_INCLUDE), and, if you want to use NiTE in your project, enter $(NITE2_INCLUDE) too on a new line and then click on **OK**.

19. Locate the **Linker** section and expand it.

20. Select the **General** node, edit **Additional Library Directories**, then add $(OPENNI2_LIB), and, if you want to use NiTE in your project, enter $(NITE2_LIB) too on a new line and then click on **OK**.

21. Select **Input** node in the same section (**Linker**), edit **Additional Dependencies**, then add OpenNI2.lib, and, if you want to use NiTE in your project, enter NiTE2.lib too on a new line. Then click on **OK**.

22. Navigate to **Build Events**, expand it, select the **Post-Build Event** node, edit the **Command** field from the right panel, and enter:

```
xcopy "%OPENNI2_REDIST%*" "$(OutDir)" /y /s /e /i /d
```

23. And if you want to use NiTE2 in your project, enter the following line too:

```
xcopy "%NITE2_REDIST%*" "$(OutDir)" /y /s /e /i /d
```

24. Click on **OK** and then in the parent window click on **Apply**.

25. Now we need to set some of settings that are going to be used for both platforms. So select the **All Configurations** option from the top-right dropdown (the **Configuration** dropdown) and **All Platforms** from the top-right dropdown (the **Platform** dropdown). Then select the **Debugging** node in the left panel and edit **Working Directory** from the right panel. Replace its value with $ (OutDir) and click on **OK**.

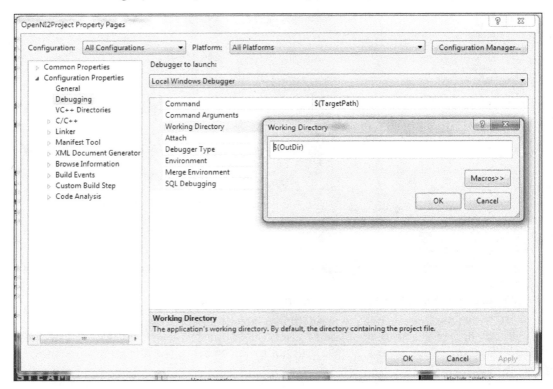

26. We are done with the **Project Property** window, so you can close it by clicking on **OK**.

27. Back in the main window of Visual Studio, we need to include OpenNI header files in our source code too; to do this, open the main source file of your project and enter these lines at the top of everything in the editor:

Downloading the example code:

You can download the example code files for all Packt books you have purchased from your account at http://www.packtpub.com. If you purchased this book elsewhere, you can visit http://www.packtpub.com/support and register to have the files e-mailed directly to you.

```
// General headers
#include <stdio.h>
// OpenNI2 headers
#include <OpenNI.h>
using namespace openni;
```

28. If you want to use NiTE2 in your project, you need to add these lines to the top of the main source file too:

```
// NiTE2 headers
#include <NiTE.h>
```

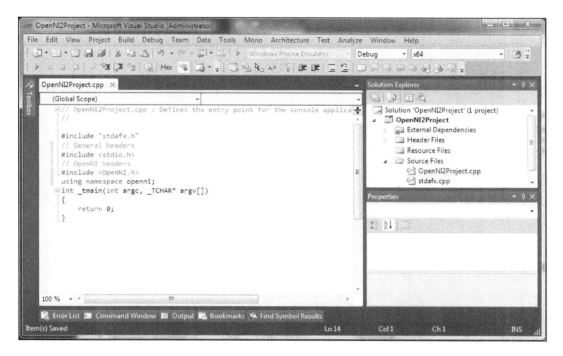

Build your project. This will tell you if any problem is found.

How it works...

First of all we need to create a project so that we can start coding:

▸ Steps 1 to 3 are about making a new C++ project using Visual Studio; we used the Win32 Console application because we don't want to create a visual user interface and only want our application to be able to execute.

▶ Step 4 is about introducing a new configuration profile for our project and asking Visual Studio to use x64 compiler when this profile is active; we used x86 settings as default values for this new profile. You actually don't need it if you want to use a 32-bit version of OpenNI.

A 32-bit application can be executed in a 64-bit environment but not vice versa. Also it doesn't matter if you are using or targeting a 32-bit or 64-bit version of OS, but you can't use a 64-bit version of OpenNI when creating a 32-bit application.

▶ Because we want to work with OpenNI framework and NiTE, we need to have access to their APIs, so we need to show Visual Studio how to use them; steps 8 to 12 and steps 17 to 21 are about introducing the needed libraries and header files to Visual Studio.

Unlike the OpenNI 1.x and NiTE 1.x era when there was only one global version of OpenNI and NiTE on a system, now OpenNI 2.x and NiTE 2.x offer the possibility to have different versions of OpenNI and NiTE on the same system. You can even have one version of OpenNI 1.x along with the different versions of OpenNI 2.x working together for different applications. Actually this is because each application must have its own version of OpenNI libraries in OpenNI 2; so we don't need to worry about version compatibility any more. But currently we are the developers, so we need to copy a version of OpenNI 2.x in our project too.

▶ In steps 13 to 14 and 22 to 23 we asked the compiler to copy the needed OpenNI and NiTE libraries and files to our project's output library after the compiling process has finished successfully. This is so we can have our version of OpenNI next to the executable file of our project.

▶ Steps 27 and 28 ask the source editor to load OpenNI and NiTE header files so we can use their APIs in our code. The last line in step 27 lets us use OpenNI's API without writing `openni::` before any class and object in that namespace (for example, we can write `Status` instead of `openni::Status`).

Please note that steps 5 and 7 to 15 are for x64 compiling and steps 16 to 23 are needed only if you want to develop a 32-bit version of your software. But we highly recommend doing all the steps and then you can select the desired target CPU using the top solution platform dropdown. Note that you need to have the same version of OpenNI on your system before compiling.

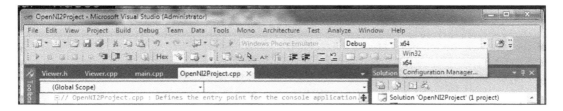

There's more...

You can use the `OpenNI2Project - Empty Project` and `OpenNI2Project - Empty Project with NiTE` projects as templates for starting. These projects are available in the Packt Publishing website for free download. Please note that when using these templates for writing different projects you can't import two or more of them into one solution; that's because they use the same GUID and you need to change their GUID to something unique before importing them in one solution.

See also

▸ The *OpenNI class and error handling* recipe

▸ The *Configuring Visual Studio 2010 to use OpenGL* recipe in *Chapter 3, Using Low-level Data*

OpenNI class and error handling

We will show how to create and initialize a context object in C++ and how to use the `openni::Status` datatype to handle errors thrown by OpenNI core. We will use `openni::Status` very often in the later recipes and it is a very important part of any successful application.

In this recipe, we try to show the version number of the current OpenNI environment and then initialize the OpenNI framework. This will ask OpenNI to search for any connected device and load their modules and drivers.

Getting ready

Create a project in Visual Studio 2010 and prepare it for working with OpenNI using the *Creating a project in Visual Studio 2010* recipe in this chapter.

How to do it...

Have a look at the following steps:

1. Open your project and then the project's main source code file. Locate this line:

```
int _tmain(int argc, _TCHAR* argv[])
{
```

2. Write the following code snippet above the preceding line of code:

```
char ReadLastCharOfLine()
{
  int newChar = 0;
  int lastChar;
  fflush(stdout);
  do
  {
    lastChar = newChar;
    newChar = getchar();
  }
  while ((newChar != '\n') && (newChar != EOF));
  return (char)lastChar;
}
```

3. Locate this line again:

```
int _tmain(int argc, _TCHAR* argv[])
{
```

4. Write the following code snippet below the preceding line of code:

```
printf("OpenNI Version is %d.%d.%d.%d",
    OpenNI::getVersion().major,
    OpenNI::getVersion().minor,
    OpenNI::getVersion().maintenance,
    OpenNI::getVersion().build);
printf("Scanning machine for devices and loading "
        "modules/drivers ...\r\n");
Status status = STATUS_OK;
status = OpenNI::initialize();
if (status != STATUS_OK){
  printf("ERROR: #%d, %s", status,
        OpenNI::getExtendedError());
  return 1;
}
printf("Completed.\r\n");
```

```
// Requesting device and creating sensor stream, then
// reading data goes here

printf("Press ENTER to exit.\r\n");

ReadLastCharOfLine();

OpenNI::shutdown();
return 0;
```

How it works...

In the first step we defined a new method named `ReadLastCharOfLine()`. This function will wait until the user presses the *Enter* key and will return the last character typed by the user before *Enter* or 0 if nothing. We will use this function to wait for the user input or ask the user to make a decision. In this example, we used it for preventing our application from closing before the user command. We will not describe it line by line because this function is not a part of our topic but it is simple and easy to understand.

In the second step we used the `openni::OpenNI::getVersion()` method from the `openni::OpenNI` class to get the version of the used OpenNI framework. The return value of this function is of the type `openni::Version` (the other name for OniVersion). Using different fields of this structure we can access different version number categories.

```
printf("OpenNI Version is %d.%d.%d.%d",
    OpenNI::getVersion().major,
    OpenNI::getVersion().minor,
    OpenNI::getVersion().maintenance,
    OpenNI::getVersion().build);
```

Then we used `openni::OpenNI` to initialize OpenNI. The initializing process includes initializing and preloading different modules and drivers by OpenNI. We don't need to create an object from the `openni::OpenNI` class because all methods are static.

```
status = OpenNI::initialize();
```

Also, we checked if the initializing process ended without error, by creating a variable of type `openni::Status`.

```
Status status = STATUS_OK;
    ...
if (status != STATUS_OK)
```

`openni::Status` will inform us if any error exists but it can't give us more information about this error. But on other hand OpenNI gives us a method that will return the latest error message. This method is `openni::OpenNI::getExtendedError()`.

```
printf("ERROR: #%d, %s", status,
        OpenNI::getExtendedError());
```

If everything is ok, we can proceed to other steps including requesting and reading data from the device or file. These parts will be discussed in later recipes. And at last when we are done with OpenNI it is better to ask it to turn all devices down and release all resources. For doing so we need to execute `openni::OpenNI::shutdown()`.

```
OpenNI::shutdown();
```

In our code we used the `printf()` function for printing messages and variable's values to console.

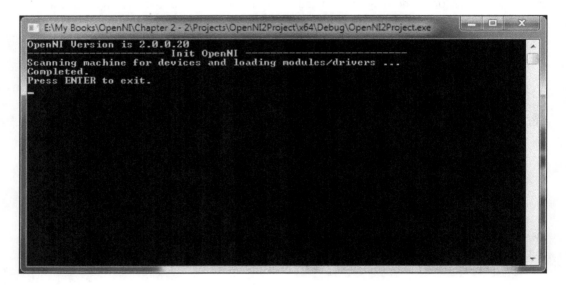

Defining a method for displaying error message

From now on we will create and use a function in our project to handle `openni::Status`, returned from different methods of OpenNI. This will help us reduce the number of conditions in our code and improve it by making it more readable and understandable. The following is the function that we will use in the later recipes:

```
bool HandleStatus(Status status)
{
```

```
  if (status == STATUS_OK)
    return true;
  printf("ERROR: #%d, %s", status,
    OpenNI::getExtendedError());
  ReadLastCharOfLine();
  return false;
}
```

This function will return `false` in case of an error and will print an error message to the console. There is nothing new to describe here.

Possible values of openni::Status

Our status variable in the previous code is of the type `openni::Status`. This `enum` has different possible values that we will try to explain as follows:

-   `openni::Status::STATUS_OK`: This specifies that there is no problem or error
-   `openni::Status::STATUS_ERROR`: This specifies that an error has happened in the process of execution of the requested method or function
-   `openni::Status::STATUS_NOT_IMPLEMENTED`: This specifies that the method or the function you called or used is not implemented yet
-   `openni::Status::STATUS_NOT_SUPPORTED`: This specifies that the requested task is not supported or not possible
-   `openni::Status::STATUS_BAD_PARAMETER`: This specifies that the parameter of the method or function is incorrect, null, or irrelevant
-   `openni::Status::STATUS_OUT_OF_FLOW`: In other words, overflow usually means a problem with the memory/device or stack
-   `openni::Status::STATUS_NO_DEVICE`: This specifies that no device is connected and available to use

Enumerating a list of connected devices

We learned how to initialize OpenNI and how to retrieve the version number of OpenNI using the `openni::OpenNI::getVersion()` method and how to ask OpenNI to read all modules and drivers by calling `openni::OpenNI::initialize()` in the last recipe. In this recipe we will get the list of all the connected devices, their hardware Uri (location), and product ID (that can be used to identify the device).

Getting ready

Create a project in Visual Studio 2010 and prepare it for working with OpenNI using the *Creating a project in Visual Studio 2010* recipe in this chapter.

How to do it...

Open your project and then the project's main source code file. Locate this line:

```
int _tmain(int argc, _TCHAR* argv[])
{
```

Write the following code snippet above the preceding line of code:

```
char ReadLastCharOfLine()
{
  int newChar = 0;
  int lastChar;
  fflush(stdout);
  do
  {
    lastChar = newChar;
    newChar = getchar();
  }
  while ((newChar != '\n') && (newChar != EOF));
  return (char)lastChar;
}


bool HandleStatus(Status status)
{
  if (status == STATUS_OK)
    return true;
  printf("ERROR: #%d, %s", status,
    OpenNI::getExtendedError());
  ReadLastCharOfLine();
    return false;
}
```

Locate this line again:

```
int _tmain(int argc, _TCHAR* argv[])
{
```

Write the following code snippet below the preceding line of code:

```
Status status = STATUS_OK;
printf("Scanning machine for devices and loading "
      "" modules/drivers ...\r\n");
status = OpenNI::initialize();
if (!HandleStatus(status)) return 1;
printf("Completed.\r\n");
```

```
openni::Array<openni::DeviceInfo> listOfDevices;
openni::OpenNI::enumerateDevices(&listOfDevices);
int numberOfDevices = listOfDevices.getSize();
if (numberOfDevices > 0){
  printf("%d Device(s) are available to use.\r\n\r\n",
      numberOfDevices);
  for (int i = 0; i < numberOfDevices; i++)
  {
    openni::DeviceInfo device = listOfDevices[i];
    printf("%d. %s->%s (VID: %d | PID: %d) is connected "
        " at %s\r\n",
      i,
      device.getVendor(),
      device.getName(),
      device.getUsbVendorId(),
      device.getUsbProductId(),
      device.getUri());
  }
}else{
  printf("No device connected to this machine.");
  }

printf("Press ENTER to exit.\r\n");
ReadLastCharOfLine();
OpenNI::shutdown();
return 0;
```

How it works...

In the first two steps we defined a new method named `ReadLastCharOfLine()`. This function will wait until the user presses the *Enter* key and will return the last character typed by the user before *Enter* or 0 if nothing. We will use this function to wait for user input or ask the user to make a decision. In this example we used it for preventing our application from closing before the user command. We will not describe it line by line because this function is not a part of our topic.

We also defined another method named `HandleStatus()`. This method will check if an `openni::Status` object shows an error and if so it will get the last reported error message using `openni::OpenNI::getExtendedError()` and print it to the console. Then it will wait for the user input and in the end it will return `false` if any error is found and `true` if there was no problem. This function will help us to reduce the code we need to write in our main program.

Step four contains our main code. Just as in the last recipe we defined a variable of type `openni::Status` and then used `openni::OpenNI` class to initialize OpenNI; the return value of `openni::OpenNI::initialize()` is an `openni::Status` object that we sent to `HandleStatus()` to find out if any error has occurred in the initializing process. And if any error has occurred (`HandleStatus()` will return `false` in case of error), we will end the program execution process by returning `1` (any value except `0` means an error to the OS) in the main function.

```
Status status = STATUS_OK;
...
status = OpenNI::initialize();
if (!HandleStatus(status)) return 1;
```

After that our main part of code starts. For getting the number of connected devices we need to send an array to OpenNI that can be filled with information of all connected devices. Because arrays are a little messy in C++ compared to high-level languages like C# (mainly because the size of an array is unknown) OpenNI itself tries to present a template class named `openni::Array` to us. A template class lets us extend different datatypes without rewriting code for each datatype separately. In this example we can use the `openni::Array` class with any datatype including `char`, `int` and so on.

> **Template classes** are known as **Generic classes** in other languages such as C#, Java, or VB.Net.

Using an array of the `openni::DeviceInfo` class and by passing this array to the `openni::OpenNI::enumerateDevices()` method, we can gain access to the list of currently connected devices.

The following is the code we used to define an array of `openni::DeviceInfo` using the `openni::Array` class and passing it to the `openni::OpenNI::enumerateDevices()` function to be filled with data.

```
openni::Array<openni::DeviceInfo> listOfDevices;
openni::OpenNI::enumerateDevices(&listOfDevices);
```

Then we saved the size of this array in an `int` variable to be used by other parts of our code.

```
int numberOfDevices = listOfDevices.getSize();
```

Following this line we try to make sure that the size of this array or, in other words, the number of connected devices is not 0. If there is no device connected (`numberOfDevices == 0`) we will inform the user, but if not and there was one or more devices connected to the machine then we use a loop to access each device's information one by one.

```
if (numberOfDevices > 0){
    printf("%d Device(s) are available to use.\r\n\r\n",
```

```
        numberOfDevices);
    for (int i = 0; i < numberOfDevices; i++)
    {
        ...
    }
}else{
    printf("No device connected to this machine.");
}
```

In our loop we defined a variable of type `openni::DeviceInfo` to store our current `openni::DeviceInfo` object temporarily and then filled it with one of our array items.

```
openni::DeviceInfo device = listOfDevices[i];
```

Currently, we have no use for this information so our only goal is to show this device's information to the user using the `printf()` function.

```
printf("%d. %s->%s (VID: %d | PID: %d) is connected "
    "at %s\r\n",
    i,
    device.getVendor(),
    device.getName(),
    device.getUsbVendorId(),
    device.getUsbProductId(),
    device.getUri());
```

As you can see we used different methods of the `openni::DeviceInfo` class here. The following is the description of each method's return value:

- `openni::DeviceInfo.getVendor()`: It specifies that the returned value is the name of the device driver vendor company.

- `openni::DeviceInfo.getName()`: It specifies that the returned value is the name of the device given by the device driver.

- `openni::DeviceInfo.getUsbVendorId()`: It specifies that the returned value is an `int16` containing the ID number of the device driver vendor company. This value is valuable when we want to determinate the device's company or the device's model series. Read the *There's more...* section for more information.

- `openni::DeviceInfo.getUsbProductId()`: It specifies that the returned value is an `int16` containing the ID number of the device given by the device driver. This value is valuable when we want to determine the device model. Read the *There's more...* section for more info.

- `openni::DeviceInfo.getUri()`: The most important value here is a string containing the hardware location of the device. We can use this value later to select our desired device when there is more than one device available. Read the later recipes for more information.

When we are done with showing all the information to the user, we will ask him/her to press *Enter* and then wait for it.

```
printf("Press ENTER to exit.\r\n");
ReadLastCharOfLine();
```

After pressing *Enter* we will shut down OpenNI and return 0, which means the program executed successfully without any errors.

```
OpenNI::shutdown();
return 0;
```

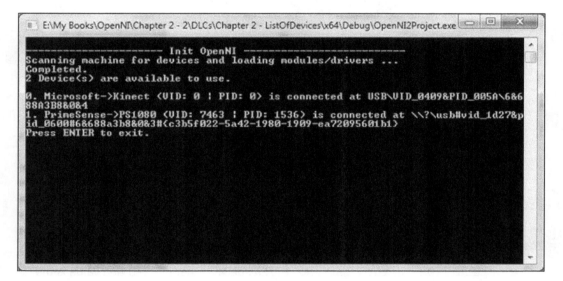

There's more...

List of known Product IDs and Vendor IDs at the time of writing of this book

The following is a list of Vendor IDs and Product IDs of known devices:

Device	Vendor ID	Product ID
Asus Xtion	7463	1536
	7463	1537
PimeSense Sensor	7463	512
	7463	768
	7463	1024
	7463	1280
	7463	4763
	7463	8448
	7463	8704
	7463	63963
Kinect	1118	688
	1118	685
	1118	686
Kinect for Windows	1118	702
	1118	703

Please note that in the current version, OpenNI returns Product IDs and Vendor IDs of Kinect and Kinect for Windows as 0. We believe this is going to be solved in the later versions of OpenNI.

See also

▶ The _Selecting a specific device for accessing depth stream_ recipe

▶ The _Listening to the device connect and disconnect events_ recipe

Accessing video streams (depth/IR/RGB) and configuring them

In OpenNI 2 there is only one class that is responsible for giving us access to the output of all video-based sensors (depth/IR/RGB) that have made our work very simple compared to the OpenNI 1.x era, where we needed to use three different classes to access sensors. In this recipe we will show you how to access the depth sensor and initialize it. For accessing the IR sensor and RGB sensor we need to follow the same procedure that we will discuss more in the _How It Works..._ section of this recipe. We will show you how to select an output video mode for a sensor too. Also we will show you how to ask a device to see if an output is supported or not.

We will not cover other configurable properties of the `openni::VideoStream` class including cropping and mirroring in this recipe; read *Chapter 4, More about Low-level Outputs* about this topic.

Getting ready

Create a project in Visual Studio 2010 and prepare it for working with OpenNI using the *Creating a project in Visual Studio 2010* recipe in this chapter.

How to do it...

Have a look at the following steps:

1. Open your project and then the project's main source code file. Locate this line:

```
int _tmain(int argc, _TCHAR* argv[])
{
```

2. Write the following code snippet above the preceding line of code:

```
char ReadLastCharOfLine()
{
  int newChar = 0;
  int lastChar;
  fflush(stdout);
  do
  {
    lastChar = newChar;
    newChar = getchar();
  }
  while ((newChar != '\n') && (newChar != EOF));
  return (char)lastChar;
}


bool HandleStatus(Status status)
{
  if (status == STATUS_OK)
    return true;
  printf("ERROR: #%d, %s", status,
    OpenNI::getExtendedError());
  ReadLastCharOfLine();
  return false;
}
```

3. Locate this line again:

```
int _tmain(int argc, _TCHAR* argv[])
{
```

4. Write the following code snippet below the preceding line of code:

```
Status status = STATUS_OK;
printf("Scanning machine for devices and loading "
    "modules/drivers ...\r\n");
status = OpenNI::initialize();
if (!HandleStatus(status)) return 1;
printf("Completed.\r\n");

printf("Press ENTER to continue.\r\n");
ReadLastCharOfLine();

printf("Opening any device ...\r\n");
Device device;
status = device.open(ANY_DEVICE);
if (!HandleStatus(status)) return 1;
printf("%s Opened, Completed.\r\n",
  device.getDeviceInfo().getName());

printf("Press ENTER to continue.\r\n");
ReadLastCharOfLine();

printf("Checking if depth stream is supported ...\r\n");
if (!device.hasSensor(SENSOR_DEPTH))
{
  printf("Depth stream not supported by this device. "
      "Press ENTER to exit.\r\n");
  ReadLastCharOfLine();
  return 1;
}

printf("Asking device to create a depth stream ...\r\n");
VideoStream sensor;
status = sensor.create(device, SENSOR_DEPTH);
if (!HandleStatus(status)) return 1;
printf("Completed.\r\n");

printf("Changing sensor video mode to 640x480@30fps.\r\n");
VideoMode depthVM;
depthVM.setFps(30);
```

```
depthVM.setResolution(640,480);
depthVM.setPixelFormat(PIXEL_FORMAT_DEPTH_1_MM);
status = sensor.setVideoMode(depthVM);
if (!HandleStatus(status)) return 1;
printf("Completed.\r\n");

printf("Asking sensor to start receiving data ...\r\n");
status = sensor.start();
if (!HandleStatus(status)) return 1;
printf("Completed.\r\n");

printf("Press ENTER to exit.\r\n");
ReadLastCharOfLine();
sensor.destroy();
device.close();
OpenNI::shutdown();
return 0;
```

How it works...

First we defined our `ReadLastCharOfLine()` and `HandleStatus()` methods just like we did previously; read the previous recipe about that.

Then in the first line of the second step we used the `openni::OpenNI::initialize()` method to initialize OpenNI and load modules and drivers. Again you can read the previous recipe for more information.

Our main code actually started when we defined a variable of type `openni:Device`. Then, using this variable we opened access to the first driver in the list of OpenNI's connected devices. We also checked (with the `HandleStatus()` function) to see if this process ended without any error message so as to continue or write the error to the console and `return 1` if there was any error.

```
Device device;
status = device.open(ANY_DEVICE);
if (!HandleStatus(status)) return 1;
```

From now, using the `device` variable we can request access to a depth sensor (or any other type we want), but before that it is a good idea to check if this type of sensor is even supported by this device or not.

```
if (!device.hasSensor(SENSOR_DEPTH))
{
  printf("Depth stream not supported by this device. "
      "Press ENTER to exit.\r\n");
  ReadLastCharOfLine();
  return 1;
}
```

Note `SensorType` enum in the code; currently there are three types of video sensors that we can use or send a request for:

▶ `openni::SensorType::SENSOR_COLOR`: RGB camera

▶ `openni::SensorType::SENSOR_DEPTH`: Depth data

▶ `openni::SensorType::SENSOR_IR`: IR output from IR camera

Any line after the previous condition will run only if our desired sensor type is supported by the device. And if the sensor is supported by the device, we can request an access to this sensor; for doing so we need to create a variable from `openni::VideoStream` type, ask it to initialize for our device's depth stream, and of course if any error happens we need to handle that.

```
VideoStream sensor;
status = sensor.create(device, SENSOR_DEPTH);
if (!HandleStatus(status)) return 1;
```

This will give us access to the depth sensor with default settings; but we want to use a specific video mode for the output of this sensor so we need to change this configuration.

For doing so we need to create a variable of type `openni::VideoMode`, change it the way we want, and then pass it to our sensor. Again we must take care of any error in this process.

```
VideoMode depthVM;
depthVM.setFps(30);
depthVM.setResolution(640,480);
depthVM.setPixelFormat(PIXEL_FORMAT_DEPTH_1_MM);
status = sensor.setVideoMode(depthVM);
if (!HandleStatus(status)) return 1;
```

The code will request the output with a resolution of `(640,480)` at `30` frames per second and with `PIXEL_FORMAT_DEPTH_1_MM` pixel format. Read more about pixel formats in the *There's more...* section.

When we are done with configuring our sensor, we can ask it to start receiving data. This process includes requesting the device to start the sensor and send the required data to the machine. We didn't have any real communication with the physical device before this part of our code.

```
status = sensor.start();
if (!HandleStatus(status)) return 1;
```

Then we need to read data from the sensor so as to use or display it. We don't cover this topic here; we simply wait for the user input and then we will end our application. And of course, we would ask `sensor` and `device` to release resources and then `openni:OpenNI` to `shutdown()` before ending.

```
ReadLastCharOfLine();
sensor.destroy();
device.close();
OpenNI::shutdown();
return 0;
```

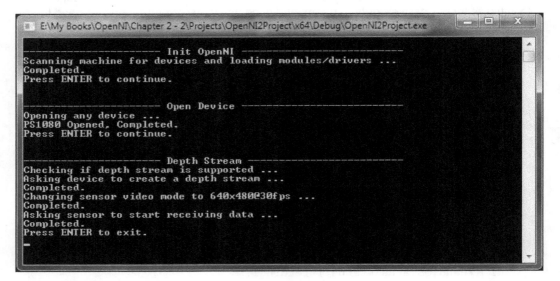

There's more...

Read the *How it works...* section of this recipe about how to use `openni::SensorType` enum to select the desired sensor when creating the `openni::VideoSensor` object. You also need to select a supported `openni::PixelFormat` for the type of sensor you selected; for example, you can't request for `openni::PixelFormat::PIXEL_FORMAT_DEPTH_1_MM` as the format for receiving data from the color sensor. Read the next topic for more information.

You can also define different variables of type `openni::VideoSensor` and use more than one sensor at a time. But you must keep in mind that creating (or in other words, requesting) the same sensor twice will result in having the same underlying object with two wrappers; that means any change to one will mirror to the other one.

Also it is impossible to have both IR and color stream active; you must stop one before using another one. It seems that this limitation comes from limited USB 2 bandwidth. Also it is important to know that depth output is based on IR CMOS sensor so you can't have both IR and depth active with different resolutions. You must always keep their resolutions same. There is only one exception when using IR with 1280x1024 resolution; in this case, depth must be in 640x480 with 30 fps. The exception is only correct when we use Asus Xtion or PrimeSense sensors.

Pixel formats

In the current version of OpenNI (V2.2) there are ten types of pixel formats that can be used to read data from video streams; we will describe some of them more specifically in the later chapters (when we really need them to read data from streams), but now you can get an idea from the following table:

Name	Used for	Description
openni::PixelFormat::PIXEL_FORMAT_DEPTH_1_MM	Depth stream	This is the usual way to read depth data from the stream. The values are in depth pixel with 1mm accuracy
openni::PixelFormat::PIXEL_FORMAT_DEPTH_100_UM	Depth stream	This is same as openni::PixelFormat::PIXEL_FORMAT_DEPTH_1_MM but with 0.1mm (100 micrometres) accuracy. It is not supported by any currently released sensor (at the time of writing of this book),
openni::PixelFormat::PIXEL_FORMAT_SHIFT_9_2	Depth stream	It is the value of displacement between the projected pattern and the device's view of projected pattern to the environment.
		This is the RAW output of depth stream. This output is used for creating openni::PixelFormat::PIXEL_FORMAT_DEPTH_1_MM by driver.
openni::PixelFormat::PIXEL_FORMAT_SHIFT_9_3	Depth stream	This is same as openni::PixelFormat::PIXEL_FORMAT_SHIFT_9_2 but with more accuracy.
		This output is used for creating openni::PixelFormat::PIXEL_FORMAT_DEPTH_100_UM by driver.
		Not supported by any currently released sensor (at the time of writing of this book).

Name	Used for	Description
`openni::PixelFormat::PIXEL_FORMAT_RGB888`	Color and IR streams	This can be used for color and IR streams to generate data with a 24-bit bitmap format. Usually used for color stream as the main usable output format and rarely used for IR, because using Grayscale 16-bit gives us a more detailed output when reading from the IR stream but with less bandwidth and memory usage.
`openni::PixelFormat::PIXEL_FORMAT_YUV422`	Color stream	YCbCr (commonly called as YUV422) is a way to encode RGB data to reduce redundancy of data by reducing the size of an image (using YUV422) to 2/3 of RGB bitmap size. Using this output format that is supported by color stream, we can use less memory to manipulate it and also the device needs less bandwidth to send it. But for displaying to the user, this format is not very useable as we need to do a number of calculations until it becomes ready (getting it converted to RGB value). In YUV422, the byte order is UY_1VY_2.
`openni::PixelFormat::PIXEL_FORMAT_GRAY8`	Color stream	Grayscale 8-bit contains the average of all three RGB values, which is displayed as one single value. Useable when we don't need to know colors; so we can prevent wasting memory and bandwidth for receiving and manipulating unneeded data.
`openni::PixelFormat::PIXEL_FORMAT_GRAY16`	IR stream	Grayscale 16-bit is usable only for reading data from the IR stream. Grayscale 16-bit has more details than Grayscale 8-bit (256 times more).
`openni::PixelFormat::PIXEL_FORMAT_JPEG`	Not supported yet	This is not supported by any currently released device (at the time of writing of this book) It is expected to be used with color sensor to receive JPEG directly from the device.
`openni::PixelFormat::PIXEL_FORMAT_YUYV`	Color stream	This is same as `openni::PixelFormat::PIXEL_FORMAT_YUV422` but with different byte order. Byte order of YUYV (also known as YUV2) is Y_1UY_2V.

Known supported list of resolutions of each sensor in different devices

The following is a list of known supported resolutions of each sensor along with their fps in different devices:

Device	Sensor	Resolution	Frames per second
Asus Xtion PrimeSense Sensor	Depth	320x240	25/30/60
		640x480	25/30
	Image IR	320x240	25/30/60
		640x480	25/30
		1280x1024	30
Kinect Kinect for Windows	Depth	80x60	30
		320x240	30
		640x480	30
	Image	640x480	30
	IR	1280x960	12

See also

▸ The *Reading and showing a frame from the depth sensor* recipe in *Chapter 3, Using Low-level Data*

▸ The *Reading and showing a frame from the image sensor (color / IR)* recipe in *Chapter 3, Using Low-level Data*

Retrieving a list of supported video modes for depth stream

From the previous recipe we learned that we can use different video modes for the sensor's output, different resolutions, fps, and pixel formats. We also wrote a table of known supported resolutions and pixel formats. But in case you want to be sure about the list of supported types or if you have a new device and want to know the possible resolutions and pixel formats of one of its sensors, you can easily ask device driver. OpenNI gives us this possibility to retrieve a list of supported video modes for each sensor from the driver itself. In this recipe, we will try to show you how to retrieve a list of supported video modes for the Depth sensor and we will let the user select what video mode to use for our sensor.

Getting ready

Create a project in Visual Studio 2010 and prepare it for working with OpenNI using the *Creating a project in Visual Studio 2010* recipe in this chapter.

How to do it...

Have a look at the following steps:

1. Open your project and then the project's main source code file. Locate this line:

```cpp
int _tmain(int argc, _TCHAR* argv[])
{
```

2. Write the following code snippet above the preceding line of code:

```cpp
char ReadLastCharOfLine()
{
  int newChar = 0;
  int lastChar;
  fflush(stdout);

  do
  {
    lastChar = newChar;
    newChar = getchar();
  }
  while ((newChar != '\n') && (newChar != EOF));
  return (char)lastChar;
}

bool HandleStatus(Status status)
{
  if (status == STATUS_OK)
    return true;
  printf("ERROR: #%d, %s", status,
    OpenNI::getExtendedError());
  ReadLastCharOfLine();
  return false;
}
```

3. Locate this line again:

```cpp
int _tmain(int argc, _TCHAR* argv[])
{
```

4. Write the following code snippet below the preceding line of code:

```
Status status = STATUS_OK;
printf("Scanning machine for devices and loading "
    "modules/drivers ...\r\n");
status = OpenNI::initialize();
if (!HandleStatus(status)) return 1;
printf("Completed.\r\n");

printf("Press ENTER to continue.\r\n");
ReadLastCharOfLine();

printf("Opening any device ...\r\n");
Device device;
status = device.open(ANY_DEVICE);
if (!HandleStatus(status)) return 1;
printf("%s Opened, Completed.\r\n",
  device.getDeviceInfo().getName());

printf("Press ENTER to continue.\r\n");
ReadLastCharOfLine();

printf("Checking if depth stream is supported ...\r\n");
if (false && !device.hasSensor(SENSOR_DEPTH))
{
  printf("Depth stream not supported by this device. "
      "Press ENTER to exit.\r\n");
  ReadLastCharOfLine();
  return 1;
}

printf("Asking device to create a depth stream ...\r\n");
VideoStream sensor;
status = sensor.create(device,SENSOR_DEPTH);
if (!HandleStatus(status)) return 1;
printf("Completed.\r\n");

printf("Retrieving list of possible video modes for this "
      "stream ...\r\n");
const Array<VideoMode> *supportedVideoModes =
  &(sensor.getSensorInfo().getSupportedVideoModes());
int numOfVideoModes = supportedVideoModes->getSize();
if (numOfVideoModes == 0)
{
```

```
        printf("No supported video mode available, press ENTER "
              "to exit.\r\n");
        ReadLastCharOfLine();
        return 1;
    }

    for (int i = 0; i < numOfVideoModes; i++)
    {
        VideoMode vm = (*supportedVideoModes)[i];
        printf("%c. %dx%d at %dfps with %d format \r\n",
              'a' + i,
              vm.getResolutionX(),
              vm.getResolutionY(),
              vm.getFps(),
              vm.getPixelFormat());
    }
    printf("Completed.\r\n");

    int selected = 0;
    do
    {
        printf("Select your desired video mode and then press "
              "ENTER to continue.\r\n");
        selected = ReadLastCharOfLine() - 'a';
    } while (selected < 0 || selected >= numOfVideoModes);

    VideoMode vm = (*supportedVideoModes)[selected];
    printf("%dx%d at %dfps with %d format selected. "
          "Requesting video mode ... \r\n",
        vm.getResolutionX(),
        vm.getResolutionY(),
        vm.getFps(),
        vm.getPixelFormat());
    status = sensor.setVideoMode(vm);
    if (!HandleStatus(status)) return 1;

    printf("Accepted. Starting stream ...\r\n");
    status = sensor.start();
    if (!HandleStatus(status)) return 1;
    printf("Completed.\r\n");

    printf("Press ENTER to exit.\r\n");
    ReadLastCharOfLine();
    sensor.destroy();
    device.close();
    OpenNI::shutdown();
    return 0;
```

How it works...

We defined our `ReadLastCharOfLine()` and `HandleStatus()` methods just like we did previously; read the previous recipes about that.

In the first line of the fourth step, we used the `openni::OpenNI::initialize()` method to initialize OpenNI and load modules and drivers. Again you can read previous recipes for more information.

Then we used the `openni::Device::hasSensor()` method to become sure if accessing the depth stream is possible and if so, then we use a variable of type `openni::VideoStream` to have access to the sensor's stream. These lines are just like the ones in the previous recipe, which talk about how to access a depth stream. Read it for a line-by-line description of code.

Our main code actually started when we defined a variable of type `Array<VideoMode>*` named `supportedVideoModes`. We talked a lot about the `openni::Array` template class in previous recipes, so I don't want to speak too much about it here.

For getting the list of supported video modes we need to call the `openni::SensorInfo::getSupportedVideoModes()` method that is located in the `openni::SensorInfo` class, but actually we don't have the `openni::SensorInfo` object associated with our `openni::VideoStream` that we created previously. So we need to use one of the `openni::VideoStream` methods named `openni::VideoStream::getSensorInfo()` that return the associated `openni::SensorInfo` object for our selected sensor and then using the return value of `openni::SensorInfo::getSupportedVideoModes()`, we can put our hand on the list of supported video modes of our desired sensor:

```
const Array<VideoMode> *supportedVideoModes =
    &(sensor.getSensorInfo().getSupportedVideoModes());
```

Then to make sure that there is at least one supported video mode, we use `openni::Array::getSize()` to get the size of the returned array, and store it in a variable of type `int` named `numOfVideoModes`. If `numOfVideoModes` was equal to 0, there will be no supported video mode and we will show an error to the user and ask to press the *Enter* key. Then it returns 1 so as to terminate the program execution; but if it wasn't 0, then we can loop through this array and show its members to the user and ask him/her to select the desired video mode.

```
int numOfVideoModes = supportedVideoModes->getSize();
if (numOfVideoModes == 0)
{
  printf("No supported video mode available, press ENTER "
        "to exit.\r\n");
  ReadLastCharOfLine();
  return 1;
}
```

```
for (int i = 0; i < numOfVideoModes; i++)
{
  ...
}
```

In this loop we used a variable of type `openni::VideoMode` to temporarily store one of array's members , so as to show it to the user. Then using its method to return its properties and using `printf()`, we displayed different properties of this video mode to the user.

```
VideoMode vm = (*supportedVideoModes)[i];
printf("%c. %dx%d at %dfps with %d format \r\n",
    'a' + i,
    vm.getResolutionX(),
    vm.getResolutionY(),
    vm.getFps(),
    vm.getPixelFormat());
```

You may question why we used `'a' + i` here. Actually the reason behind doing this is related to the ASCII code of characters. We know that the ASCII code for `'a'` is 97 and other characters in the table follow this number (`'b'` is 98 and so on); so using this code (and keeping in mind that the value of `i` increases during the loop) we can print a character for each item in the list. So we can use these characters later to recognize the user's selection.

Going more deeply into the code you can see the usage of different methods of the `openni::VideoMode` class. Their names are self-describing and we don't see any reason to describe them one by one.

You can guess now that our next move is to ask the user to input one of these characters to show which video mode he/she selected.

```
int selected = 0;
do
{
  printf("Select your desired video mode and then press "
         "ENTER to continue.\r\n");
  selected = ReadLastCharOfLine() - 'a';
} while (selected < 0 || selected >= numOfVideoModes);
```

As you can see we put our question and calling of `ReadLastCharOfLine()` method in a `do while` loop; we did that because we want to make sure that the user selects a character in the range of our options; and if he/she puts an incorrect input, we can ask him/her to do it again.

Here we have the same point as the last part of the code; we used `'a'` character again but this time for reading the user input. As we know, the `ReadLastCharOfLine()` method will return the last character typed before the user presses the *Enter* key. This character can be converted to `int`. On the other hand, we don't need a character but we need to know the index of the selected video mode in the array. This is achieved using a simple subtraction of returned values of the `ReadLastCharOfLine()` method and the `'a'` character. We can extract the index of the selected video mode by this method. You may ask how, so read the last 20 lines and think about the ASCII table and the order of characters again.

Anyway, using this number, which is an index of the selected video mode in our array, we can show the user his/her chosen item and then ask the sensor to use this video mode.

```
VideoMode vm = (*supportedVideoModes)[selected];
printf("%dx%d at %dfps with %d format selected. "
       "Requesting video mode ... \r\n",
    vm.getResolutionX(),
    vm.getResolutionY(),
    vm.getFps(),
    vm.getPixelFormat());
status = sensor.setVideoMode(vm);
if (!HandleStatus(status)) return 1;
```

Then we will ask the sensor to start generating data and after that we need to read the data, but reading the data is not part of this topic so we end it without really using the sensor's data.

```
printf("Accepted. Starting stream ...\r\n");
status = sensor.start();
if (!HandleStatus(status)) return 1;
printf("Completed.\r\n");

printf("Press ENTER to exit.\r\n");
```

```
ReadLastCharOfLine();
sensor.destroy();
device.close();
OpenNI::shutdown();
return 0;
```

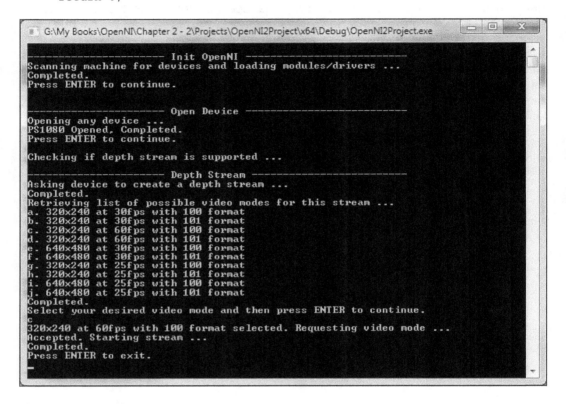

See also

▶ The *Reading and showing a frame from the depth sensor* recipe in *Chapter 3, Using Low-level Data*

Selecting a specific device for accessing depth stream

We discussed about how to retrieve a list of connected devices but we never used this data to select one of those devices; we always used ANY_DEVICE as the parameter for the openni::Device::open() method without even asking ourselves what this parameter is.

In this recipe, we will show you how to select your desired device and open it. Then create `openni::VideoStream` for the depth sensor of this device.

But first let's talk about the `openni::Device::open()` method. Actually this method has a parameter of type string (actually a character array) containing the hardware location (Uri) of the desired device. We always used `ANY_DEVICE` as the parameter of this method until now, but actually `ANY_DEVICE` is equal to `null` and is used only for better reading of code. When passing `null` as the parameter of this method, OpenNI automatically selects the first device in the list of loaded and recognized devices. So if we want to select our desired device we need to use its `Uri` as the parameter of this method. On the other hand, we need to know our device Uri and the only way to know it is to get the list of connected devices from OpenNI that we did in the earlier recipe.

We will talk more about code in the later sections, but for now let's see how we can do it in code.

Also we recommend reading the *Enumerating the list of connected devices* recipe of this chapter before reading the *How it works...* section of this recipe.

Getting ready

Create a project in Visual Studio 2010 and prepare it for working with OpenNI using the *Creating a project in Visual Studio 2010* recipe in this chapter.

How to do it...

Have a look at the following steps:

1. Open your project and then the main source code file. Locate this line:

    ```
    int _tmain(int argc, _TCHAR* argv[])
    {
    ```

2. Write the following code snippet above the preceding line of code:

    ```
    char ReadLastCharOfLine()
    {
      int newChar = 0;
      int lastChar;
      fflush(stdout);
      do
      {
        lastChar = newChar;
        newChar = getchar();
      }
    ```

```
    while ((newChar != '\n') && (newChar != EOF));
    return (char)lastChar;
  }


bool HandleStatus(Status status)
{
  if (status == STATUS_OK)
    return true;
  printf("ERROR: #%d, %s", status,
    OpenNI::getExtendedError());
  ReadLastCharOfLine();
  return false;
}
```

3. Locate this line again:

```
int _tmain(int argc, _TCHAR* argv[])
{
```

4. Write the following code snippet below the preceding line of code:

```
Status status = STATUS_OK;
printf("Scanning machine for devices and loading "
    "modules/drivers ...\r\n");
status = OpenNI::initialize();
if (!HandleStatus(status)) return 1;
printf("Completed.\r\n");
printf("Press ENTER to continue.\r\n");
ReadLastCharOfLine();

printf("Retrieving list of connected devices ...\r\n");
openni::Array<openni::DeviceInfo> listOfDevices;
openni::OpenNI::enumerateDevices(&listOfDevices);
int numberOfDevices = listOfDevices.getSize();
if (numberOfDevices > 0){
printf("%d Device(s) are available to use.\r\n\r\n",
    numberOfDevices);
  for (int i = 0; i < numberOfDevices; i++)
  {
    openni::DeviceInfo device = listOfDevices[i];
    printf("%c. %s->%s (VID: %d | PID: %d) is connected "
        "at %s\r\n", 'a' + i,
      device.getVendor(),
      device.getName(),
      device.getUsbVendorId(),
      device.getUsbProductId(),
```

```
        device.getUri());
    }
  }else{
    printf("No device connected to this machine.");
  }

  int selected = 0;
  do
  {
    printf("Select your desired device and then press "
        "ENTER to continue.\r\n");
    selected = ReadLastCharOfLine() - 'a';
  } while (selected < 0 || selected >= numberOfDevices);

  DeviceInfo di = listOfDevices[selected];
  printf("%s->%s (VID: %d | PID: %d) Selected\r\n",
    di.getVendor(),
    di.getName(),
    di.getUsbVendorId(),
    di.getUsbProductId());

  printf("Opening device at %s ...\r\n", di.getUri());
  Device device;
  status = device.open(di.getUri());
  if (!HandleStatus(status)) return 1;
  printf("%s Opened, Completed.\r\n",
    device.getDeviceInfo().getName());

  printf("Press ENTER to continue.\r\n");
  ReadLastCharOfLine();

  printf("Checking if depth stream is supported ...\r\n");
  if (false && !device.hasSensor(SENSOR_DEPTH))
  {
    printf("Depth stream not supported by this device. "
        "Press ENTER to exit.\r\n");
    ReadLastCharOfLine();
    return 1;
  }
  printf("Asking device to create a depth stream ...\r\n");
  VideoStream sensor;
  status = sensor.create(device, SENSOR_DEPTH);
  if (!HandleStatus(status)) return 1;
  printf("Completed.\r\n");
```

```
printf("Starting stream ...\r\n");
status = sensor.start();
if (!HandleStatus(status)) return 1;
printf("Completed.\r\n");

printf("Press ENTER to exit.\r\n");
ReadLastCharOfLine();
OpenNI::shutdown();
sensor.destroy();
device.close();
return 0;
```

How it works...

We defined our `ReadLastCharOfLine()` and `HandleStatus()` methods just like we did previously; read the previous recipes about that.

In the first line of the second step we used the `openni::OpenNI::initialize()` method to initialize OpenNI and load modules and drivers. Again you can read the last recipes for more information.

As you can see, most of the lines are same as in the previous recipe code but with some major changes; we will not list video modes, but we will list all devices and ask the user to select one of the devices to access its depth sensor.

Read the previous recipes to see how to retrieve and show the list of connected devices and how to request data stream of the depth sensor.

As you can see we used `openni::Array<openni:DeviceInfo>` to create an array that can be used as a parameter of the `openni::OpenNI::enumerateDevices()` method to get the list of connected devices.

```
openni::Array<openni::DeviceInfo> listOfDevices;
openni::OpenNI::enumerateDevices(&listOfDevices);
```

Then we printed the name and other properties of each device along with a unique character before the name of each device, which will help us recognize the user input later.

```
openni::DeviceInfo device = listOfDevices[i];
printf("%c. %s->%s (VID: %d | PID: %d) is connected "
    "at %s\r\n",
  'a' + i,
  device.getVendor(),
  device.getName(),
  device.getUsbVendorId(),
  device.getUsbProductId(),
  device.getUri());
```

Just like in the previous recipe, we used a `do while` loop to read the user input.

```
int selected = 0;
do
{
printf("Select your desired device and then press "
        "ENTER to continue.\r\n");
  selected = ReadLastCharOfLine() - 'a';
} while (selected < 0 || selected >= numberOfDevices);
```

Using the user input we can calculate the selected index in our array of devices, then we can show the selected device to the user, and use its information to open a device.

```
DeviceInfo di = listOfDevices[selected];
printf("%s->%s (VID: %d | PID: %d) Selected\r\n",
  di.getVendor(),
  di.getName(),
  di.getUsbVendorId(),
  di.getUsbProductId());

printf("Opening device at %s ...\r\n", di.getUri());
Device device;
status = device.open(di.getUri());
if (!HandleStatus(status)) return 1;
printf("%s Opened, Completed.\r\n",
  device.getDeviceInfo().getName());
```

Please note that `listOfDevices` is an array of `openni::DeviceInfo`, so we can't use this object to access sensors or other information. This object only contains information about connected devices such as product identification and hardware Uri. But we can use the hardware Uri of a device to initialize and open access to it. This is what we did in the code.

After that we will define a variable of type `openni::VideoStream` and ask it to associate to the data stream of device's depth sensor; then we ask the variable to start generating data, just like how we did in the _Accessing video streams (depth/IR/RGB) and configuring them_ recipe of this chapter.

And of course we don't want to speak about how to use the output of the `openni::VideoStream` in this chapter, so we can shut OpenNI down and terminate our application by returning 0.

```
printf("Checking if depth stream is supported ...\r\n");
if (false && !device.hasSensor(SENSOR_DEPTH))
{
  printf("Depth stream not supported by this device. "
      "Press ENTER to exit.\r\n");
  ReadLastCharOfLine();
```

```
    return 1;
}

printf("Asking device to create a depth stream ...\r\n");
VideoStream sensor;
status = sensor.create(device, SENSOR_DEPTH);
if (!HandleStatus(status)) return 1;
printf("Completed.\r\n");

printf("Starting stream ...\r\n");
status = sensor.start();
if (!HandleStatus(status)) return 1;
printf("Completed.\r\n");

printf("Press ENTER to exit.\r\n");
ReadLastCharOfLine();
sensor.destroy();
device.close();
OpenNI::shutdown();
return 0;
```

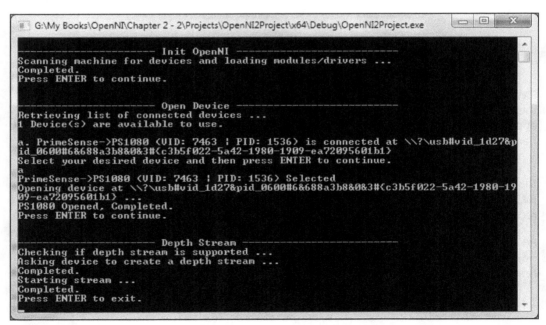

See also

- ▸ The *Enumerating a list of connected devices* recipe
- ▸ The *Listening to the device connect and disconnect events* recipe
- ▸ The *Reading and showing a frame from the depth sensor* recipe in *Chapter 3, Using Low-level Data*

Listening to the device connect and disconnect events

We learned how to get a list of connected devices from OpenNI, but here we want to use one of the new features of OpenNI 2. OpenNI 2 lets us introduce two methods that we want to be executed when there is any new device connected or disconnected. Using this ability we want to define two methods and introduce them to OpenNI as a callback for these two events (connect and disconnect). Our methods will only print a line to the console to show the user what happened, but you can use this feature to wait until the user connects a device or warn the user when a device is disconnected; or you can at least update the list of connected devices without using a timer to refresh it.

Getting ready

Create a project in Visual Studio 2010 and prepare it for working with OpenNI using the *Creating a project in Visual Studio 2010* recipe in this chapter.

How to do it...

Have a look at the following steps:

1. Open your project and then the project's main source code file. Locate this line:

```
int _tmain(int argc, _TCHAR* argv[])
{
```

2. Write the following code snippet above the preceding line of code:

```
char ReadLastCharOfLine()
{
  int newChar = 0;
  int lastChar;
  fflush(stdout);
  do
  {
    lastChar = newChar;
```

```
      newChar = getchar();
   }
   while ((newChar != '\n') && (newChar != EOF));
   return (char)lastChar;
  }


bool HandleStatus(Status status)
{
  if (status == STATUS_OK)
    return true;
  printf("ERROR: #%d, %s", status,
    OpenNI::getExtendedError());
  ReadLastCharOfLine();
  return false;
}
  struct OurOpenNIEventMonitorer :
  public OpenNI::DeviceDisconnectedListener,
    public OpenNI::DeviceConnectedListener
  void onDeviceConnected(const DeviceInfo* device){
    printf("%d. %s->%s (VID: %d | PID: %d) Connected "
        "to %s\r\n",
      clock(),
      device->getVendor(),
      device->getName(),
      device->getUsbVendorId(),
      device->getUsbProductId(),
      device->getUri());
  }
  void onDeviceDisconnected(const DeviceInfo* device){
    printf("%d. %s->%s (VID: %d | PID: %d) Disconnected "
        "from %s\r\n",
      clock(),
      device->getVendor(),
      device->getName(),
      device->getUsbVendorId(),
      device->getUsbProductId(),
      device->getUri());
  }
};
```

3. Locate this line again:

```
int _tmain(int argc, _TCHAR* argv[])
{
```

4. Write the following code snippet below the preceding line of code:

```
Status status = STATUS_OK;
printf("Scanning machine for devices and loading "
       "modules/drivers ...\r\n");
status = OpenNI::initialize();
if (!HandleStatus(status)) return 1;
printf("Completed. Adding listener ...\r\n");

  OurOpenNIEventMonitorer eventMonitorer;
  status =
    OpenNI::addDeviceConnectedListener(&eventMonitorer);
  if (!HandleStatus(status)) return 1;
  status =
    OpenNI::addDeviceDisconnectedListener(&eventMonitorer);
  if (!HandleStatus(status)) return 1;

printf("Done. Listening to OpenNI's event, Press ENTER "
       "to exit.\r\n");
ReadLastCharOfLine();
OpenNI::shutdown();
return 0;
```

How it works...

We defined our `ReadLastCharOfLine()` and `HandleStatus()` methods just like we did previously; you can read the previous recipes about that.

For the first time in this chapter you can see other lines next to the definition of these two methods. Actually you can see that we defined a structure and two methods within that.

So we defined a structure named `OurOpenNIEventMonitorer`; but wait a minute, let's forget this structure and speak about the procedure of listening to an event. Prior to OpenNI 2, when we wanted to listen to an event, we were required to define a function and then introduce it to OpenNI as a callback method for that event. This procedure in OpenNI 2 is slightly different. We don't need to introduce methods to OpenNI; instead; we must introduce structures or classes to OpenNI as the listener for each event.

That's why we defined a new structure named `OurOpenNIEventMonitorer`. This structure inherits the `OpenNI::DeviceDisconnectedListener` and `OpenNI::DeviceConnectedListener` classes. The reason for the relationship between our new structure and these two classes is that we need to send our structure as a parameter to the `openni::OpenNI::addDeviceConnectedListener()` and `openni::OpenNI::addDeviceDisconnectedListener()` methods later and these methods accept only a parameter of these two types or their child. This is because OpenNI needs to know a way to recognize methods and using a virtual class is the best way to do it.

> Here we mean a class with virtual methods; we don't have anything named virtual class by definition in C++ — don't confuse it with virtual base class or pure virtual class (abstract class).

`OpenNI::DeviceDisconnectedListener`, `OpenNI::DeviceConnectedListener`, and `openni::OpenNI::DeviceStateChangedListener` each contains one method: `openni::OpenNI::DeviceDisconnectedListener::onDeviceDisconnected()`, `openni::OpenNI::DeviceConnectedListener::onDeviceConnected()`, and `openni::OpenNI::DeviceStateChangedListener::onDeviceStateChanged()`, respectively. These methods are virtual methods, meaning that they are changeable by child class (or structure); so, when we inherit from these classes, we can override these methods and write our own methods.

> If you are a .Net or Java developer, you may ask how a structure can inherit a class. Actually, in C++ there is no difference between a structure and a class except in the default access modifier of members. So you can change the definition of `OurOpenNIEventMonitorer` to class if you want. The only reason we used structure to define `OurOpenNIEventMonitorer` is to show you that you can use structures too.

```cpp
struct OurOpenNIEventMonitorer :
    public OpenNI::DeviceDisconnectedListener,
    public OpenNI::DeviceConnectedListener
{
void onDeviceConnected(const DeviceInfo* device){
    printf("%d. %s->%s (VID: %d | PID: %d) Connected "
        "to %s\r\n",
        clock(),
        device->getVendor(),
        device->getName(),
```

```
                device->getUsbVendorId(),
                device->getUsbProductId(),
                device->getUri());
      }
      void onDeviceDisconnected(const DeviceInfo* device){
        printf("%d. %s->%s (VID: %d | PID: %d) Disconnected "
            "from %s\r\n",
            clock(),
            device->getVendor(),
            device->getName(),
            device->getUsbVendorId(),
            device->getUsbProductId(),
            device->getUri());
      }
   };
```

As you can see, our structure has two methods and both of them do a simple write to the console about any change that occurs.

The clock() function is used to show the order of events. clock() returns the number of milliseconds from the time the program execution started in Windows and the number of milliseconds you used for CPU time in Linux.

In the second step we initialized OpenNI using openni:OpenNI:initialize() just like always and then we defined a variable of type OurOpenNIEventMonitorer named eventMonitorer. We sent this newly created variable as a parameter to both openni::OpenNI::addDeviceConnectedListener() and openni::OpenNI::addDeviceDisconnectedListener() methods.

```
      OurOpenNIEventMonitorer eventMonitorer;
      status =
        OpenNI::addDeviceConnectedListener(&eventMonitorer);
      if (!HandleStatus(status)) return 1;
      status =
        OpenNI::addDeviceDisconnectedListener(&eventMonitorer);
      if (!HandleStatus(status)) return 1;
```

If the returned `openni::Status` shows no error, we are already listening to device events and there is nothing to do after that except to prevent the program from terminating. The best way to do it is to ask the user to press *Enter* to terminate the execution of the application. And until that time, OpenNI will execute our methods in the `OurOpenNIEventMonitorer` structure when any device connects or disconnects.

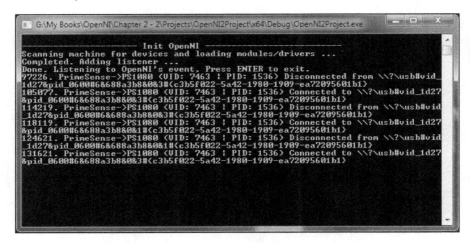

There's more...

Apart from the two events we discarded, there is another event named `DeviceChangedStatus`. Also it is possible to stop listening to an event. Read more about these two topics.

Device state changed event

There is another listener for the OpenNI class named `openni::OpenNI::DeviceStateChangedListener`. You can inherit this class, override its `openni::OpenNI::DeviceStateChangedListener::onDeviceStateChanged()` method, and listen to this event.

You can add and remove listening to this event using the `openni::OpenNI::addDeviceStateChangedListener()` and `openni::OpenNI::removeDeviceStateChangedListener()` methods.

Stop listening to events

We can use the `openni::OpenNI::removeDeviceConnectedListener()`, `openni::OpenNI::removeDeviceDisconnectedListener()`, and `openni::OpenNI::removeDeviceStateChangedListener()` methods to remove our structure (or class) from the list of listeners of events. This will stop listening events. This method has the same signature as `openni::OpenNI::addDeviceConnectedListener()`, `openni::OpenNI::addDeviceDisconnectedListener()`, and `openni::OpenNI::addDeviceStateChangedListener()`.

See also

▶ The *Event-based reading of data* recipe in *Chapter 3, Using Low-level Data*

▶ The *Enumerating a list of connected devices* recipe

Opening an already recorded file (ONI file) instead of a device

Prior to the *Selecting a specific device for accessing depth stream* recipe of this chapter we used ANY_DEVICE as the parameter of the openni::Device::open() method to open the first device and access its sensors. In the *Selecting a specific device for accessing depth stream* recipe of this chapter we learned that we can select what device to open by sending its hardware Uri to the openni::OpenNI::open() method. And in this recipe, we will learn another use of the openni::OpenNI::open() method.

You will find out how to record data from different sensors of a device to a file in the later sections of the chapter, but now we want to show how to re-open them as an individual device (just like when we open a physical device) and access saved data streams).

Getting ready

Create a project in Visual Studio 2010 and prepare it for working with OpenNI using the *Creating a project in Visual Studio 2010* recipe in this chapter.

You can find a sample file in the downloadable content of this book. Refer to the recipe's directory for the source code and **ONI file**.

How to do it...

Have a look at the following steps:

1. Open your project and then the project's main source code file. Locate this line:

```
int _tmain(int argc, _TCHAR* argv[])
{
```

2. Write the following code snippet above the preceding line of code:

```
char ReadLastCharOfLine()
{
  int newChar = 0;
  int lastChar;
  fflush(stdout);
  do
```

```
      {
        lastChar = newChar;
        newChar = getchar();
      }
      while ((newChar != '\n') && (newChar != EOF));
      return (char)lastChar;
    }


  bool HandleStatus(Status status)
  {
    if (status == STATUS_OK)
      return true;
    printf("ERROR: #%d, %s", status,
      OpenNI::getExtendedError());
    ReadLastCharOfLine();
    return false;
  }
```

3. Locate this line again:

```
  int _tmain(int argc, _TCHAR* argv[])
  {
```

4. Write the following code snippet below the preceding line of code:

```
    Status status = STATUS_OK;
    printf("Scanning machine for devices and loading "
        "modules/drivers ...\r\n");
    status = OpenNI::initialize();
    if (!HandleStatus(status)) return 1;
    printf("Completed.\r\n");

    printf("Press ENTER to continue.\r\n");
    ReadLastCharOfLine();

    char* addressOfFile =
        "C:\\\\MultipleHands_From_OpenNIorg.oni";
    printf("Opening ONI file from %s as device ...\r\n",
        addressOfFile);
    Device device;
    status = device.open(addressOfFile);
    if (!HandleStatus(status)) return 1;
    printf("%s Opened, Completed.\r\n",
      device.getDeviceInfo().getName());

    printf("Press ENTER to continue.\r\n");
```

```
ReadLastCharOfLine();

printf("Checking if depth stream is supported ...\r\n");
if (false && !device.hasSensor(SENSOR_DEPTH))
{
  printf("Depth stream not supported by this device. "
      "Press ENTER to exit.\r\n");
  ReadLastCharOfLine();
  return 1;
}

printf("Asking device to create a depth stream ...\r\n");
VideoStream sensor;
status = sensor.create(device, SENSOR_DEPTH);
if (!HandleStatus(status)) return 1;
printf("Completed.\r\n");

printf("Starting stream ...\r\n");
status = sensor.start();
if (!HandleStatus(status)) return 1;
printf("Completed.\r\n");

printf("Press ENTER to exit.\r\n");
ReadLastCharOfLine();
sensor.destroy();
device.close();
OpenNI::shutdown();
return 0;
```

How it works...

We defined our `ReadLastCharOfLine()` and `HandleStatus()` methods just like we did previously; read the previous recipes about that.

As you can see, most of the lines in the code are the same as the ones in the older recipes such as the *Accessing video stream (depth/IR/RGB) and configuring them* recipe or the *Selecting a specific device for accessing depth stream* recipe. There is only one minor change in the opening device:

```
char* addressOfFile =
    "C:\\\\MultipleHands_From_OpenNIorg.oni";
printf("Opening ONI file from %s as device ...\r\n",
      addressOfFile);
Device device;
status = device.open(addressOfFile);
```

As it is brightly visible, we used the address of our file instead of the hardware Uri as the parameter of the openni::OpenNI::open() method.

```
G:\My Books\OpenNI\Chapter 2 - 2\Projects\OpenNI2Project\x64\Debug\OpenNI2Project.exe

---------------------- Init OpenNI ----------------------
Scanning machine for devices and loading modules/drivers ...
Completed.
Press ENTER to continue.


---------------------- Open Device ----------------------
Opening ONI file from C:\\MultipleHands_From_OpenNIorg.oni as device ...
 Opened, Completed.
Press ENTER to continue.


---------------------- Depth Stream ----------------------
Checking if depth stream is supported ...
Asking device to create a depth stream ...
Completed.
Starting stream ...
Completed.
Press ENTER to exit.
```

There's more...

Actually ONI files are like multichannel video files that can be used later to read color, IR, or depth data streams. Thinking from this perspective, we can guess that it is possible to change the speed of playing, even skip some frames, and so on; and actually it is possible and the way to do these customizations is via using the openni::PlaybackControl class. You can read more about this class and a sample code in *Chapter 3, Using Low-level Data*.

See also

- ▶ The *Recording streams to file (ONI file)* recipe in *Chapter 3, Using Low-level Data*
- ▶ The *Controlling the player when opening a device* from file recipe in *Chapter 3, Using Low-level Data*

3
Using Low-level Data

In this chapter, we will cover the following recipes:

- ► Configuring Visual Studio 2010 to use OpenGL
- ► Initializing and preparing OpenGL
- ► Reading and showing a frame from the image sensor (color/IR)
- ► Reading and showing a frame from the depth sensor
- ► Controlling the player when opening a device from file
- ► Recording streams to file (ONI file)
- ► Event-based reading of data

Introduction

In the previous chapter, we learned how to initialize sensors and configure their output in the way we want. In this chapter, we will introduce ways to read this data and show it to the user.

This chapter is not about advanced or high-level (middleware) outputs. For now, we are going to talk only about native OpenNI outputs: color, IR, and depth.

But before anything, we need to know about some of OpenNI's related classes.

VideoFrameRef object

Unlike the OpenNI 1.x era, where there were different classes for reading frames of data from sensors, known as **MetaData** types, here we have only one class to read data from any sensor, called openni::VideoFrameRef. This is just as in the previous chapter, where we had the openni::VideoStream class for accessing different sensors instead of one Generator class per sensor.

But let's forget about OpenNI 1.x. We are here to talk about OpenNI 2.x. In OpenNI 2.x, you don't need different classes to access frames; the only thing you need is the `openni::VideoFrameRef` class.

Every time we want to read one frame from a sensor's stream, we need to ask its `openni::VideoStream` object to read that frame from the device and give us access to it. This can be done by calling the `openni::VideoStream::readFrame()` method. The return value of this method is `openni::Status`, which can be used to find out whether the operation ended successfully or not. And if so, we can use the `openni::VideoFrameRef` variable, which we sent to this method as a parameter before, to access the frame data.

That's it. Simple enough; but you need to know that this operation may not finish immediately if there is no information available to read. For understanding this behavior, it is better to think about network streams (sockets) in socket programming. In socket programming, sockets have 2 different modes: the blocking and non-blocking modes. When you are in the blocking mode, a read request will wait until there is some data to return. In OpenNI 2.x, we have the same behavior. When we request to read a frame from `openni::VideoStream` as proxy for the physical sensor, OpenNI will wait for a frame to become ready or it may return the last unread frame instantly, if there was one.

Let's talk a bit more about `openni::VideoFrameRef`. `openni::VideoFrameRef` has a number of methods that can be used to get more information about the returned frame but the most important one is `openni::VideoFrameRef::getData()`. This method returns a pointer with the undefined data type (`void*`) to the first pixel of the frame.

The data type of the returned data must be known before reading and processing it. To find out what the data type of the data is, we can use the `openni::VideoFrameRef::getVideoMode()` method. We can also request another data type by setting a new `VideoMode` class for the sensor. Following is a list of data types for different pixel formats:

- `unsigned char`: It is usable when we want to read from a frame with the `openni::PixelFormat::PIXEL_FORMAT_GRAY8` pixel format. Each pixel in 8-bit grayscale is 1 byte (in C++ we know bytes as chars) with a range of 0-255.

- `OniDepthPixel`: From its name, it is clear that this data type is the main data type when we want to read depth data from a frame with the `openni::PixelFormat::PIXEL_FORMAT_DEPTH_1_MM` or `openni::PixelFormat::PIXEL_FORMAT_DEPTH_100_UM` pixel format. `OniDepthPixel` is actually an `unsigned short` data type(also known as `UINT16` or `uint16_t`).

- `OniRGB888Pixel`: It is a structure containing 3 `unsigned char` data types for representing the color of a pixel and is used when the pixel format of a frame is `openni::PixelFormat::PIXEL_FORMAT_RGB888`. Blue, green, and red are the three values of this structure.

- ▶ `OniGrayscale16Pixel:` Just as with `OniDepthPixel`, this data type is only an alias to `unsigned short` (also known as `UINT16` or `uint16_t`) when the frame has the `openni::PixelFormat::PIXEL_FORMAT_GRAY16` pixel format.

- ▶ `OniYUV422DoublePixel:` It is a structure containing four `unsigned char` data types for representing colors of two pixels and is used when the pixel format of a frame is `openni::PixelFormat::PIXEL_FORMAT_YUV422`.

After knowing the data type of the returned frame, you can increase the pointer with the size of the returned data type and retrieve the following pixels one by one.

> The most important method is `openni::VideoFrameRef::getData()`, which returns a pointer with the undefined data type (`void*`) to the first pixel of the frame.

One of the other useful methods is `openni::VideoFrameRef::getStrideInBytes();` the return value of this method is of the `int` type and shows the number of bytes each row of image has, including padding if any. To understand this better, let's review how images can be stored in memory; going against what we know about an image as a two-dimensional array of pixels, they are actually stored in a one-dimensional array of pixels in memory and there is no sign where a row ends and a new row begins. The program itself must take care of that by knowing the width and height of the image before starting to read its data. This is simple and can be done by multiplying the image width with the size of the image's pixel format in bytes. Each pixel holds a number of bytes in memory depending upon the image's pixel format; for example, an image in RGB24 has 3 bytes of data per pixel in memory. So an image with a size of 640 x 480 in RGB24 (also called RGB888) has 921600 (`ImageWidth x Image Height x SizeOfEachPixel`) bytes of data and each row starts after 1920 (`ImageWidth x SizeOfEachPixel`) bytes of data. This is a simple approach, but that's not always the case. An image can have padding after each row (unused bytes) and this can break our code. Actually, no one can be sure about padding and the size of padding except the program that wrote this image to memory; and in this case, only OpenNI knows how we need to read data from memory. That's why we have `openni::VideoFrameRef::getStrideInBytes()`. As we had previously said, this method will return the number of bytes that you must add to the current row's first pixel position to have the next row's first pixel; and even though this number is equal to `ImageWidth x SizeOfEachPixel` most of the time, it is much safer to use this method instead.

> One of the other useful methods is `openni::VideoFrameRef::get StrideInBytes();` the return value of this method is of the `int` type and it shows the number of bytes each row of the image has, including padding if any.

There are other methods too, such as the following:

- `openni::VideoFrameRef::getDataSize()`: Here, the returned value is equal to the number of bytes of the frame.
- `openni::VideoFrameRef::getSensorType()`: Here, the returned value is an `openni::SensorType` object showing the type of parent sensor (depth, IR, or color).
- `openni::VideoFrameRef::getWidth()`: This returns the number of pixels in each row of the frame.
- `openni::VideoFrameRef::getHeight()`: This returns the number of rows of the frame.
- `openni::VideoFrameRef::getVideoMode()`: This returns an object of type `openni::VideoMode`, which holds the current frame's video mode information, including expected width, height, pixel format, and fps. But the only important value is pixel format, because values of width and height are not trustable. It is better to use `openni::VideoFrameRef::getWidth()` and `openni::VideoFrameRef::getHeight()` instead.
- `openni::VideoFrameRef::getTimestamp()`: This returns the frame generation time in milliseconds from the start of the sensor.
- `openni::VideoFrameRef::getFrameIndex()`: This returns the index of the returned frame from the start of the sensor.

There are plenty of other methods that we will discuss in other chapters.

For now, let's take a look at the following image to get an idea about each method's return value:

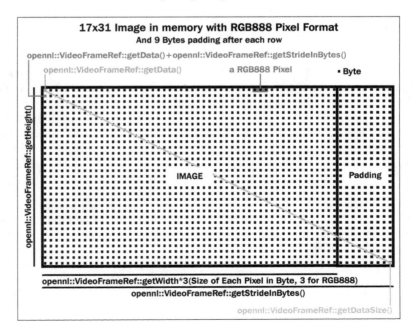

Please note that this image has a width of 17 pixels, a height of 31 pixels, and an RGB888 (also called RGB24) pixel format, meaning that every 3 bytes is equivalent to 1 pixel. Also, the previous sample has 9 bytes of padding after each pixel; in reality, though, it may have no padding at all.

Back to the OpenNI object again

We already know about the `openni::OpenNI` object from the previous chapter. We are going to introduce a method of `openni::OpenNI` here that we have never talked about before.

In the previous section, we had seen that when using `openni::VideoStream::readFrame()`, we can't be sure about the immediate response from this method. This is not a big problem if you want to use one thread for each receiving process; for example, a thread for receiving depth and another for receiving color frames along with a thread to get input from the user and control the other two. In this case, two threads wait for a new frame to become available independent of each other and the third thread. But what if you want to wait for a new frame from two different sources (different sensors or different devices) in the same thread? In this case, one operation may block another and this may create a big frame-rate drop. This can become worse if you decide to receive the user's input in the same thread too. But this is exactly what we want to do in all the recipes of this chapter. And yes, we know writing a multithread application is good in current multicore PCs, but it is not always necessary, especially in this case when there is no big calculation in any thread and they are idle most of the time, waiting for a new frame; also, we don't want to make our code hard to read or understand by using third-party libraries for performing multithread operations.

For solving this problem, we need to have a method to tell us if one of the streams has new data to read. And we have a method with the same functionality here in OpenNI, named `openni::OpenNI::waitForAnyStream()`. This method receives one or more `openni::VideoStream` objects and tells you which one has any new data to read. This method also has a time-out parameter that can be used to wait until one of the streams has any data. For example, if you want to read from two or more `openni::VideoStream` objects and want to know which one has a new frame, you can call `openni::OpenNI::waitForAnyStream()` in a loop with a high time-out value, since you don't need to do anything else except read frames. But if you want to do something else (for example, check user input and at the same time wait for a new frame to become ready), you can call `openni::OpenNI::waitForAnyStream()` with 0 or a very small time-out parameter. We will be doing this in the recipes of this chapter.

<h1>Configuring Visual Studio 2010 to use OpenGL</h1>

As we need to show the result of the color, IR, and/or depth sensors to the user, we must use an interface. Here we choose to use OpenGL to show data to the user because it is multiplatformed and you can convert your code to other platforms easily later on, if you want to. OpenNI's samples use OpenGL too. But you can also go for **DirectX** or other types of interfaces capable of displaying 2D images, such as **Graphics Device Interface** (**GDI**).

Follow this recipe to add OpenGL to a Microsoft Visual Studio 2010 C++ project.

Getting ready

Create and configure a project using the *Creating a project in Visual Studio 2010* recipe of *Chapter 2, Open NI and C++.*

In this recipe we used the OpenGL Utility Toolkit to make working with OpenGL easier. You can download the GLUT library and header files from this website or use the `glut.zip` file in this chapter's downloadable content. Unfortunately, the official site offers 32-Bit binaries only which can be downloaded at:

`http://user.xmission.com/~nate/glut.html`

Apart from these, GLUT is available at the following addresses for download too:

32-Bit and 64-Bit: `http://www.falahati.net/opengl/glut.zip`

32-Bit and 64-Bit: `http://www.idfun.de/glut64/`

Follow this recipe for instructions on how to install and use it.

How to do it...

We need to open our **Project Property** window and introduce glut libraries and headers to our project and Visual Studio 2010 (actually to the compiler, linker, and debugger).

For doing so, open the project created in the *Creating a project in Visual Studio 2010* recipe of *Chapter 2, Open NI and C++* , with Visual Studio 2010 and then carry out the following steps:

1. Create a folder somewhere and extract `glut.zip` there. We created a folder named GLUT in `C:` and extracted the archive there but you can extract it anywhere you want to. Then you need to change this recipe a little. Let's assume you did what we did and used `C:\GLUT` as an extraction folder.

2. Right-click on the project name from the **Solution Explorer** window, which is usually located at the top-right, and click on **Properties**.

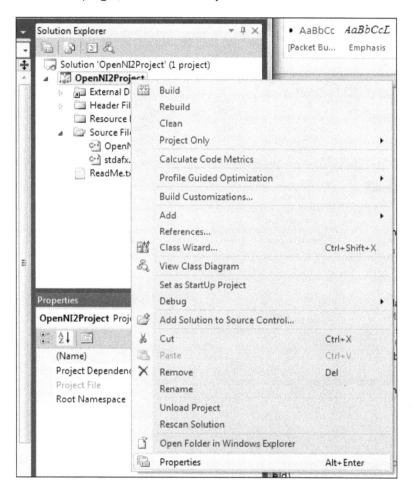

3. Select **All Configurations** from the top-left dropdown (the **Configuration** dropdown) and **x64** from the top-right dropdown (the **Platform** dropdown).

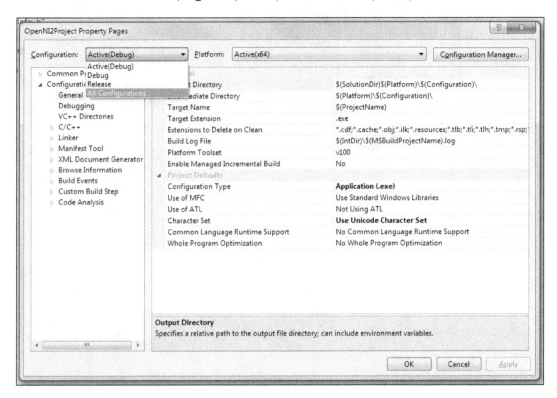

4. Locate the **C/C++** section and expand it. Select the **General** node and edit **Additional Include Directories** (using the down arrow located to the right of this field), add C:\GLUT, and then click on **OK**.

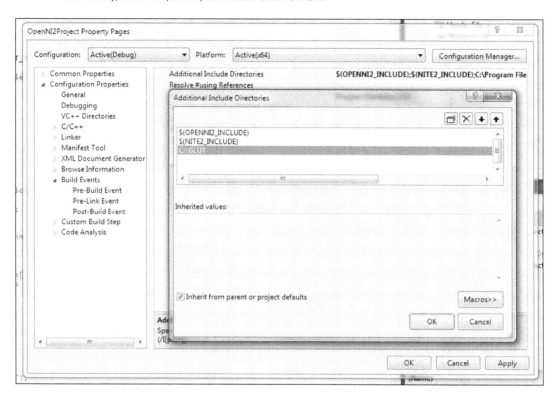

5. Locate the **Linker** section and expand it. Select the **General** node and edit **Additional Library Directories**, add C:\GLUT, and then click on **OK**.

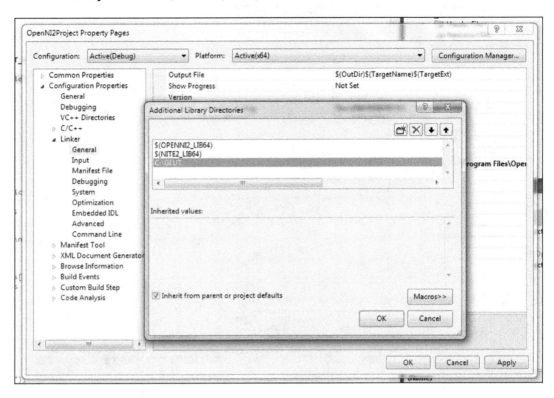

6. Select the **Input** node (in the same section as **Linker**), edit **Additional Dependencies**, add `glut64.lib`, and then click on **OK**.

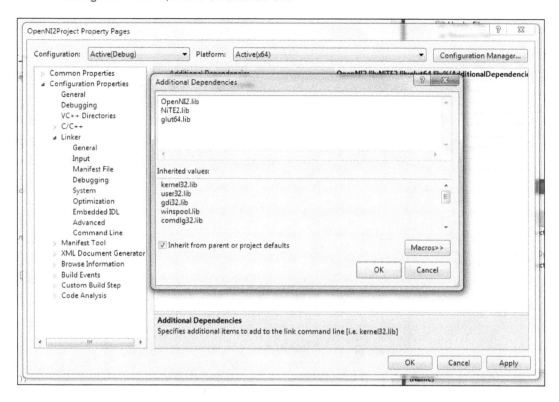

7. Navigate to **Build Events** and expand it. Select the **Post-Build Event** node, edit the **Command Line** field from the panel to the right and add `xcopy "C:\GLUT\ glut64.dll" "$(OutDir)" /y /d`. Then click on **OK** and in the parent window click on **Apply**.

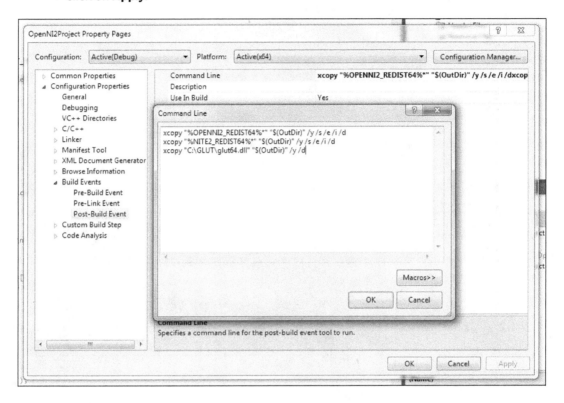

8. Now we must set the needed options for a 32-bit platform in case we want to compile 32-bit binary too (or if we only want to compile 32-bit binary). Select **All Configurations** from the top-left dropdown (the **Configuration** dropdown) and **Win32** from the top-right dropdown (the **Platform** dropdown). We will ignore images for each part from now on because the settings are much like the previous steps, with small changes.

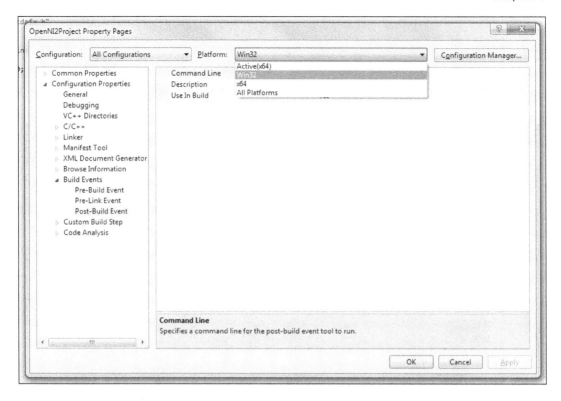

9. Locate the **C/C++** section and expand it. Select the **General** node and edit **Additional Include Directories** (using the down arrow located to the right of this field), add C:\GLUT, and then click on **OK**.

10. Locate the **Linker** section and expand it. Select the **General** node and edit **Additional Library Directories**, add C:\GLUT, and then click on **OK**.

11. Select the **Input** node (in the same section as **Linker**) and edit **Additional Dependencies**, add glut32.lib, and then click on **OK**.

12. Navigate to **Build Events** and expand it. Select the **Post-Build Event** node, edit the **Command Line** field from the panel to the right, and add xcopy "C:\GLUT\glut32.dll" "$(OutDir)" /y /d.

13. Then click on **OK**, and in the parent window click on **Apply**.

14. We are done with the **Project Property** window, so you can close it by clicking on **OK**.

15. Back at the Visual Studio 2010 main window, we need to include the GLUT header file in our source code too. For doing this, open the main source file of your project and enter the following lines at the bottom of everything else in the editor:

```
// GLUT headers
#include <gl/glut.h>
```

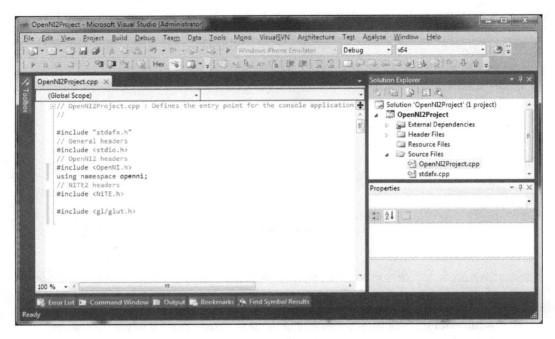

Build your project. This will tell you if any problem was found.

How it works...

In the `glut.zip` file, we have different files that we need to introduce to Visual Studio 2010 before using OpenGL.

After the extraction of this file, you can clearly see 2 `.dll` files: `glut32.dll` for using in 32-bit applications and `glut64.dll` for using in 64-bit applications. We need to use these 2 `.dll` files in our code, but first of all Visual Studio 2010 and the compiler must know the functions and other contents of these files. Here is where we need to introduce header files in Visual Studio 2010 (actually, the C++ compiler). We did it in steps 4 and 9, when telling Visual Studio 2010 to search for header files in the `GL` directory.

After compiling Visual Studio 2010, and especially the linker process, we need to know which function points to which .dll file (and exactly what point in .dll). For doing so, we need to introduce directories containing .lib and .dll files along with the name of the .lib files, as we did it in steps 5, 6, 10, and 11.

At the end, we need to have a copy of glut32.dll or glut64.dll (depending on our project target CPU's architecture) next to our application's executable file. For doing so, we added a command to Visual Studio 2010's post build event in steps 7 and 12. This command ran the xcopy application after the building of the project ended successfully, to copy one .dll file to our project output directory.

And then, in step 14, we asked the source editor to load the GLUT header files so that we can use its APIs in our code.

Please note that steps 3 to 7 are for x64 compiling and steps 8 to 12 are needed only if you want to develop a 32-bit version of your software. But we highly recommend doing all the steps so that you can select the desired target CPU using the solution platform dropdown at the top.

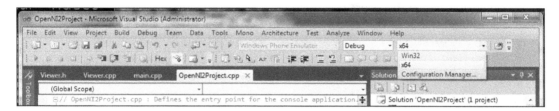

There's more...

You can use the OpenNI2Project-Empty Project with GLUT and OpenNI2Project-Empty Project with NiTE and GLUT projects as templates for starting. These projects are available on the Packt website for download. Please note that, when using these templates for writing different projects, you can't import two or more of them into one solution because they use the same GUID; thus, you will need to change their GUID to something unique before importing them into one solution.

There is no need to download and extract GLUT files for using these templates.

GLUT alternatives

As GLUT itself is a little old (development stopped in 1998), you can use freeGLUT or OpenGLUT too. These two open source alternatives are available to replace GLUT and can be used in almost the same way. Also, they are compatible with the code of this chapter, offer more functionality, and have solved a number of problems with the original GLUT.

Check the following websites for more information:

```
http://freeglut.sourceforge.net/
```

```
http://openglut.sourceforge.net/
```

Initializing and preparing OpenGL

If we want to use OpenGL for showing frames and other data to the user, we must know how to implement OpenGL's main functionalities in our project. This recipe is about how to initialize and prepare OpenGL to be used in other recipes.

Getting ready

Create a project in Visual Studio 2010 and prepare it for working with OpenNI using the *Creating a project in Visual Studio 2010* recipe of *Chapter 2, Open NI and C++*. Then, configure Visual Studio 2010 to use OpenGL using the *Configuring Visual Studio 2010 to use OpenGL* recipe of this chapter.

How to do it...

Open your project and then your project's main source code file.

1. Add the following lines above your source code (just below the #include lines):

```
int window_w = 640;
int window_h = 480;
OniRGB888Pixel* gl_texture;

void gl_KeyboardCallback(unsigned char key, int x, int y)
{
  if (key == 27) // ESC Key
    exit(1);
}

void gl_IdleCallback()
{
  glutPostRedisplay();
}

void gl_DisplayCallback()
{
  // Clear the OpenGL buffers
  glClear (GL_COLOR_BUFFER_BIT | GL_DEPTH_BUFFER_BIT);
```

```
// Setup the OpenGL viewpoint
glMatrixMode(GL_PROJECTION);
glPushMatrix();
glLoadIdentity();
glOrtho(0, window_w, window_h, 0, -1.0, 1.0);

// UPDATING TEXTURE

// Create the OpenGL texture map
glTexParameteri(GL_TEXTURE_2D,
    0x8191, GL_TRUE); // 0x8191 = GL_GENERATE_MIPMAP
glTexImage2D(GL_TEXTURE_2D, 0, GL_RGB, window_w, window_h,
    0, GL_RGB, GL_UNSIGNED_BYTE, gl_texture);

glBegin(GL_QUADS);
glTexCoord2f(0.0f, 0.0f);
glVertex3f(0.0f, 0.0f, 0.0f);
glTexCoord2f(0.0f, 1.0f);
glVertex3f(0.0f, (float)window_h, 0.0f);
glTexCoord2f(1.0f, 1.0f);
glVertex3f((float)window_w, (float)window_h, 0.0f);
glTexCoord2f(1.0f, 0.0f);
glVertex3f((float)window_w, 0.0f, 0.0f);
glEnd();

glutSwapBuffers();
}
```

2. Then locate the following lines of code:

```
int _tmain(int argc, _TCHAR* argv[])
{
```

3. Write the following code snippet below the preceding lines of code:

```
gl_texture = (OniRGB888Pixel*)malloc(
    window_w * window_h * sizeof(OniRGB888Pixel));
glutInit(&argc, (char**)argv);
glutInitDisplayMode(GLUT_RGB | GLUT_DOUBLE | GLUT_DEPTH);
glutInitWindowSize(window_w, window_h);
glutCreateWindow ("OpenGL | OpenNI 2.x CookBook Sample");
glutKeyboardFunc(gl_KeyboardCallback);
glutDisplayFunc(gl_DisplayCallback);
glutIdleFunc(gl_IdleCallback);
glDisable(GL_DEPTH_TEST);
glEnable(GL_TEXTURE_2D);
glutMainLoop();
```

How it works...

In the first step, we defined the size of our texture and also defined a pointer to the location in the memory where we want to store the output texture (we will allocate the required size in the memory later). This texture is of type `OniRGB888Pixel`, which is a simple 3-byte structure (red-green-blue). Please note that, no matter what the source of data and pixel format of OpenNI's outputs or any other outputs are, we need to convert it to RGB for saving it temporarily in the buffer before using it for being rendered by OpenGL.

```
int window_w = 640;
int window_h = 480;
OniRGB888Pixel* gl_texture;
```

GLUT can let us capture all keyboard events from the OpenGL window by introducing a keyboard callback function. Here, we define our custom function for handling keyboard events from the OpenGL window.

```
void gl_KeyboardCallback(unsigned char key, int x, int y)
{
  if (key == 27) // ESC Key
    exit(1);
}
```

Currently, in this example, we only want a way to close the OpenGL window from the keyboard and so our function is only sensitive to the *Esc* key. We may add more keys later on in other recipes.

We don't want to display our output only once because our output is not just a frame (as with a picture), but a video created from frames of data. But OpenGL doesn't do that automatically. You may think of putting a `while (true)` loop or any other loop in the buffer-filling process and this will actually work, but this is a bad idea as it will block our application as well as the OpenGL core completely and make the application irresponsive to any outer event such as keyboard events or Windows events. But there is a correct way too. The correct way to update OpenGL output without blocking it is to use OpenGL's `idle` callback and ask GLUT to recall the `gl_DisplayCallback()` function each time it becomes idle. This is possible by defining a function and introducing it to OpenGL as the `idle` callback.

```
void gl_IdleCallback()
{
  glutPostRedisplay();
}
```

The `glutPostRedisplay()` function will call the display function once again, giving us the ability to update and redraw the output texture.

The next step is to define the `gl_DisplayCallback()` function (the one that will be called each time OpenGL needs a new frame).

```
void gl_DisplayCallback()
{
```

In this function, we will try to clear OpenGL's buffer as well as write new data to the texture and show it. Let's start with clearing OpenGL's buffers. This can be done with one line of code.

```
glClear (GL_COLOR_BUFFER_BIT | GL_DEPTH_BUFFER_BIT);
```

This will clear OpenGL's depth and color buffer. Then we set the position of the camera and the view point.

```
glMatrixMode(GL_PROJECTION);
glPushMatrix();
glLoadIdentity();
glOrtho(0, window_w, window_h, 0, -1.0, 1.0);
```

After that, we must clear and update the texture buffer. We will do it later on in other recipes depending on what we want to show to the user.

After updating the texture, we need to tell OpenGL to show our temporary texture.

```
glTexParameteri(GL_TEXTURE_2D,
   0x8191, GL_TRUE); // 0x8191 = GL_GENERATE_MIPMAP
glTexImage2D(GL_TEXTURE_2D, 0, GL_RGB, window_w, window_h,
   0, GL_RGB, GL_UNSIGNED_BYTE, gl_texture);
```

The first line of the code snippet forces OpenGL to generate MipMap and the second line tells it to use the texture buffer as an image texture.

 0x8191 is the value of GL_GENERATE_MIPMAP. It seems that GLUT did not define GL_GENERATE_MIPMAP; maybe because it is an extension of OpenGL. Anyway, using a numeric value will work without any issues.

Then we must define the position of our texture. The following lines are for positioning our texture:

```
glBegin(GL_QUADS);
glTexCoord2f(0.0f, 0.0f);
glVertex3f(0.0f, 0.0f, 0.0f);
glTexCoord2f(0.0f, 1.0f);
glVertex3f(0.0f, (float)window_h, 0.0f);
glTexCoord2f(1.0f, 1.0f);
glVertex3f((float)window_w, (float)window_h, 0.0f);
```

```
glTexCoord2f(1.0f, 0.0f);
glVertex3f((float)window_w, 0.0f, 0.0f);
glEnd();
```

After all configurations are done, we tell OpenGL to swap buffers and move the current buffer to the front (we are using double buffering).

```
glutSwapBuffers();
```

The next step is to initialize OpenGL and pass these functions (`Idle`, `Display`, and `Keyboard`) to it. But before that, we need to allocate the required memory for our texture in memory (RAM actually), because what we defined first was just a pointer.

```
gl_texture = (OniRGB888Pixel*)malloc(
  window_w * window_h * sizeof(OniRGB888Pixel));
```

As you can see, we requested an allocation of 1612800 bytes here. 640 x 480 is the resolution of our texture buffer, which contains 307200 pixels, and since each pixel needs 3 bytes (one for each primary color), we need a total of 1612800 bytes.

Then we can go for OpenGL initializing.

```
glutInit(&argc, (char**)argv);
glutInitDisplayMode(GLUT_RGB | GLUT_DOUBLE | GLUT_DEPTH);
```

This will initialize OpenGL and force it to use both the color and depth buffer as well as double buffering. Then we need to initialize the OpenGL window.

```
glutInitWindowSize(window_w, window_h);
glutCreateWindow ("OpenGL | OpenNI 2.x CookBook Sample");
```

We created a window of a specific size and with a specific caption. It is now time to tell OpenGL which functions to use:

```
glutKeyboardFunc(gl_KeyboardCallback);
glutDisplayFunc(gl_DisplayCallback);
glutIdleFunc(gl_IdleCallback);
```

Then we need to enable 2D display of the texture, disable depth buffer updating, and start the whole process of rendering.

```
glDisable(GL_DEPTH_TEST);
glEnable(GL_TEXTURE_2D);
glutMainLoop();
```

The last line of the previous code snippet will put our program in an infinite loop of OpenGL. Any code after this line will not be executed.

The output for these lines of code is shown in the following screenshot:

See also

▸ The *Reading and showing a frame from the image sensor (color/IR)* recipe

▸ The *Reading and showing a frame from the depth sensor* recipe

▸ The *Overlaying the depth frame over the image frame* recipe of *Chapter 4, More About Low-level Outputs*

Reading and showing a frame from the image sensor (color/IR)

There is no doubt that the output of the image/color sensor in an RGB camera is useful. Here, we will teach you how to read frames from this sensor and show it to the user through OpenGL. Because showing and reading data from the IR sensor have the same procedure, we have tried to cover both of these sensors (Color and IR) in one example.

Getting ready

Create a project in Visual Studio 2010 and prepare it for working with OpenNI using the *Creating a project in Visual Studio 2010* recipe of *Chapter 2, OpenNI and C++* and then configure Visual Studio 2010 to use OpenGL using the *Configuring Visual Studio 2010 to use OpenGL* recipe of this chapter.

How to do it...

1. Add the following lines above your source code (just below the #include lines):

```
int window_w = 640;
int window_h = 480;
OniRGB888Pixel* gl_texture;
VideoStream selectedSensor;
Device device;

char ReadLastCharOfLine()
{
  int newChar = 0;
  int lastChar;
  fflush(stdout);
  do
  {
    lastChar = newChar;
    newChar = getchar();
  }
  while ((newChar != '\n')
    && (newChar != EOF));
  return (char)lastChar;
}

bool HandleStatus(Status status)
{
  if (status == STATUS_OK)
```

```
      return true;
    printf("ERROR: #%d, %s", status,
      OpenNI::getExtendedError());
    ReadLastCharOfLine();
    return false;
}

void SetActiveSensor(SensorType sensorType, Device* device)
{
    Status status = STATUS_OK;
    if (sensorType == SENSOR_DEPTH)
    {
      printf("Not supported with this example.\r\n");
      return;
    }
    printf("Checking if stream is supported ...\r\n");
    if (!device->hasSensor(sensorType))
    {
      printf("Stream not supported by this device.\r\n");
      return;
    }
    if (selectedSensor.isValid())
    {
      printf("Stop and destroy old stream.\r\n");
      selectedSensor.stop();
      selectedSensor.destroy();
    }
    printf("Asking device to create a stream ...\r\n");
    status = selectedSensor.create(*device, sensorType);
    if (!HandleStatus(status)) return;

    printf("Setting video mode to 640x480x30 RGB24 ...\r\n");
    VideoMode vmod;
    vmod.setFps(30);
    vmod.setPixelFormat(PIXEL_FORMAT_RGB888);
    vmod.setResolution(640, 480);
    status = selectedSensor.setVideoMode(vmod);
    if (!HandleStatus(status)) return;
    printf("Done.\r\n");

    printf("Starting stream ...\r\n");
    status = selectedSensor.start();
    if (!HandleStatus(status)) return;
    printf("Done.\r\n");
```

```
    }

    void gl_KeyboardCallback(unsigned char key, int x, int y)
    {
      if (key == 27) // ESC Key
      {
        selectedSensor.destroy();
        OpenNI::shutdown();
        exit(0);
      }
      else if (key == 'C' || key == 'c')
      {
        if (device.isValid())
        {
          printf("\r\n-->Setting active sensor to COLOR\r\n");
          SetActiveSensor(SENSOR_COLOR, &device);
        }
      }
      else if (key == 'I' || key == 'i')
      {
        if (device.isValid())
        {
          printf("\r\n-->Setting active sensor to IR\r\n");
          SetActiveSensor(SENSOR_IR, &device);
        }
      }
    }

    void gl_IdleCallback()
    {
      glutPostRedisplay();
    }

    void gl_DisplayCallback()
    {
      if (selectedSensor.isValid())
      {
        Status status = STATUS_OK;
        VideoStream* streamPointer = &selectedSensor;
        int streamReadyIndex;
        status = OpenNI::waitForAnyStream(&streamPointer, 1,
          &streamReadyIndex, 500);
        if (status == STATUS_OK && streamReadyIndex == 0)
        {
```

```
VideoFrameRef newFrame;
status = selectedSensor.readFrame(&newFrame);
if (status == STATUS_OK && newFrame.isValid())
{
  // Clear the OpenGL buffers
  glClear (
    GL_COLOR_BUFFER_BIT | GL_DEPTH_BUFFER_BIT);

  // Setup the OpenGL viewpoint
  glMatrixMode(GL_PROJECTION);
  glPushMatrix();
  glLoadIdentity();
  glOrtho(0, window_w, window_h, 0, -1.0, 1.0);

  // UPDATING & RESIZING TEXTURE (RGB888 TO RGB888)

  double resizeFactor = min(
    (window_w / (double)newFrame.getWidth()),
    (window_h / (double)newFrame.getHeight()));
  unsigned int texture_x = (unsigned int)(window_w -
    (resizeFactor * newFrame.getWidth())) / 2;
  unsigned int texture_y = (unsigned int)(window_h -
    (resizeFactor * newFrame.getHeight())) / 2;

  for  (unsigned int y = 0;
    y < (window_h - 2 * texture_y); ++y)
  {
    OniRGB888Pixel* texturePixel = gl_texture +
      ((y + texture_y) * window_w) + texture_x;
    for  (unsigned int x = 0;
      x < (window_w - 2 * texture_x);
      ++x)
    {
      OniRGB888Pixel* streamPixel =
        (OniRGB888Pixel*)(
          (char*)newFrame.getData() +
            ((int)(y / resizeFactor) *
              newFrame.getStrideInBytes())
          ) + (int)(x / resizeFactor);
      memcpy(texturePixel, streamPixel,
        sizeof(OniRGB888Pixel));
    texturePixel += 1; // Moves variable by 3 bytes

    }
```

```
            }


            // Create the OpenGL texture map
            glTexParameteri(GL_TEXTURE_2D,
              0x8191, GL_TRUE);
              glTexImage2D(GL_TEXTURE_2D, 0, GL_RGB,
              window_w, window_h,     0, GL_RGB,
              GL_UNSIGNED_BYTE, gl_texture);


            glBegin(GL_QUADS);
            glTexCoord2f(0.0f, 0.0f);
            glVertex3f(0.0f, 0.0f, 0.0f);
            glTexCoord2f(0.0f, 1.0f);
            glVertex3f(0.0f, (float)window_h, 0.0f);
            glTexCoord2f(1.0f, 1.0f);
            glVertex3f((float)window_w,
              (float)window_h, 0.0f);
            glTexCoord2f(1.0f, 0.0f);
            glVertex3f((float)window_w, 0.0f, 0.0f);
            glEnd();


            glutSwapBuffers();
          }
        }
      }
    }
```

2. Then locate the following lines of code:

```
int _tmain(int argc, _TCHAR* argv[])
{
```

3. Write the following lines of code below the preceding lines of code:

```
Status status = STATUS_OK;
printf("Scanning machine for devices and loading "
  "modules/drivers ...\r\n");

status = OpenNI::initialize();
if (!HandleStatus(status)) return 1;
printf("Completed.\r\n");

printf("Opening first device ...\r\n");
status = device.open(ANY_DEVICE);
if (!HandleStatus(status)) return 1;
```

```
printf("%s Opened, Completed.\r\n",
  device.getDeviceInfo().getName());

printf("Initializing OpenGL ...\r\n");
gl_texture = (OniRGB888Pixel*)malloc(
  window_w * window_h * sizeof(OniRGB888Pixel));
glutInit(&argc, (char**)argv);
glutInitDisplayMode(GLUT_RGB | GLUT_DOUBLE | GLUT_DEPTH);
glutInitWindowSize(window_w, window_h);
glutCreateWindow ("OpenGL | OpenNI 2.x CookBook Sample");
glutKeyboardFunc(gl_KeyboardCallback);
glutDisplayFunc(gl_DisplayCallback);
glutIdleFunc(gl_IdleCallback);
glDisable(GL_DEPTH_TEST);
glEnable(GL_TEXTURE_2D);
printf("Starting OpenGL rendering process ...\r\n");
SetActiveSensor(SENSOR_COLOR, &device);
printf("Press C for color and I for IR.\r\n");
glutMainLoop();
```

How it works...

Let's start with step one. As you can see, we defined a number of functions and variables here. Lets take a look at the list of these functions and variables:

- ▶ `window_w`: This variable is used as OpenGL's window width.

- ▶ `window_h`: This variable is used as OpenGL's window height.

- ▶ `gl_texture`: This variable is used as the texture buffer for OpenGL.

- ▶ `selectedSensor`: Instead of declaring our `VideoStream` variable in the `main` function, we defined it here to be sure we have access to it in all functions.

- ▶ `device`: This is the same variable that we always declared in our `main` function earlier (*Chapter 2, OpenNI and C++*), but this time we defined it here for the same reason as `selectedSensor`.

- ▶ `ReadLastCharOfLine`: You know this function from the earlier recipes in *Chapter 2, Open NI and C++*. This function will wait for the user to press the *Enter* key in the console and then return the character that was last entered (except the *Enter* key itself). We used this function only once this time in the `HandleStatus` function (the following function).

- ▶ `HandleStatus`: You should be aware of this function by now. We have used it a lot earlier and are going to use it here too. This function will check the `openni::Status` variable's status; if it means error, it will show the error that occured last and ask the user to press the *Enter* key to continue or exit.

- ▶ `SetActiveSensor`: This is one of the important functions in this example. We defined this function to separate our code, for changing the current active sensor, from other parts. In other words, in this function we will change the `selectedSensor` variable with the desired sensor. IR and color are the available options in this example. We will talk a bit more about this function.

- ▶ `gl_KeyboardCallback`: You know this function from the previous recipe. We used this function to check user input in the OpenGL window. In the previous recipe, we only checked for the *Esc* key and the exiting code. But here we extended this function to support more keys for different commands, such as changing the active sensor.

- ▶ `gl_IdleCallback`: This function will also be familiar if you have read the previous recipe. This function will get executed when OpenGL has nothing to do, and in this function we ask OpenGL to run the `display` function again.

- ▶ `gl_DisplayCallback`: This is another important function in this example. We are going to fill the texture buffer for OpenGL for each frame from our sensor's output here. We will talk more about this function in the following paragraph.

Let's go deeper into the `SetActiveSensor`, `gl_KeyboardCallback`, and `gl_DisplayCallback` functions.

We have already mentioned `SetActiveSensor` in the previous list. This function is used to change the current active sensor's `VideoStream` object. In other words, it will change the `selectedSensor` variable to the `VideoStream` object of either the depth or the IR sensor depending on its arguments.

As you can clearly see in the signature of this function, it will accept the `openni::SensorType` and `openni::Device` variables, then try to create an `openni::VideoStream` class of the specified type from the specified device, and finally store it in `selectedSensor`.

```
void SetActiveSensor(SensorType sensorType, Device* device)
{
```

In the first line of this function, we defined a variable of type `openni::Status`, which we used for storing the return values of OpenNI's methods (these will be checked later). After that, we checked the value of the `sensorType` argument. As this example doesn't support depth, we must be sure that the request is not for the depth sensor, and if so return, with an error.

```
Status status = STATUS_OK;
if (sensorType == SENSOR_DEPTH)
{
  printf("Not supported with this example.\r\n");
  return;
}
```

After this part, we have another `if` condition to see if the sent device is active and valid. If not, we will return, and print an error.

```
if (!device->hasSensor(sensorType))
{
  printf("Stream not supported by this device.\r\n");
  return;
}
```

Then we will check if the currently active `openni::VideoStream` object is valid or not. In other words, check if we are currently showing any sensor's output to the user or not. This condition is `false` when we call `SetActiveSensor()` for the first time but after that it will always be `true`.

If this condition was `true` and there was an active `openni::VideoStream` object already, we will stop it and release its resources. This will be done by calling `openni::VideoStream::stop()` and `openni::VideoStream::destroy()`.

```
if (selectedSensor.isValid())
{
  printf("Stop and destroy old stream.\r\n");
  selectedSensor.stop();
  selectedSensor.destroy();
}
```

After that, we will try to use the same `openni::VideoStream` variable to request the desired sensor's output by calling `openni::VideoStream.create()` with almost the same parameters as in the main function and then check if this ended successfully or not.

```
status = selectedSensor.create(*device, sensorType);
if (!HandleStatus(status)) return;
```

We will then change `VideoMode` of the newly created stream. The main reason for doing so is to make sure the output of this stream will be `PIXEL_FORMAT_RGB888` so that we can read both the color and IR outputs in the same way.

```
VideoMode vmod;
vmod.setFps(30);
vmod.setPixelFormat(PIXEL_FORMAT_RGB888);
vmod.setResolution(640, 480);
status = selectedSensor.setVideoMode(vmod);
if (!HandleStatus(status)) return;
```

And then we will start the newly created `openni::VideoStream` class:

```
status = selectedSensor.start();
if (!HandleStatus(status)) return;
```

This function has nothing else. But lets see what we have in the `gl_KeyboardCallback` function. Recall from the previous recipe about OpenGL and introducing callback functions for different events of OpenGL. We know of `gl_KeyboardCallback` from there, as we defined this function to receive keyboard events from OpenGL's window. There, we just checked to see whether the *Esc* key was pressed and whether it ended the program or not. But here we have extended its functionalities.

First of all, as we did earlier, we will check if the pressed key is the *Esc* key or not, but this time we will release any resource held by the `openni::VideoStream` and `openni::Device` objects, then ask `openni::OpenNI` to shut down, and at last terminate our program. Carrying out these steps ensures that OpenNI ends in a correct way and releases all devices and resources.

```cpp
if (key == 27) // ESC Key
{
  selectedSensor.destroy();
  OpenNI::shutdown();
  exit(0);
}
```

But if the pressed key was the *C* or *c* key, we need to make the color sensor active. But before changing the active `openni::VideoStream` object, we need to make sure our device is open and valid. Only then can we change the active sensor using the `SetActiveSensor()` function that we had defined earlier.

```cpp
else if (key == 'C' || key == 'c')
{
  if (device.isValid())
  {
    printf("\r\n-->Setting active sensor to COLOR\r\n");
    SetActiveSensor(SENSOR_COLOR, &device);
  }
}
```

We are going to do the same thing when the *I* or *i* key is pressed, but this time for the IR sensor:

```cpp
else if (key == 'I' || key == 'i')
{
  if (device.isValid())
  {
    printf("\r\n-->Setting active sensor to IR\r\n");
    SetActiveSensor(SENSOR_IR, &device);
  }
}
```

Now that we are done with this function, we can talk about the `gl_DisplayCallback` function – the function that was last defined in step 1. In this function, we are going to fill the texture buffer and ask OpenGL to show this buffer. You know this function from the previous recipe and also the lines required to make a texture buffer visible in the OpenGL window. So here we will only talk about how to fill this buffer from the sensor's output.

Right from the beginning and before anything else, we must be sure that the currently active `openni::VideoStream` object is valid and related to an actual sensor (physical or file).

```
void gl_DisplayCallback()
{
  if (selectedSensor.isValid())
  {
```

If so, we need to make sure there is a frame available to read too, as we don't want our `openni::VideoStream::readFrame()` call to block the execution of code. For doing so, we need to use the `openni::OpenNI::waitForAnyStream()` method. The first argument of this method is of the double pointer type `openni::VideoStream`; in other words, an array of `openni::VideoStream` objects. But here we have only one `openni::VideoStream` object to check, and so we saved the pointer of our `openni::VideoStream` object in a variable named `streamPointer` and then sent the pointer of this variable to `openni::OpenNI::waitForAnyStream()`. This will create an array, but only with one element. The second parameter of `openni::OpenNI:waitForAnyStream()` is the number of elements in the array, which is 1 in this example, as you can clearly see. The third parameter of this method is a pointer to the `int` variable to store the index of the ready stream. We defined a variable named `streamReadyIndex` and sent its pointer as the third parameter. We need to check the value of this variable later to make sure our stream is ready and we have a frame available to read. The last argument of this method is the number of milliseconds it will wait for a new frame to become available. We decided to put a 500 millisecond time-out here, meaning 0.5 seconds. By selecting this number, we can be sure that our code will get executed at least twice each second even if there is no data to read. From this, we can be sure that our keyboard callback and OpenGL's loop can work without waiting a long time for data availability.

The return value of this method is of type `openni::Status` and shows us how this process ended; that is, with error, with time out, or maybe everything went correctly and we have a new frame to read. If everything was fine, we can check `streamReadyIndex` to see which `openni::VideoStream` object has new data for us. In this case, we have only one and so can check if `streamReadyIndex` is equal to 0 (the index of our `openni::VideoStream` object in the array). Then we can proceed to read data from it.

```
Status status = STATUS_OK;
VideoStream* streamPointer = &selectedSensor;
int streamReadyIndex;
status = OpenNI::waitForAnyStream(&streamPointer, 1,
  &streamReadyIndex, 500);
if (status == STATUS_OK && streamReadyIndex == 0)
{
```

For reading from the sensor, we need to have access to the frame object, known as
`openni::VideoFrameRef`. Using this object, we can access the newly received frame data
and its properties, including height, width, and row size in bytes. But first, we need to get
`openni::VideoFrameRef` from `openni::VideoStream` by calling the `openni::Vide
oStream::readFrame()` method. This method accepts an argument of the type pointer
`openni::VideoFrameRef` and will fill that variable with a valid `openni::VideoFrameRef`
object. Also, the return value of this method is again of `openni::Status` type and indicates
if the process ended successfully or not and the returned frame is valid or not.

```
VideoFrameRef newFrame;
status = selectedSensor.readFrame(&newFrame);
if (status == STATUS_OK && newFrame.isValid())
{
```

Until now, we have made sure that we have a valid `openni::VideoStream` object and it has
a new frame that is valid too. Currently, we have access to this frame and all its data. It is time
to copy it to our texture buffer variable, which is called `gl_texture`. But before that, we need
to prepare OpenGL for it. We talked about this in the previous recipe, regarding clearing the
buffer of OpenGL and setting the position of the camera and view point of the window.

```
// Clear the OpenGL buffers
glClear (
  GL_COLOR_BUFFER_BIT | GL_DEPTH_BUFFER_BIT);

// Setup the OpenGL viewpoint
glMatrixMode(GL_PROJECTION);
glPushMatrix();
glLoadIdentity();
glOrtho(0, window_w, window_h, 0, -1.0, 1.0);
```

Now we need to copy data from the `openni::VideoFrameRef` object to the `gl_texture`
variable. This is one of the most important parts of the code.

The first step is calculating the resize factor of the resizing process by comparing the width
and height of both the newly generated frame and our texture buffer (that has the same size
as OpenGL's window). After that, you can see where we used a size for this buffer. Then, from
this `resizeFactor` value, we can calculate the X and Y padding required for the frame to fit
into our texture buffer when they don't have the same ratio.

```
double resizeFactor = min(
  (window_w / (double)newFrame.getWidth()),
  (window_h / (double)newFrame.getHeight()));
unsigned int texture_x = (unsigned int)(window_w -
  (resizeFactor * newFrame.getWidth())) / 2;
unsigned int texture_y = (unsigned int)(window_h -
  (resizeFactor * newFrame.getHeight())) / 2;
```

Let's show what these variables mean with the aid of a figure. Assume you have a texture buffer with a resolution of 1280 x 1024 and a frame from the color sensor with a resolution of 640 x 480. We want to fit this frame into our texture buffer so that the user can see the entire image without cropping. The following figure shows the values of the preceding variables in this scenario in a visual manner:

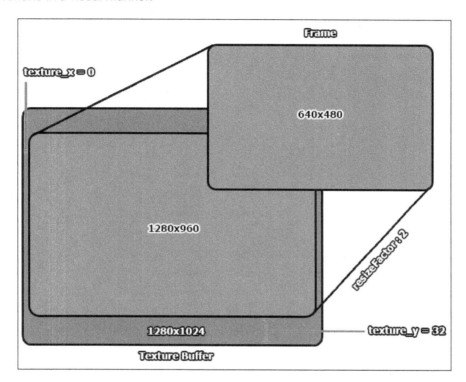

This picture shows how variables will be in that scenario. But think about our code here. We asked the sensor to create an output with a resolution of 640 x 480 and initialized OpenGL with a window size of 640 x 480 and a texture buffer of the same size. So, in our code here, the resizeFactor value is 1 and both texture_x and texture_y are 0 because the frame will fill up all parts of the buffer, and so there is no need to calculate any of these three variables normally.

But the reason we did this was to write a global code that can be used with any size and ratio of the sensor's frame data and texture buffer.

After doing so, we need to fill each pixel of our texture buffer. For doing that, we need to loop through our texture buffer row by row and then pixel by pixel. This can be done with two `for` loops, one for each row and another for each pixel of the texture buffer. After the first `for` loop that loops through each row, we need to calculate the position of the first pixel of that row. Then, in the second `for` loop, we move forward and fill the other pixels of that row too. For filling each pixel, we need to calculate the position of the responsible pixel in the sensor's frame data, convert each pixel, and copy it to the texture buffer.

Let's take a look at the code.

```
for  (unsigned int y = 0;
  y < (window_h - 2 * texture_y); ++y)
{
  OniRGB888Pixel* texturePixel = gl_texture +
    ((y + texture_y) * window_w) + texture_x;
  for  (unsigned int x = 0;
    x < (window_w - 2 * texture_x);
    ++x)
  {
    OniRGB888Pixel* streamPixel =
      (OniRGB888Pixel*)(
        (char*)newFrame.getData() +
          ((int)(y / resizeFactor) *
            newFrame.getStrideInBytes())
        ) + (int)(x / resizeFactor);
    memcpy(texturePixel, streamPixel,
      sizeof(OniRGB888Pixel));
      texturePixel += 1; // Moves variable by 3 bytes
  }
}
```

First of all, keep in mind that all operations here are about the texture buffer except for one line, which I will be mentioning separately.

As you can see, we have a loop starting from `0` till the end of the calculated height of the data being copied (`window_h - 2 * texture_y`).

In this loop, we need to calculate the position of the first pixel of that row.

```
OniRGB888Pixel* texturePixel = gl_texture +
        ((y + texture_y) * window_w) + texture_x;
```

We defined a pointer of type `openni::OniRGB888Pixel`, which is a structure of 3 bytes. The value of this pointer (or in other words, the position of the first pixel of that row) is equal to the sum of the position of the first pixel of the whole buffer (`gl_texture`), the first pixel of the actual required row in the texture buffer (`(y + texture_y) * window_w`), and the calculated horizontal padding of the image being copied (`texture_x`).

Then, in the second loop, we will go to the next pixel by calling `texturePixel+=1;` at the end of the `for` definition. Please note that adding a number to a pointer doesn't always increase its value by 1 byte. It will increase the value by the number of bytes of data type multiplied by your number. So `texturePixel+=1;` will add 3 bytes (because `openni::OniRGB888Pixel` is a structure of 3 bytes) and move exactly to the next pixel.

In the body of the second loop, we have the address of the responsible pixel in the texture buffer. Now we need to copy data from the output frame data to the texture buffer. For doing this, we need to have the address of the related pixel in the output frame. Moreover, we want to resize the image at the same time too. So we need to calculate the position of the related pixel in the output frame data from the position of the pixel in the texture buffer. This can be done easily because we know the exact resize factor. If x and y are the positions of a pixel in the stream data, we can guess that x / `resizeFactor` and y / `resizeFactor` are the positions of the related pixel in the texture data. Then we need to calculate the position of this pixel in memory.

```
OniRGB888Pixel* streamPixel =
    (OniRGB888Pixel*)(
        (char*)newFrame.getData() +
        ((int)(y / resizeFactor) *
            newFrame.getStrideInBytes())
    ) + (int)(x / resizeFactor);
```

This code may seem hard to understand at first, but the logic behind it is simple. `newFrame.getData()` will return the position of the first pixel of the first row. As we need to calculate the position of the yth row, we need to add the `(y / resizeFactor) * newFrame.getStrideInBytes()` byte to it. Again, as we want the xth pixel of that row, we need to add the `(x / resizeFactor)` pixel to it.

Note the difference between adding bytes and adding pixels. In calculating the position of a pixel in the texture buffer, there was no word about bytes. We always used pixels because increasing a pointer of type `openni::OniRGB888Pixel` would increase it by the number of bytes held by its data type, and we need not worry about bytes as it will be done automatically in C++. But here we need to add the number of bytes for each row in **bytes** and then add the number of pixels in that row in **pixels**. But how can we add two different pointer types?

We do this by converting `newFrame.getData()` to the `char` pointer (in C++ we know bytes as chars), adding `((int)(y / resizeFactor) * newFrame.getStrideInBytes())` to it, and then converting the whole part again into the `openni:: OniRGB888Pixel` pointer. At the end, add `(int)(x / resizeFactor)` to it. This way, we can be sure that the first addition happens in bytes and the second happens in pixels.

Now that we have the position of the pixels in both places, we need to convert and copy data from `streamPixel` to `texturePixel` but, as this time both pixel formats are RGB888 or RGB24, we can copy data without converting it.

```
memcpy(texturePixel, streamPixel,
    sizeof(OniRGB888Pixel));
```

It is simple enough. The only important part in the previous code is `sizeof(OniRGB888Pixel)`. This will return 3 because the size of the `openni::OniRGB888Pixel` structure is 3; one byte per color for blue, green, and red. The `memcpy()` function needs three arguments: destination pointer, source pointer, and number of bytes to copy.

Now that we are almost done with the texture, we only need to put our texture in OpenGL and tell it to render the scene.

```
// Create the OpenGL texture map
glTexParameteri(GL_TEXTURE_2D,
    0x8191, GL_TRUE);
glTexImage2D(GL_TEXTURE_2D, 0, GL_RGB,
    window_w, window_h, 0, GL_RGB,
    GL_UNSIGNED_BYTE, gl_texture);

glBegin(GL_QUADS);
glTexCoord2f(0.0f, 0.0f);
glVertex3f(0.0f, 0.0f, 0.0f);
glTexCoord2f(0.0f, 1.0f);
glVertex3f(0.0f, (float)window_h, 0.0f);
glTexCoord2f(1.0f, 1.0f);
glVertex3f((float)window_w,
    (float)window_h, 0.0f);
glTexCoord2f(1.0f, 0.0f);
glVertex3f((float)window_w, 0.0f, 0.0f);
glEnd();

glutSwapBuffers();
```

Now about steps 2 and 3.

You know the `main` function. This function will be executed when our application starts. In other words, it is the starting point of our application. So we need to put our initializing code of OpenNI and OpenGL here.

As always, we first need to initialize OpenNI and then open a device.

```
status = OpenNI::initialize();
if (!HandleStatus(status)) return 1;
..
status = device.open(ANY_DEVICE);
if (!HandleStatus(status)) return 1;
```

Then we have to initialize OpenGL and allocate the needed space in memory for the texture buffer.

```
gl_texture = (OniRGB888Pixel*)malloc(
  window_w * window_h * sizeof(OniRGB888Pixel));
```

We next need to initialize OpenGL windows with GLUT and set the needed settings.

```
glutInit(&argc, (char**)argv);
glutInitDisplayMode(GLUT_RGB | GLUT_DOUBLE | GLUT_DEPTH);
glutInitWindowSize(window_w, window_h);
glutCreateWindow ("OpenGL | OpenNI 2.x CookBook Sample");
glutKeyboardFunc(gl_KeyboardCallback);
glutDisplayFunc(gl_DisplayCallback);
glutIdleFunc(gl_IdleCallback);
glDisable(GL_DEPTH_TEST);
glEnable(GL_TEXTURE_2D);
```

Now we need to select the color sensor as the default sensor and inform the user that he/she can switch between the color sensor and IR sensor with the help of the keyboard.

```
SetActiveSensor(SENSOR_COLOR, &device);
printf("Press C for color and I for IR.\r\n");
```

Then we will start OpenGL's main rendering loop as the last step.

```
glutMainLoop();
```

After that, the `SetActiveSensor`, `gl_KeyboardCallback`, and `gl_DisplayCallback` functions will control our application behavior.

The output of our application will be as shown in the following screenshot:

After switching to the IR sensor, we will get an output resembling the following screenshot:

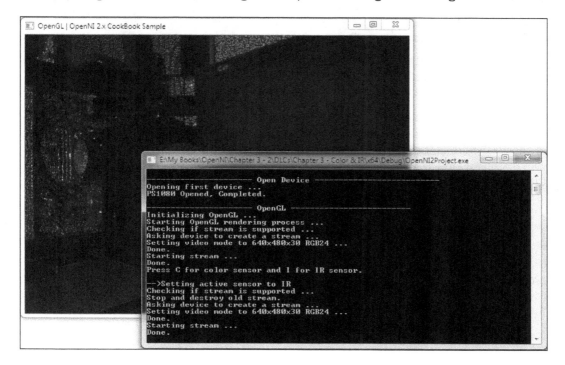

See also

▶ The *Reading and showing a frame from the depth sensor* recipe

▶ The *Overlaying the depth frame over the image frame* recipe of *Chapter 4, More About Low-level Outputs*

▶ The *Enabling/disabling auto exposure and auto white balance* recipe of *Chapter 4, More About Low-level Outputs*

Reading and showing a frame from the depth sensor

Who doesn't agree that the output of the depth sensor is the most important output of OpenNI and compatible devices? In this recipe, we will show you how to use OpenGL and OpenNI to show OpenNI's depth sensor output to the user.

We highly recommend reading the previous recipe of this chapter, *Reading and showing a frame from the image sensor (color/IR)*, to have a background about how we can use OpenGL to show a picture to the user and how we can copy a picture from OpenNI to our texture buffer with resizing on-the-fly; especially the *How it works...* section, as we are not going to cover all the lines in detail in this recipe (as we did in the previous recipe). But don't worry. This recipe is simpler than the last one—at least at first glance!

Getting ready

Create a project in Visual Studio 2010, prepare it for working with OpenNI using the *Create a project in Visual Studio 2010* recipe of *Chapter 2*, *Open NI and C++*, and then configure Visual Studio 2010 to use OpenGL using the *Configuring Visual Studio 2010 to use OpenGL* recipe of this chapter.

How to do it...

1. Add the following lines above your source code (just below the `#include` lines):

```
int window_w = 640;
int window_h = 480;
OniRGB888Pixel* gl_texture;
VideoStream depthSensor;
Device device;

char ReadLastCharOfLine()
{
  int newChar = 0;
  int lastChar;
  fflush(stdout);
  do
  {
    lastChar = newChar;
    newChar = getchar();
  }
  while ((newChar != '\n')
    && (newChar != EOF));
```

```
    return (char)lastChar;
}

bool HandleStatus(Status status)
{
  if (status == STATUS_OK)
    return true;
  printf("ERROR: #%d, %s", status,
    OpenNI::getExtendedError());
  ReadLastCharOfLine();
  return false;
}

void gl_KeyboardCallback(unsigned char key, int x, int y)
{
  if (key == 27) // ESC Key
  {
    depthSensor.destroy();
    OpenNI::shutdown();
    exit(0);
  }
}

void gl_IdleCallback()
{
  glutPostRedisplay();
}

void gl_DisplayCallback()
{
  if (depthSensor.isValid())
  {
    Status status = STATUS_OK;
    VideoStream* streamPointer = &depthSensor;
    int streamReadyIndex;
    status = OpenNI::waitForAnyStream(&streamPointer, 1,
      &streamReadyIndex, 500);
    if (status == STATUS_OK && streamReadyIndex == 0)
    {
      VideoFrameRef newFrame;
      status = depthSensor.readFrame(&newFrame);
      if (status == STATUS_OK && newFrame.isValid())
      {
        // Clear the OpenGL buffers
```

```
glClear (
  GL_COLOR_BUFFER_BIT | GL_DEPTH_BUFFER_BIT);

// Setup the OpenGL viewpoint
glMatrixMode(GL_PROJECTION);
glPushMatrix();
glLoadIdentity();
glOrtho(0, window_w, window_h, 0, -1.0, 1.0);

// UPDATING TEXTURE (DEPTH 1MM TO RGB888)
unsigned short maxDepth = 0;
for  (int y = 0; y < newFrame.getHeight(); ++y)
{
  DepthPixel* depthCell = (DepthPixel*)(
    (char*)newFrame.getData() +
    (y * newFrame.getStrideInBytes())
    );
  for  (int x = 0; x < newFrame.getWidth();
        ++x, ++depthCell)
  {
    if (maxDepth < *depthCell){
      maxDepth = *depthCell;
    }
  }
}

double resizeFactor = min(
  (window_w / (double)newFrame.getWidth()),
  (window_h / (double)newFrame.getHeight()));
unsigned int texture_x = (unsigned int)(window_w -
  (resizeFactor * newFrame.getWidth())) / 2;
unsigned int texture_y = (unsigned int)(window_h -
  (resizeFactor * newFrame.getHeight())) / 2;

for  (unsigned int y = 0;
  y < (window_h - 2 * texture_y); ++y)
{
  OniRGB888Pixel* texturePixel = gl_texture +
    ((y + texture_y) * window_w) + texture_x;
  for  (unsigned int x = 0;
    x < (window_w - 2 * texture_x);
    ++x)
  {
    DepthPixel* streamPixel =
      (DepthPixel*)(
          (char*)newFrame.getData() +
```

```
                    ((int)(y / resizeFactor) *
                       newFrame.getStrideInBytes())
                  ) + (int)(x / resizeFactor);
              if (*streamPixel != 0){
                char depthValue = ((float)*streamPixel /
                  maxDepth) * 255;
                texturePixel->b = 255 - depthValue;
                texturePixel->g = 255 - depthValue;
                texturePixel->r = 255 - depthValue;
              }
              else
              {
                texturePixel->b = 0;
                texturePixel->g = 0;
                texturePixel->r = 0;
              }
    texturePixel += 1; // Moves variable by 3 bytes
            }
          }


        // Create the OpenGL texture map
        glTexParameteri(GL_TEXTURE_2D,
          0x8191, GL_TRUE);
        glTexImage2D(GL_TEXTURE_2D, 0, GL_RGB,
          window_w, window_h, 0, GL_RGB,
          GL_UNSIGNED_BYTE, gl_texture);

        glBegin(GL_QUADS);
        glTexCoord2f(0.0f, 0.0f);
        glVertex3f(0.0f, 0.0f, 0.0f);
        glTexCoord2f(0.0f, 1.0f);
        glVertex3f(0.0f, (float)window_h, 0.0f);
        glTexCoord2f(1.0f, 1.0f);
        glVertex3f((float)window_w,
          (float)window_h, 0.0f);
        glTexCoord2f(1.0f, 0.0f);
        glVertex3f((float)window_w, 0.0f, 0.0f);
        glEnd();

        glutSwapBuffers();
      }
    }
  }
}
```

2. Then locate the following lines of code:

```
int _tmain(int argc, _TCHAR* argv[])
{
```

3. Write the following lines of code below the preceding lines of code:

```
Status status = STATUS_OK;
printf("Scanning machine for devices and loading "
    "modules/drivers ...\r\n");

status = OpenNI::initialize();
if (!HandleStatus(status)) return 1;
printf("Completed.\r\n");

printf("Opening first device ...\r\n");
status = device.open(ANY_DEVICE);
if (!HandleStatus(status)) return 1;
printf("%s Opened, Completed.\r\n",
  device.getDeviceInfo().getName());

printf("Checking if stream is supported ...\r\n");
if (!device.hasSensor(SENSOR_DEPTH))
{
  printf("Stream not supported by this device.\r\n");
  return 1;
}

printf("Asking device to create a depth stream ...\r\n");
status = depthSensor.create(device, SENSOR_DEPTH);
if (!HandleStatus(status)) return 1;

printf("Setting video mode to 640x480x30 Depth 1MM..\r\n");
VideoMode vmod;
vmod.setFps(30);
vmod.setPixelFormat(PIXEL_FORMAT_DEPTH_1_MM);
vmod.setResolution(640, 480);
status = depthSensor.setVideoMode(vmod);
if (!HandleStatus(status)) return 1;
printf("Done.\r\n");

printf("Starting stream ...\r\n");
status = depthSensor.start();
if (!HandleStatus(status)) return 1;
printf("Done.\r\n");
```

```
    printf("Initializing OpenGL ...\r\n");
    gl_texture = (OniRGB888Pixel*)malloc(
      window_w * window_h * sizeof(OniRGB888Pixel));
    glutInit(&argc, (char**)argv);
    glutInitDisplayMode(GLUT_RGB | GLUT_DOUBLE | GLUT_DEPTH);
    glutInitWindowSize(window_w, window_h);
    glutCreateWindow ("OpenGL | OpenNI 2.x CookBook Sample");
    glutKeyboardFunc(gl_KeyboardCallback);
    glutDisplayFunc(gl_DisplayCallback);
    glutIdleFunc(gl_IdleCallback);
    glDisable(GL_DEPTH_TEST);
    glEnable(GL_TEXTURE_2D);
    printf("Starting OpenGL rendering process ...\r\n");
    glutMainLoop();
```

How it works...

Lets start with step one.

Just as in the previous recipe, we used the first step to define our required variables and functions, including `window_w` and `window_h` for setting OpenGL's window size and `gl_texture` to hold our texture buffer in memory, along with an `openni::VideoStream` variable named `depthSensor` and an `openni::Device` variable named `device` to let us access the depth sensor's data and the device from different functions.

Functions are almost the same too. You know about `ReadLastCharOfLine()` and `HandleStatus()` from the previous recipe and even before that, we have seen `gl_KeyboardCallback()`, `gl_IdleCallback()`, and `gl_DisplayCallback()`, but there is no `SetActiveSensor()` anymore because we merged it with the `main` function.

It is clear at first glance that `gl_KeyboardCallback()` and `gl_DisplayCallback()` changed when compared to the previous recipe. Let's start with the changes in `gl_KeyboardCallback()`. As you can see, there is no check for the *C* or *I* key anymore, as we don't need to change the active sensor output stream. This function now supports only the *Esc* key for exiting.

```
    if (key == 27) // ESC Key
    {
      depthSensor.destroy();
      OpenNI::shutdown();
      exit(0);
    }
```

In the function that was last defined in step 1, `gl_DisplayCallback`, we will fill the texture buffer and ask OpenGL to show this buffer, just as we did in the previous recipe, but this time for the depth sensor.

You know what we are going to do if you have read the previous recipe's *How it works...*
section. The only change between these two is the part about converting and filling the texture
buffer. This part starts at line 24 of the function, after the UPDATING TEXTURE line. In this
line, you can see that, instead of starting the copying process, we decided to loop through
the output frame data because we wanted to find out the upper bound of data in order to
normalize the range of colors later. As you can see, there is nothing special here. We defined
a variable named maxDepth to store the upper bound of data and then looped through the
data to find out which is a bigger value.

```
unsigned short maxDepth = 0;
for  (int y = 0; y < newFrame.getHeight(); ++y)
{
  DepthPixel* depthCell = (DepthPixel*)(
    (char*)newFrame.getData() +
    (y * newFrame.getStrideInBytes())
  );
  for  (int x = 0; x < newFrame.getWidth();
        ++x, ++depthCell)
  {
    if (maxDepth < *depthCell){
      maxDepth = *depthCell;
    }
  }
}
```

The only notable line in this code is the one about defining the depthCell
variable. In this code, we converted newFrame.getData() to char (originally it is in type
openni::DepthPixel) because we can then increase the value of the pointer by bytes.
After that, we added the number of bytes required to move the pointer to the first pixel of the
next row and converted the entire line into the openni::DepthPixel type pointer again and
finally stored it in depthCell variable.

```
DepthPixel* depthCell = (DepthPixel*)(
            (char*)newFrame.getData() +
            (y * newFrame.getStrideInBytes())
            );
```

Then, just as we did in the previous recipe, we try to calculate the resizeFactor value and
pad the frame data before copying it to the texture buffer.

```
double resizeFactor = min(
  (window_w / (double)newFrame.getWidth()),
  (window_h / (double)newFrame.getHeight()));
unsigned int texture_x = (unsigned int)(window_w -
  (resizeFactor * newFrame.getWidth())) / 2;
unsigned int texture_y = (unsigned int)(window_h -
  (resizeFactor * newFrame.getHeight())) / 2;
```

Next, we start to loop through the height of the texture and calculate the position of each row's first pixel.

```
for  (unsigned int y = 0;
  y < (window_h - 2 * texture_y); ++y)
{
  OniRGB888Pixel* texturePixel = gl_texture +
    ((y + texture_y) * window_w) + texture_x;
```

`gl_texture` is the first pixel of the texture buffer that we added the `((y + texture_y) * window_w)` pixels to (representing the number of pixels from the first row to the current row) and then added `texture_x`, which represents horizontal padding.

Next we need to loop through the width of the image using another loop and increase `texturePixel` by one pixel, calculate the related pixel's position in the frame data, and then convert and copy data from there.

```
for  (unsigned int x = 0;
  x < (window_w - 2 * texture_x);
  ++x)
{
  DepthPixel* streamPixel =
    (DepthPixel*)(
        (char*)newFrame.getData() +
        ((int)(y / resizeFactor) *
          newFrame.getStrideInBytes())
    ) + (int)(x / resizeFactor);
  if (*streamPixel != 0){
    char depthValue = ((float)*streamPixel /
      maxDepth) * 255;
    texturePixel->b = 255 - depthValue;
    texturePixel->g = 255 - depthValue;
    texturePixel->r = 255 - depthValue;
  }
  else
  {
    texturePixel->b = 0;
    texturePixel->g = 0;
    texturePixel->r = 0;
  }
    texturePixel += 1; // Moves variable by 3 bytes
}
```

As you can see, increasing the value of `texturePixel` is done before the end of the `for` body; inside its body, we have a variable named `streamPixel` with the `openni::DepthPixel` pointer type, which is going to be the related pixel in the depth frame data. As earlier, where we converted `newFrame.getData()` (the address of the first pixel of frame data) to a pointer of type `char`, here too, we can increase its pointer by `(y / resizeFactor) * newFrame.getStrideInBytes()` bytes and again convert it into a pointer of `openni::DepthPixel` type to increase it by pixels, and finally increase it by `(x / resizeFactor)` pixels.

```
DepthPixel* streamPixel =
    (DepthPixel*)(
        (char*)newFrame.getData() +
        ((int)(y / resizeFactor) *
          newFrame.getStrideInBytes())
    ) + (int)(x / resizeFactor);
```

Now we have both pixels but they are in two different formats. One is the depth pixel and the other is the RGB pixel. We need to find a way to convert each depth pixel into a reasonable RGB value.

A pixel depth can have a range of 0-65535 (it is actually an `unsigned short` data type), but an RGB value (one among red, green, or blue) can be in the range of 0-255; so we can't fit our data completely in an RGB color space. This means we are going to lose 256 levels of detail.

You may ask why we said the range of each RGB pixel is 0-255. Actually, an RGB pixel has 3 bytes, which means it has a range of 0-16777215. But a lot of these colors are the darker and lighter versions of each other. We want to show our output in grayscale, which means all the bytes will have the same value. Therefore, we have a maximum range of 0-255.

But don't forget that the `openni::VideoStream::getMaxPixelValue()` method returns 10000 for the depth sensor. If we consider this value as the maximum possible value of a depth pixel, we need to fit 0-10000 in our limited 0-255 RGB range. This means we need to lose almost 40 levels of detail, which is better than the previous one but still not a very good option.

In our search for finding the real range of data, we found that the `PixelFormat::PIXEL_FORMAT_DEPTH_1_MM` pixel format actually has 11 bits of data, which means it has a maximum of 2048 different values. But again, this number is not too reliable either. This is because, firstly, `PixelFormat::PIXEL_FORMAT_DEPTH_100_UM` has 12 bits of data, which means it can have up to 4096 different values; and secondly, it seems that OpenNI changes these values a little (actually, we know that `PixelFormat::PIXEL_FORMAT_SHIFT_9_2` and `PixelFormat::PIXEL_FORMAT_SHIFT_9_3` are the only unchanged raw data of the device and so we expect that). From our experiments, it seems that we can expect data in the range of 300-4000 when using `PixelFormat::PIXEL_FORMAT_DEPTH_1_MM` as the pixel format.

As you can see, all the values are unreliable and we need to calculate the upper bound of data in each frame manually (that's what we did earlier too; read the preceding lines of this part) and then fit our data in the 0-255 range for showing it as RGB. As we had said earlier, the upper bound of data was normally under 4000 in our experiments, and so on average we were going to lose more than 15 levels of detail. If you need to see other methods of conversion and better outputs, check the *There's more* part of this recipe. We didn't want to make it difficult in the main code.

Using the previously given information and the upper bound of data (we knew this), we tried to convert (or, in other words, fit) our data into the texture buffer.

```
char depthValue = ((float)*streamPixel /
  maxDepth) * 255;
texturePixel->b = 255 - depthValue;
texturePixel->g = 255 - depthValue;
texturePixel->r = 255 - depthValue;
```

As you can see, it is a simple calculation for changing the range of data. Then we inverse the output by writing `255 - depthValue`. We do this because data is actually in the form of near-black and far-white and we need to change it to near-white and far-black before displaying to the user.

You may notice that, before writing the previous code snippet, we used a condition to see if `*streamPixel` is equal to 0. If it is, we skipped our code and put a 0 in all the bytes of our pixel in the texture buffer. This is because, in depth frame data, 0 means there is no data to show; if so, we want to fill these pixels with black in the end result too.

The other parts of the code are like the previous recipes.

Now let's talk about step 3. You know the `main` function. This function will be executed when our application starts. So we need to put our initializing code of OpenNI and OpenGL here.

As always, we first need to initialize OpenNI and then open a device.

```
status = OpenNI::initialize();
if (!HandleStatus(status)) return 1;
...
status = device.open(ANY_DEVICE);
if (!HandleStatus(status)) return 1;
```

Then create `openni::VideoStream` for the depth sensor and request the desired `openni::VideoMode` object. At last, start the newly created `openni::VideoStream` class:

```
printf("Asking device to create a depth stream ...\r\n");
status = depthSensor.create(device, SENSOR_DEPTH);
if (!HandleStatus(status)) return 1;

printf("Setting video mode to 640x480x30 Depth 1MM..\r\n");
VideoMode vmod;
vmod.setFps(30);
vmod.setPixelFormat(PIXEL_FORMAT_DEPTH_1_MM);
vmod.setResolution(640, 480);
status = depthSensor.setVideoMode(vmod);
if (!HandleStatus(status)) return 1;
printf("Done.\r\n");

printf("Starting stream ...\r\n");
status = depthSensor.start();
if (!HandleStatus(status)) return 1;
printf("Done.\r\n");
```

Our next task is to initialize OpenGL and allocate the required space in memory for the texture buffer:

```
gl_texture = (OniRGB888Pixel*)malloc(
  window_w * window_h * sizeof(OniRGB888Pixel));
```

Then initialize the OpenGL windows with GLUT and configure the required settings:

```
glutInit(&argc, (char**)argv);
glutInitDisplayMode(GLUT_RGB | GLUT_DOUBLE | GLUT_DEPTH);
glutInitWindowSize(window_w, window_h);
glutCreateWindow ("OpenGL | OpenNI 2.x CookBook Sample");
glutKeyboardFunc(gl_KeyboardCallback);
glutDisplayFunc(gl_DisplayCallback);
glutIdleFunc(gl_IdleCallback);
glDisable(GL_DEPTH_TEST);
glEnable(GL_TEXTURE_2D);
```

Now we start OpenGL's main rendering loop.

```
glutMainLoop();
```

After that, gl_KeyboardCallback and mainly the gl_DisplayCallback function will control our application behavior.

The output of our application is shown in the following screenshot:

There's more...

There are some enhancements for this output that we will cover in this section.

Histogram equalization – better details in the same color space

Using the main code, we tried to show data directly from the sensor without many changes (except fitting it into our color space) but now we are going to use a few lines of code to improve the result without adding more colors or changing color space. We will use a simple histogram-equalization method.

Let's say we have an image with different colors of grayscale color space; that is, we have different colors between white and black. But, for example, in the previous picture you can see that a lot of these colors are similar to each other and there are a lot of other colors that are rarely used. Using histogram equalization, we can use all of our color space by dynamically changing the contrast of the image to show more important data with much more detail.

Let's talk about histograms. Histograms are 2D graphs for showing the distribution of colors in an image. You can read more about image histograms on Wikipedia at:

```
http://en.wikipedia.org/wiki/Image_histogram
```

For example, for our previous image (the output of our program in the previous code), we have the following histogram:

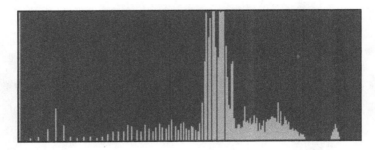

As you can clearly see, the majority of the colors used are in a specific range and most of the color space is never really used. Using histogram equalization, we can change that somewhat, to use all parts of the color space. The following is the same histogram after correction:

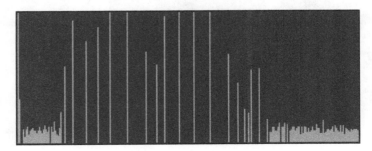

Histogram equalization is a good way to increase the contrast of important parts of an image that use very limited parts of a color space. But its main advantage reveals itself when you are going to fit an image with a bigger color palette into a smaller one, because in addition to showing important parts of an image more clearly, it will add more detail to the image by converting only the useful parts of color palette into a new color space.

This is our case here too. Our depth frame data is using 16 bits for each pixel but our texture buffer has a smaller color palette of 8 bits per pixel (as we said before, RGB is 24-bit but we need to use only 8 bits of it for grayscale). So we can expect a huge difference.

Read more about histogram equalization on Wikipedia at:

```
http://en.wikipedia.org/wiki/Histogram_equalization
```

Enough talk; let's check it out in code now. For doing so, you need to use the same code as in this recipe but replace the entire `gl_DisplayCallback` function with the following lines of code:

```
void gl_DisplayCallback()
{
  if (depthSensor.isValid())
  {
    Status status = STATUS_OK;
    VideoStream* streamPointer = &depthSensor;
    int streamReadyIndex;
    status = OpenNI::waitForAnyStream(&streamPointer, 1,
      &streamReadyIndex, 500);
    if (status == STATUS_OK && streamReadyIndex == 0)
    {
      VideoFrameRef newFrame;
      status = depthSensor.readFrame(&newFrame);
      if (status == STATUS_OK && newFrame.isValid())
      {
        // Clear the OpenGL buffers
        glClear (
          GL_COLOR_BUFFER_BIT | GL_DEPTH_BUFFER_BIT);

        // Setup the OpenGL viewpoint
        glMatrixMode(GL_PROJECTION);
        glPushMatrix();
        glLoadIdentity();
        glOrtho(0, window_w, window_h, 0, -1.0, 1.0);

        // UPDATING TEXTURE (DEPTH 1MM TO RGB888)
        int depthHistogram[65536];
        int numberOfPoints = 0;
```

```cpp
memset(depthHistogram, 0,
  sizeof(depthHistogram));
for  (int y = 0;
     y < newFrame.getHeight(); ++y)
{
  DepthPixel* depthCell = (DepthPixel*)(
    (char*)newFrame.getData() +
    (y * newFrame.getStrideInBytes())
    );
  for  (int x = 0; x < newFrame.getWidth();
       ++x, ++depthCell)
  {
    if (*depthCell != 0)
      {
      depthHistogram[*depthCell]++;
      numberOfPoints++;
      }
  }
}

for (int nIndex=1;
nIndex < sizeof(depthHistogram) / sizeof(int);
nIndex++)
{
  depthHistogram[nIndex] +=
    depthHistogram[nIndex-1];
}

double resizeFactor = min(
  (window_w / (double)newFrame.getWidth()),
  (window_h / (double)newFrame.getHeight()));
unsigned int texture_x = (unsigned int)(window_w -
  (resizeFactor * newFrame.getWidth())) / 2;
unsigned int texture_y = (unsigned int)(window_h -
  (resizeFactor * newFrame.getHeight())) / 2;

for  (unsigned int y = 0;
  y < (window_h - 2 * texture_y); ++y)
{
  OniRGB888Pixel* texturePixel = gl_texture +
    ((y + texture_y) * window_w) + texture_x;
  for  (unsigned int x = 0;
    x < (window_w - 2 * texture_x);
    ++x, ++texturePixel)
```

```
    {
      DepthPixel* streamPixel =
        (DepthPixel*)(
          (char*)newFrame.getData() +
          ((int)(y / resizeFactor) *
            newFrame.getStrideInBytes())
        ) + (int)(x / resizeFactor);
      if (*streamPixel != 0)
      {
        char depthValue =
        ((float)depthHistogram[*streamPixel] /
        numberOfPoints) * 255;
        texturePixel->b = 255 - depthValue;
        texturePixel->g = 255 - depthValue;
        texturePixel->r = 255 - depthValue;
      }
      else
      {
        texturePixel->b = 0;
        texturePixel->g = 0;
        texturePixel->r = 0;
      }
    }
  }
}


// Create the OpenGL texture map
glTexParameteri(GL_TEXTURE_2D,
  0x8191, GL_TRUE);
glTexImage2D(GL_TEXTURE_2D, 0, GL_RGB,
  window_w, window_h, 0, GL_RGB,
  GL_UNSIGNED_BYTE, gl_texture);

glBegin(GL_QUADS);
glTexCoord2f(0.0f, 0.0f);
glVertex3f(0.0f, 0.0f, 0.0f);
glTexCoord2f(0.0f, 1.0f);
glVertex3f(0.0f, (float)window_h, 0.0f);
glTexCoord2f(1.0f, 1.0f);
glVertex3f((float)window_w,
  (float)window_h, 0.0f);
glTexCoord2f(1.0f, 0.0f);
glVertex3f((float)window_w, 0.0f, 0.0f);
glEnd();
```

```
        glutSwapBuffers();
      }
    }
  }
}
```

As you can see, a lot of the parts are similar. We put in conditions to check if `openni::VideoStream` is valid, waited for a new frame, then checked whether the new frame is valid, and so on. After that, we cleared the OpenGL buffer, set some options, filled texture data, provided the texture buffer to OpenGL, and swapped the buffers.

The only change here is in the filling part (as always), which starts after the `UPDATING TEXTURE (DEPTH 1MM TO RGB888)` line and ends before `// Create the OpenGL texture map` line.

Here, we first tried to create a histogram of 16-bit depth data using the following code snippet:

```
int depthHistogram[65536];
int numberOfPoints = 0;
memset(depthHistogram, 0,
  sizeof(depthHistogram));
for  (int y = 0;
      y < newFrame.getHeight(); ++y)
{
  DepthPixel* depthCell = (DepthPixel*)(
    (char*)newFrame.getData() +
    (y * newFrame.getStrideInBytes())
    );
  for  (int x = 0; x < newFrame.getWidth();
      ++x, ++depthCell)
  {
    if (*depthCell != 0)
      {
      depthHistogram[*depthCell]++;
      numberOfPoints++;
    }
  }
}
```

In this code, we first declared a variable of type `int` and an array named `depthHistogram` to store our histogram. Then we declared another variable named `numberOfPoints` to keep the number of all valid pixels (pixels with data) of the entire data.

Our main process starts with the first loop through the height of our depth frame data and then we calculate the position of each row's first pixel in the next line.

```
DepthPixel* depthCell = (DepthPixel*)(
    (char*)newFrame.getData() +
    (y * newFrame.getStrideInBytes())
    );
```

Again, we converted `newFrame.getData()` to the `char` pointer and increased it by `(y * newFrame.getStrideInBytes())` bytes, then converted it back to the `openni::DepthPixel` pointer, and stored it in the `depthCell` variable. In the next `for` loop, we looped through each pixel of that row by increasing `depthCell` and checked whether the value of the current pixel is greater than 0. If so, we will add 1 to the number of points and to its position in the histogram array.

Using these 2 loops, we will analyze the whole picture and extract the distribution of colors; in other words, we will create the image's histogram.

For histogram equalization, we need to perform two operations. First, we need to change our histogram to a cumulative histogram and then calculate the new pixel value from that histogram. Currently, we need to convert our histogram to a cumulative histogram (also known as an accumulated histogram).

```
for (int nIndex=1;
nIndex < sizeof(depthHistogram) / sizeof(int);
nIndex++)
{
  depthHistogram[nIndex] +=
    depthHistogram[nIndex-1];
}
```

Read more about cumulative histograms at:
`http://en.wikipedia.org/wiki/Histogram#Cumulative_histogram`
And why we need to use it at:
`http://en.wikipedia.org/wiki/Histogram_equalization#Implementation`

Now we are almost done. In the last step, we need an alternate copying process too. Just as we did earlier, here too we have codes for the calculation of `resizeFactor` and paddings, and right after that we have two loops.

```
for  (unsigned int y = 0;
  y < (window_h - 2 * texture_y); ++y)
{
```

```
OniRGB888Pixel* texturePixel = gl_texture +
  ((y + texture_y) * window_w) + texture_x;
for  (unsigned int x = 0;
  x < (window_w - 2 * texture_x);
  ++x, ++texturePixel)
{
```

In the second loop, we need to calculate the position of the related pixel in the depth frame data and convert and copy it to our texture frame data. But now we want to change this process a little.

```
DepthPixel* streamPixel =
  (DepthPixel*)(
    (char*)newFrame.getData() +
    ((int)(y / resizeFactor) *
      newFrame.getStrideInBytes())
  ) + (int)(x / resizeFactor);
if (*streamPixel != 0)
{
  char depthValue =
  ((float)depthHistogram[*streamPixel] /
    numberOfPoints) * 255;
  texturePixel->b = 255 - depthValue;
  texturePixel->g = 255 - depthValue;
  texturePixel->r = 255 - depthValue;
}
else
{
  texturePixel->b = 0;
  texturePixel->g = 0;
  texturePixel->r = 0;
}
```

As you can see, instead of using *streamPixel in the texture buffer directly, this time we decided to use it in the bigger formula and calculate a better value depending on the image's histogram:

```
char depthValue =
((float)depthHistogram[*streamPixel] /
  numberOfPoints) * 255;
```

This was the last step. The other parts are the same as in the main recipe's code.

Let's take a look at the output of this new method and a comparison with the native data:

Please note the changes in the grayscale line below the images. It clearly shows you how the image changed.

Wider color space for showing more details

Be informed that all we try to show to you here and in the last part is about how to show data; not the data itself. We try to introduce new ways of showing data to make more details visible. Data is always the same and contains the same details and information.

In the main code, we tried to explain to you how to show a depth frame in grayscale color space using 256 colors. Now we want to expand our color space. There are a lot of options for expanding a wider color space than grayscale; one of the most famous ones is using the colors of the rainbow. This is a good option and can give us about 1536 colors, which means we can show data with less than two times loss in detail. But it is a little complicated because we need to work with HSV and then convert it back to RGB, but we don't want to make it that complicated. So we use another range of colors with a lesser number of colors.

This color space can give us 1024 different colors that can show four times more detail than a simple grayscale while still being easy to implement.

Lets take a look at the following code snippet:

```
void gl_DisplayCallback()
{
  if (depthSensor.isValid())
  {
    Status status = STATUS_OK;
    VideoStream* streamPointer = &depthSensor;
    int streamReadyIndex;
    status = OpenNI::waitForAnyStream(&streamPointer, 1,
      &streamReadyIndex, 500);
    if (status == STATUS_OK && streamReadyIndex == 0)
    {
      VideoFrameRef newFrame;
      status = depthSensor.readFrame(&newFrame);
      if (status == STATUS_OK && newFrame.isValid())
      {
        // Clear the OpenGL buffers
        glClear (
          GL_COLOR_BUFFER_BIT | GL_DEPTH_BUFFER_BIT);

        // Setup the OpenGL viewpoint
        glMatrixMode(GL_PROJECTION);
        glPushMatrix();
        glLoadIdentity();
        glOrtho(0, window_w, window_h, 0, -1.0, 1.0);

        // UPDATING TEXTURE (DEPTH 1MM TO RGB888)
        unsigned short maxDepth =
          depthSensor.getMinPixelValue();
        unsigned short minDepth =
          depthSensor.getMaxPixelValue();
        for  (int y = 0; y < newFrame.getHeight(); ++y)
        {
          DepthPixel* depthCell = (DepthPixel*)(
            (char*)newFrame.getData() +
            (y * newFrame.getStrideInBytes())
            );
          for  (int x = 0; x < newFrame.getWidth();
              ++x, ++depthCell)
          {
            if (maxDepth < *depthCell)
            {
              maxDepth = *depthCell;
```

```
      }
      if (*depthCell != 0 &&
        minDepth > *depthCell)
      {
        minDepth = *depthCell;
      }
    }
  }
}

double resizeFactor = min(
  (window_w / (double)newFrame.getWidth()),
  (window_h / (double)newFrame.getHeight()));
unsigned int texture_x = (unsigned int)(window_w -
  (resizeFactor * newFrame.getWidth())) / 2;
unsigned int texture_y = (unsigned int)(window_h -
  (resizeFactor * newFrame.getHeight())) / 2;

for  (unsigned int y = 0;
  y < (window_h - 2 * texture_y); ++y)
{
  OniRGB888Pixel* texturePixel = gl_texture +
    ((y + texture_y) * window_w) + texture_x;
  for  (unsigned int x = 0;
    x < (window_w - 2 * texture_x);
    ++x, ++texturePixel)
  {
    DepthPixel* streamPixel =
      (DepthPixel*)(
        (char*)newFrame.getData() +
        ((int)(y / resizeFactor) *
          newFrame.getStrideInBytes())
      ) + (int)(x / resizeFactor);

    if (*streamPixel != 0)
    {
      float colorPaletteFactor =
        (float)1024 / maxDepth;
      int colorCode =
      (*streamPixel - minDepth) *
        colorPaletteFactor;
      texturePixel->b = (
        (colorCode > 0 && colorCode < 512)
          ? abs(colorCode - 256) : 255);
      texturePixel->g = (
```

```
                        (colorCode > 128 && colorCode < 640)
                          ? abs(colorCode - 384) : 255);
                 texturePixel->r = (
                   (colorCode > 512 && colorCode < 1024)
                     ? abs(colorCode - 768) : 255);
            }
            else
            {
              texturePixel->b = 0;
              texturePixel->g = 0;
              texturePixel->r = 0;
            }
        }
    }


    // Create the OpenGL texture map
    glTexParameteri(GL_TEXTURE_2D,
      0x8191, GL_TRUE);
    glTexImage2D(GL_TEXTURE_2D, 0, GL_RGB,
      window_w, window_h, 0, GL_RGB,
      GL_UNSIGNED_BYTE, gl_texture);

    glBegin(GL_QUADS);
    glTexCoord2f(0.0f, 0.0f);
    glVertex3f(0.0f, 0.0f, 0.0f);
    glTexCoord2f(0.0f, 1.0f);
    glVertex3f(0.0f, (float)window_h, 0.0f);
    glTexCoord2f(1.0f, 1.0f);
    glVertex3f((float)window_w,
      (float)window_h, 0.0f);
     glTexCoord2f(1.0f, 0.0f);
     glVertex3f((float)window_w, 0.0f, 0.0f);
     glEnd();

    glutSwapBuffers();
    }
   }
  }
 }
```

As you can see, there are slight changes here. The first change is in the line where we defined a variable named `minDepth` and then another named `maxDepth`. Later, we looped through all the pixels of data and extracted max and min values. We did the same thing in the recipe's main code, but this time we calculated `minDepth` too because we wanted to use all the parts of our color space without missing out a single color!

The next important change is in the main loop of the copying and converting process. Instead of using values directly from the data frame, we tried to convert it in a different way for each color of pixel (R, G, and B).

```
float colorPaletteFactor =
   (float)1024 / maxDepth;
int colorCode =
(*streamPixel - minDepth) *
   colorPaletteFactor;
texturePixel->b = (
   (colorCode > 0 && colorCode < 512)
     ? abs(colorCode - 256) : 255);
texturePixel->g = (
   (colorCode > 128 && colorCode < 640)
     ? abs(colorCode - 384) : 255);
texturePixel->r = (
   (colorCode > 512 && colorCode < 1024)
     ? abs(colorCode - 768) : 255);
```

In the first line, we defined a variable to calculate the color palette factor, showing how we need to reform colors. In the second line, we tried to fit this value within our range of 0-1024 and kept it in a variable named `colorCode` to be used in the next lines. Now that we have converted the value in this range, we can show it. But for showing it, we need to break it apart into three colors (RGB) before updating the texture buffer. The next three lines are all about converting this value into color. These lines are easy to understand and there is no need to describe them line by line. Just keep in mind that we used the `inline if` statement here (`(statement) ? true : false`) and the `abs()` function, which return the absolute value of a number regardless of its sign.

Let's take a look at the output of this new function and a comparison with the native data:

As you can see, this way we can provide more details rather than by using native data or equalizing its histogram. Check out this screenshot to know more:

It is also possible to combine the histogram-equalization method with this method for more details, but that's your choice.

Filling shadows

First of all, there is no way to fill shadows with exact values, because the Kinect, Asus Xtion, and PrimeSense sensors all use structured light to scan the depth of the 3D world; in this method, the projector and receiver are at different angles. So, we always get shadows.

There are different algorithms to fill these shadows. Frameworks such as OpenCV can do it with very good quality. But in many cases, we can simply fill shadow pixels with their left pixel's value. This is exactly what we are going to do here.

For saving space, we decided to show you only those parts that need to change in the main code, instead of repeating the entire `gl_DisplayCallback()` function.

```
for  (unsigned int y = 0;
   y < (window_h - 2 * texture_y); ++y)
  {
    OniRGB888Pixel* texturePixel = gl_texture +
      ((y + texture_y) * window_w) + texture_x;
    DepthPixel lastPixel = 0;
    for  (unsigned int x = 0;
      x < (window_w - 2 * texture_x);
      ++x, ++texturePixel)
    {
      DepthPixel* streamPixel =
        (DepthPixel*)(
            (char*)newFrame.getData() +
            ((int)(y / resizeFactor) *
              newFrame.getStrideInBytes())
          ) + (int)(x / resizeFactor);
      if (*streamPixel != 0){
        lastPixel = *streamPixel;
      }
      char depthValue = ((float)lastPixel /
        maxDepth) * 255;
      texturePixel->b = 255 - depthValue;
      texturePixel->g = 255 - depthValue;
      texturePixel->r = 255 - depthValue;
    }
  }
```

You need to replace two copying `for` loops in the main code (lines 50 to 80) with the preceding lines of code.

The difference is shown in the following screenshot:

Shadow filled   Native

See also

> ► The *Reading and showing a frame from the image sensor (color/IR)* recipe
>
> ► The *Overlaying the depth frame over the image frame* recipe of *Chapter 4, More About Low-level Outputs*
>
> ► The *Identifying and coloring users' pixels in depth map* recipe of *Chapter 5, NiTE and User Tracking*

Controlling the player when opening a device from file

In this recipe we want to introduce you to a new class, `OpenNI::PlaybackControl`. Using this class, you can seek a frame as well as repeat and change the speed of playback easily.

Getting ready

Create a project in Visual Studio 2010 and prepare it for working with OpenNI using the *Creating a project in Visual Studio 2010* recipe of *Chapter 2, Open NI and C++*. After that, configure Visual Studio 2010 to use OpenGL using the *Configuring Visual Studio 2010 to use OpenGL* recipe of this chapter.

How to do it...

1. Add the following lines above your source code (just below the `#include` lines):

```cpp
int window_w = 640;
int window_h = 480;
OniRGB888Pixel* gl_texture;
VideoStream depthSensor;
Device device;
PlaybackControl* playControl;
char ReadLastCharOfLine()
{
  int newChar = 0;
  int lastChar;
  fflush(stdout);
  do
  {
    lastChar = newChar;
    newChar = getchar();
  }
  while ((newChar != '\n')
    && (newChar != EOF));
  return (char)lastChar;
}


bool HandleStatus(Status status)
{
  if (status == STATUS_OK)
    return true;
  printf("ERROR: #%d, %s", status,
    OpenNI::getExtendedError());
  ReadLastCharOfLine();
  return false;
}


void gl_KeyboardCallback(unsigned char key, int x, int y)
{
  if (key == 27) // ESC Key
  {
    depthSensor.destroy();
    device.close();
    OpenNI::shutdown();
    exit(0);
  }
```

```
         else if (key == '<' || key == ',')
         {
           if ((*playControl).isValid())
           {
             (*playControl).seek(depthSensor, 0);
             printf("Restarting from beginning.\r\n");
           }
         }
         else if (key == '+' || key == '=')
         {
           if ((*playControl).isValid() &&
             (*playControl).getSpeed() < 5)
           {
             (*playControl).setSpeed(
               (*playControl).getSpeed() + 0.3);
             printf("Current Speed is %s\r\n",
               (*playControl).getSpeed());
           }
         }
         else if (key == '_' || key == '-')
         {
           if ((*playControl).isValid() &&
             (*playControl).getSpeed() > 0.3)
           {
             (*playControl).setSpeed(
               (*playControl).getSpeed() - 0.2);
             printf("Current Speed is %s\r\n",
               (*playControl).getSpeed());
           }
         }
         else if (key == 'R' || key == 'r')
         {
           if ((*playControl).isValid())
           {
             (*playControl).setRepeatEnabled(
               !(*playControl).getRepeatEnabled());
             printf("Repeating: %d.\r\n",
               (*playControl).getRepeatEnabled());
           }
         }
       }

       void gl_IdleCallback()
       {
```

```
    glutPostRedisplay();
}

void gl_DisplayCallback()
{
  if (depthSensor.isValid())
  {
    Status status = STATUS_OK;
    VideoStream* streamPointer = &depthSensor;
    int streamReadyIndex;
    status = OpenNI::waitForAnyStream(&streamPointer, 1,
      &streamReadyIndex, 500);
    if (status == STATUS_OK && streamReadyIndex == 0)
    {
      VideoFrameRef newFrame;
      status = depthSensor.readFrame(&newFrame);
      if (status == STATUS_OK && newFrame.isValid())
      {
        // Clear the OpenGL buffers
        glClear (
          GL_COLOR_BUFFER_BIT | GL_DEPTH_BUFFER_BIT);

        // Setup the OpenGL viewpoint
        glMatrixMode(GL_PROJECTION);
        glPushMatrix();
        glLoadIdentity();
        glOrtho(0, window_w, window_h, 0, -1.0, 1.0);

        // UPDATING TEXTURE (DEPTH 1MM TO RGB888)
        unsigned short maxDepth =
          depthSensor.getMinPixelValue();
        for  (int y = 0; y < newFrame.getHeight(); ++y)
        {
          DepthPixel* depthCell = (DepthPixel*)(
            (char*)newFrame.getData() +
            (y * newFrame.getStrideInBytes())
            );
          for  (int x = 0; x < newFrame.getWidth();
            ++x, ++depthCell)
          {
            if (maxDepth < *depthCell)
            {
              maxDepth = *depthCell;
            }
```

```
    }
  }

  double resizeFactor = min(
    (window_w / (double)newFrame.getWidth()),
    (window_h / (double)newFrame.getHeight()));
  unsigned int texture_x = (unsigned int)(window_w -
    (resizeFactor * newFrame.getWidth())) / 2;
  unsigned int texture_y = (unsigned int)(window_h -
    (resizeFactor * newFrame.getHeight())) / 2;

  for (unsigned int y = 0;
    y < (window_h - 2 * texture_y); ++y)
  {
    OniRGB888Pixel* texturePixel = gl_texture +
      ((y + texture_y) * window_w) + texture_x;
    for (unsigned int x = 0;
      x < (window_w - 2 * texture_x);
      ++x, ++texturePixel)
    {
      DepthPixel* streamPixel =
        (DepthPixel*)(
          (char*)newFrame.getData() +
          ((int)(y / resizeFactor) *
            newFrame.getStrideInBytes())
        ) + (int)(x / resizeFactor);
      if (*streamPixel != 0)
      {
        char depthValue = ((float)*streamPixel /
          maxDepth) * 255;
        texturePixel->b = 255 - depthValue;
        texturePixel->g = 255 - depthValue;
        texturePixel->r = 255 - depthValue;
      }
      else
      {
        texturePixel->b = 0;
        texturePixel->g = 0;
        texturePixel->r = 0;
      }
    }
  }

  // Create the OpenGL texture map
```

```
glTexParameteri(GL_TEXTURE_2D,
   0x8191, GL_TRUE);
glTexImage2D(GL_TEXTURE_2D, 0, GL_RGB,
   window_w, window_h, 0, GL_RGB,
   GL_UNSIGNED_BYTE, gl_texture);

glBegin(GL_QUADS);
glTexCoord2f(0.0f, 0.0f);
glVertex3f(0.0f, 0.0f, 0.0f);
glTexCoord2f(0.0f, 1.0f);
glVertex3f(0.0f, (float)window_h, 0.0f);
glTexCoord2f(1.0f, 1.0f);
glVertex3f((float)window_w,
   (float)window_h, 0.0f);
glTexCoord2f(1.0f, 0.0f);
glVertex3f((float)window_w, 0.0f, 0.0f);
glEnd();

glutSwapBuffers();
      }
    }
  }
}
```

2. Then locate the following lines of code:

```
int _tmain(int argc, _TCHAR* argv[])
{
```

3. Write the following code snippet below the preceding lines of code:

```
Status status = STATUS_OK;
printf("Scanning machine for devices and loading "
    "modules/drivers ...\r\n");

status = OpenNI::initialize();
if (!HandleStatus(status)) return 1;
printf("Completed.\r\n");

printf("Opening oni file ...\r\n");
status = device.open("C:\MultipleHands_From_OpenNIorg.oni");
if (!HandleStatus(status)) return 1;
printf("%s Opened, Completed.\r\n",
   device.getDeviceInfo().getName());

printf("Requesting play controller ...\r\n");
```

```
playControl = device.getPlaybackControl();
printf("Done.\r\n");

printf("Checking if stream is supported ...\r\n");
if (!device.hasSensor(SENSOR_DEPTH))
{
  printf("Stream not supported by this device.\r\n");
  return 1;
}

printf("Asking device to create a depth stream ...\r\n");
status = depthSensor.create(device, SENSOR_DEPTH);
if (!HandleStatus(status)) return 1;

printf("Starting stream ...\r\n");
status = depthSensor.start();
if (!HandleStatus(status)) return 1;
printf("Done.\r\n");

printf("Initializing OpenGL ...\r\n");
gl_texture = (OniRGB888Pixel*)malloc(
  window_w * window_h * sizeof(OniRGB888Pixel));
glutInit(&argc, (char**)argv);
glutInitDisplayMode(GLUT_RGB | GLUT_DOUBLE | GLUT_DEPTH);
glutInitWindowSize(window_w, window_h);
glutCreateWindow ("OpenGL | OpenNI 2.x CookBook Sample");
glutKeyboardFunc(gl_KeyboardCallback);
glutDisplayFunc(gl_DisplayCallback);
glutIdleFunc(gl_IdleCallback);
glDisable(GL_DEPTH_TEST);
glEnable(GL_TEXTURE_2D);
printf("Starting OpenGL rendering process ...\r\n");
printf("Use + key to increase and"
    " - to decrease speed.\r\n");
printf("Use Enter and Space key to pause playback.\r\n");
printf("Use < key to restart playback.\r\n");
printf("Toggle repeating by R key.\r\n");
glutMainLoop();
```

How it works...

As you can see, the code of the first part is pretty much as it was in the *Reading and showing a frame from the depth sensor* recipe of this chapter. We defined different variables and functions, and the body of all the functions except `gl_KeyboardCallback` are the same as before. Also, we have a new variable named `playControl` of type `openni::PlaybackControl` pointer too. Using this variable along with the `gl_KeyboardCallback` function, we are going to control the playback process via keyboard events.

```
PlaybackControl* playControl;
```

Let's take a look at the body of the `gl_KeyboardCallback` function:

```
if (key == 27) // ESC Key
{
  depthSensor.destroy();
  device.close();
  OpenNI::shutdown();
  exit(0);
}
else if (key == '<' || key == ',')
{
  if ((*playControl).isValid())
  {
    (*playControl).seek(depthSensor, 0);
    printf("Restarting from beginning.\r\n");
  }
}
else if (key == '+' || key == '=')
{
  if ((*playControl).isValid() &&
    (*playControl).getSpeed() < 5)
  {
    (*playControl).setSpeed(
      (*playControl).getSpeed() + 0.3);
    printf("Current Speed is %s\r\n",
      (*playControl).getSpeed());
  }
}
else if (key == '_' || key == '-')
{
```

```
        if ((*playControl).isValid() &&
          (*playControl).getSpeed() > 0.3)
        {
          (*playControl).setSpeed(
            (*playControl).getSpeed() - 0.2);
          printf("Current Speed is %s\r\n",
            (*playControl).getSpeed());
        }
    }
    else if (key == 'R' || key == 'r')
    {
        if ((*playControl).isValid())
        {
          (*playControl).setRepeatEnabled(
            !(*playControl).getRepeatEnabled());
          printf("Repeating: %d.\r\n",
            (*playControl).getRepeatEnabled());
        }
    }
```

As you can see, the first line is a condition for exiting by the *Esc* key, as always. If the pressed key was not the *Esc* key, we check whether it was the < or , key (they are the same key on the keyboard usually), and if so we change the active frame to the first frame. Using this, we can restart playback from the beginning.

```
        if ((*playControl).isValid())
        {
          (*playControl).seek(depthSensor, 0);
          printf("Restarting from beginning.\r\n");
        }
```

The first line checks if the `playControl` object is valid, and if so we try to use the `openni::PlaybackControl::seek()` method to change the active frame to `0`. We also use the `printf()` function to inform the user about the operation.

If the pressed key was not < or , either, we check whether it was + or = (again, because they are the same key on the keyboard and we don't want the user to press the *Shift* key); if so, we will increase the speed of playback.

```
        if ((*playControl).isValid() &&
          (*playControl).getSpeed() < 5)
        {
          (*playControl).setSpeed(
            (*playControl).getSpeed() + 0.2);
          printf("Current Speed is %s\r\n",
            (*playControl).getSpeed());
        }
```

Just as we did the last time, here too we check if the `playControl` object is valid, and if it was we check if the current speed is lower than five times (because we don't want the user to increase the speed too much), using `openni::PlaybackControl::getSpeed()` to get the current speed; if both the conditions are true, we use `openni::PlaybackControl::setSpeed()` to set the new speed (0.2 times higher than the current speed).

Again, just as with the last time, we inform the user using the `printf()` function.

We now need to introduce a way to decrease the speed, and that is why we try to check whether the pressed key was _ or –. If it was, we use the same logic as in the last part about increasing speed, but with some simple changes. For example, instead of checking the current speed not being higher than five times, this time we try to check if it was higher than 0.3 (because we don't want it to become lower than 0.1) and then decrease it by 0.2 times using the `openni::PlaybackControl::setSpeed()` method.

```
if ((*playControl).isValid() &&
  (*playControl).getSpeed() > 0.3)
{
  (*playControl).setSpeed(
    (*playControl).getSpeed() - 0.2);
  printf("Current Speed is %s\r\n",
    (*playControl).getSpeed());
}
```

If none of the keys mentioned above were pressed, we check if the pressed key is *r* or *R*; if it was, we will toggle the repeating mode on and off.

```
if ((*playControl).isValid())
{
  (*playControl).setRepeatEnabled(
    !(*playControl).getRepeatEnabled());
  printf("Repeating: %d.\r\n",
    (*playControl).getRepeatEnabled());
}
```

The logic behind the previous code is similar to that for changing the speed of playback. We used `openni::PlaybackControl::getRepeatEnabled()` to get the current repeating status, and then reversed and set it using `openni::PlaybackControl::setRepeatEnabled()`. And, of course, we checked if `playControl` is valid before doing anything.

There is nothing else important in step 1. In step 3, we tried to initialize OpenNI, as always, opened a file as `device`, created depth's `openni::VideoStream`, and then initialized OpenGL. The only difference here is in the comparison of the simple drawing of depth sensor output to OpenGL, where we requested access to the `openni::PlaybackControl` object of the associated device using `openni::Device::getPlaybackControl()`. The return value of this method is an `openni::PlaybackControl` object responsible for controlling the playback of the file. We filled our `playControl` variable with the return value of this method so that we can use it later, especially in our `gl_KeyboardCallback` function.

```
printf("Requesting play controller ...\r\n");
playControl = device.getPlaybackControl();
printf("Done.\r\n");
```

There is nothing special here. Let's take a look at the output of this application:

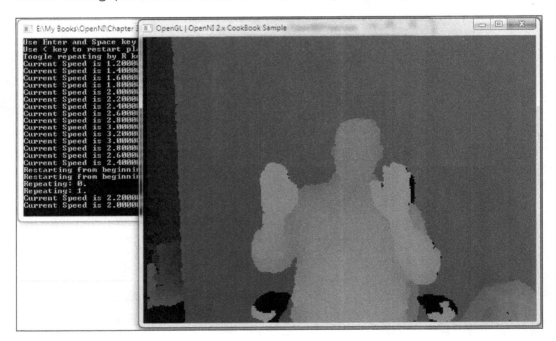

See also

▶   The *Opening an already recorded file (ONI file) instead of a device* recipe of *Chapter 2, Open NI and C++*

Recording streams to file (ONI file)

We learned about playing `ONI` files but it was only a part of this topic. You can record `ONI` files from the device's outputs yourself too. We will now introduce an `openni::Recorder` class that can be used for this purpose. This recipe is easy, as adding and starting `openni::VideoStream` involves nothing special.

Getting ready

Create a project in Visual Studio 2010 and prepare it for working with OpenNI using the *Creating a project in Visual Studio 2010* recipe of *Chapter 2, Open NI and C++*. We don't need OpenGL in this recipe.

How to do it...

1. Add the following lines above your source code (just below the `#include` lines):

```
char ReadLastCharOfLine()
{
  int newChar = 0;
  int lastChar;
  fflush(stdout);
  do
  {
    lastChar = newChar;
    newChar = getchar();
  }
  while ((newChar != '\n')
    && (newChar != EOF));
  return (char)lastChar;
}

bool HandleStatus(Status status)
{
  if (status == STATUS_OK)
    return true;
  printf("ERROR: #%d, %s", status,
    OpenNI::getExtendedError());
  ReadLastCharOfLine();
  return false;
}
```

2. Then locate the following lines of code:

```
int _tmain(int argc, _TCHAR* argv[])
{
```

3. Write the following code snippet below the preceding lines of code:

```
Status status = STATUS_OK;
printf("Scanning machine for devices and loading "
    "modules/drivers ...\r\n");

status = OpenNI::initialize();
if (!HandleStatus(status)) return 1;
printf("Completed.\r\n");

Device device;
printf("Opening first device ...\r\n");
status = device.open(ANY_DEVICE);
if (!HandleStatus(status)) return 1;
printf("%s Opened, Completed.\r\n",
  device.getDeviceInfo().getName());

printf("Checking if stream is supported ...\r\n");
if (!device.hasSensor(SENSOR_DEPTH))
{
  printf("Stream not supported by this device.\r\n");
  return 1;
}

printf("Asking device to create a depth stream ...\r\n");
VideoStream depthSensor;
status = depthSensor.create(device, SENSOR_DEPTH);
if (!HandleStatus(status)) return 1;

printf("Starting stream ...\r\n");
status = depthSensor.start();
if (!HandleStatus(status)) return 1;
printf("Done.\r\n");

printf("Creating a recorder ...\r\n");
Recorder recorder;
status = recorder.create("C:\sample.oni");
if (!HandleStatus(status)) return 1;
printf("Done.\r\n");
```

```
printf("Attaching to depth sensor ...\r\n");
status = recorder.attach(depthSensor);
if (!HandleStatus(status)) return 1;
printf("Done.\r\n");

printf("Starting recorder ...\r\n");
status = recorder.start();
if (!HandleStatus(status)) return 1;
printf("Done. Now recording ...\r\n");

ReadLastCharOfLine();
recorder.destroy();
depthSensor.destroy();
device.close();
OpenNI::shutdown();
```

How it works...

Step 1 only contains the definition of two of our basic functions, `ReadLastCharOfLine()` for waiting for user input and `HandleStatus()` for recognizing the error state and printing the error to the console. You can read more about these functions in previous chapters.

Our main code here is in step 2. As you can see, here we have the initializing process of OpenNI, as always; we then created depth by using `openni::VideoStream` and started it.

The difference in this recipe, when compared to older recipes, is where we defined a variable of type `openni::Recorder` with the name `recorder` using its `openni::Recorder::create()` method. Please note that this method accepts an argument of type `string` that will be used to create a file to save data. We selected `C:\sample.oni` as the desired name and address for our file.

```
Recorder recorder;
status = recorder.create("C:\\sample.oni");
```

Then we usually need to start the recording process just as we did with `openni::VideoStream`. But without attaching `recorder` to the depth stream, it will save nothing. We need to use the `openni::Recorder::attach()` method before starting the recording process.

```
status = recorder.attach(depthSensor);
```

We need to repeat this line for each `openni::VideoStream` object that we want to store in the recorded file.

After we add all our `openni::VideoStream` objects, we can start the recording process.

```
status = recorder.start();
```

Now we can either wait or use the output of `openni::VideoStream` objects to do something else. But because we wanted to make this recipe shorter and easier to understand, we decided to use the `ReadLastCharOfLine()` function instead of using data and waiting for the user to press a key.

At last, as the user presses the *Enter* key, we will destroy the `recorder` and `depthsensor` objects, close the device, and then shut down OpenNI. We can then return `0` to end program execution.

The output of this program is predictable. Here is a screenshot:

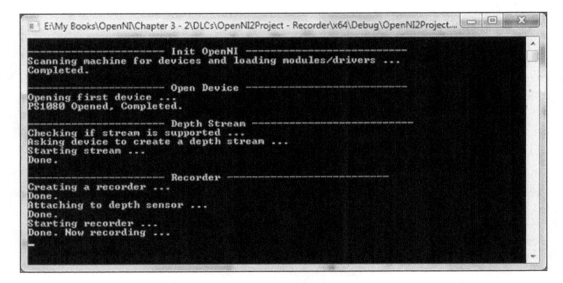

See also

▸ The *Opening an already recorded file (ONI file) instead of a device* recipe of *Chapter 2, Open NI and C++*

▸ The *Controlling the player when opening a device from file* recipe

Event-based reading of data

In OpenNI 2.x, instead of using `openni::OpenNI::waitForAnyStream()`, we can use the `openni::VideoStream` object's events for reading new frames of data. This is a more standard way than creating an infinite loop around code. In this recipe, we will try to capture this event but we are not actually going to use it in any way. Read the older recipes about how to show and read a frame from sensors.

Getting ready

Create a project in Visual Studio 2010 and prepare it for working with OpenNI using the *Creating a project in Visual Studio 2010* recipe of *Chapter 2, Open NI and C++*.We don't need OpenGL in this recipe.

How to do it...

1. Add the following lines above your source code (just below the `#include` lines):

```
char ReadLastCharOfLine()
{
  int newChar = 0;
  int lastChar;
  fflush(stdout);
  do
  {
    lastChar = newChar;
    newChar = getchar();
  }
  while ((newChar != '\n')
    && (newChar != EOF));
  return (char)lastChar;
}

bool HandleStatus(Status status)
{
  if (status == STATUS_OK)
    return true;
  printf("ERROR: #%d, %s", status,
    OpenNI::getExtendedError());
  ReadLastCharOfLine();
  return false;
}
```

```
      struct OurOpenNINewFrameMonitorer : public
      VideoStream::NewFrameListener
      {
        void onNewFrame(VideoStream& videoStream)
        {
          printf("%d. New data is available to read.\r\n",
            clock());
        }
      };
```

2. Then locate the following lines of code:

```
    int _tmain(int argc, _TCHAR* argv[])
    {
```

3. Write the following code snippet below the preceding lines of code:

```
      Status status = STATUS_OK;
      printf("Scanning machine for devices and loading "
          "modules/drivers ...\r\n");

      status = OpenNI::initialize();
      if (!HandleStatus(status)) return 1;
      printf("Completed.\r\n");

      Device device;
      printf("Opening first device ...\r\n");
      status = device.open(ANY_DEVICE);
      if (!HandleStatus(status)) return 1;
      printf("%s Opened, Completed.\r\n",
        device.getDeviceInfo().getName());

      printf("Checking if stream is supported ...\r\n");
      if (!device.hasSensor(SENSOR_DEPTH))
      {
        printf("Stream not supported by this device.\r\n");
        return 1;
      }

      printf("Asking device to create a depth stream ...\r\n");
      VideoStream depthSensor;
      status = depthSensor.create(device, SENSOR_DEPTH);
      if (!HandleStatus(status)) return 1;

      printf("Registering callback ...\r\n");
      OurOpenNINewFrameMonitorer p;
      status = depthSensor.addNewFrameListener(&p);
```

```
if (!HandleStatus(status)) return 1;

printf("Starting stream ...\r\n");
status = depthSensor.start();
if (!HandleStatus(status)) return 1;
printf("Done.\r\n");

ReadLastCharOfLine();
depthSensor.destroy();
device.close();
OpenNI::shutdown();
```

How it works...

I would recommend reading the *Listening to the device connect and disconnect events* recipe of *Chapter 2, Open NI and C++*, for knowing what listener classes are and how OpenNI implements its event callback system, because we are not going to describe it here again.

In step 1 of the previous code, we have two functions for waiting for user input, checking the `openni::Status` object, and printing error messages to the console, if any, just as in the last recipe. But right after defining these two functions, we have a definition for a structure named `OurOpenNINewFrameMonitorer`, which inherits from the `openni:VideoStream::NewFrameListener` class. If you have read the *Listening to the device connect and disconnect events* recipe of *Chapter 2, OpenNI and C++*, you will know that we need to define a class or structure from a listener class and then introduce it to OpenNI to capture OpenNI's events. Because of this logic, we defined the structure here as a child of `openni::VideoStream::NewFrameListener`. Please note that we used the `openni::VideoStream::NewFrameListener` class because we wanted to capture the `openni::VideoStream` object's events.

In this structure, we defined a method named `onNewFrame()`. The signature of this method is very important because we want to override the internal virtual method of the parent class.

In the `onNewFrame()` method, we have only one line of code for printing to the console and informing the user that there is a new frame available to be read. We don't actually want to use this data, but just inform the user and show him/her how to use this event instead of using the `openni::OpenNI::waitForAnyStream()` method.

```
struct OurOpenNINewFrameMonitorer : public
VideoStream::NewFrameListener
{
  void onNewFrame(VideoStream& videoStream)
  {
    printf("%d. New data is available to read.\r\n",
      clock());
  }
};
```

In step 3, things are pretty much the same as older recipes. Just as always, we initialized OpenNI, opened a device, and created depth by using `openni::VideoStream`. But there is a slight difference here. We used the `openni::VideoStream::addNewFrameListener()` method for the first time. This method accepts an argument of type `openni::VideoStream::NewFrameListener` and passes new frames to this class. This class is an almost empty class with only one virtual method named `onNewFrame`. But in step 1, we defined a structure from this class, named `OurOpenNINewFrameMonitorer`, and wrote our custom `onNewFrame` method. Because `OurOpenNINewFrameMonitorer` inherits from `openni::VideoStream::NewFrameListener`, we can pass it as an argument to the `openni::VideoStream::addNewFrameListener()` method without any problem. Whenever any new event is raised, this is our method that will be called.

```
OurOpenNINewFrameMonitorer p;
status = depthSensor.addNewFrameListener(&p);
```

In the first line, we created an object from the `OurOpenNINewFrameMonitorer` structure and, in the second line, we used the pointer of our new object as a parameter of the `openni::VideoStream::addNewFrameListener()` method.

Then we started the depth's `openni::VideoStream` stream and waited for new data or for the user to press the *Enter* key to end the execution process.

```
ReadLastCharOfLine();
```

After this line, we will destroy, close, and shut down everything, including OpenNI, and return 0 as a sign of the application's successful end.

> Please note that structures and classes are almost the same thing in C++ and there is little difference when we use a structure instead of a class and viceversa. So here you can use a class instead of defining a structure, and it is probably a better idea. Our reason for using a structure here is only to show you that using a structure is also possible.

The following is the output of this code at the very beginning of the run:

```
E:\My Books\OpenNI\Chapter 3 - 2\DLCs\OpenNI2Project - EventRead\x64\Debug\OpenNI2Projec...

------------------------- Init OpenNI -------------------------
Scanning machine for devices and loading modules/drivers ...
Completed.

------------------------- Open Device -------------------------
Opening first device ...
PS1080 Opened, Completed.

------------------------- Depth Stream -------------------------
Checking if stream is supported ...
Asking device to create a depth stream ...
Registring callback ...
Starting stream ...
Done.
1314. New data is available to read.
1344. New data is available to read.
1384. New data is available to read.
1414. New data is available to read.
1444. New data is available to read.
1484. New data is available to read.
1514. New data is available to read.
1544. New data is available to read.
```

4
More about Low-level Outputs

In this chapter, we will cover the following recipes:

- ▶ Cropping and mirroring frames right from the buffer
- ▶ Syncing image and depth sensors to read new frames from both streams at the same time
- ▶ Overlaying the depth frame over the image frame
- ▶ Converting the depth unit to millimetre
- ▶ Retrieving the color of the nearest point without depth-over-color registration
- ▶ Enabling/disabling auto exposure and auto white balance

Introduction

Until now we have learned how to request, read, and show outputs of sensors to a user along with how to configure each sensor to give us the desired resolution and pixel format.

But in this chapter, we are going to show you how we can do more customization, including cropping or mirroring the output of an image right from the device or, more importantly, overlaying the depth frame over the image frame.

These enhancements are scattered all over the OpenNI. Here is a list of all the classes with some information about the enhancements that are included with them.

The openni::Device object

This class contains methods to enable and disable depth and image frame syncing and depth-over-image registration. In other words, any enhancements that have an effect on two or more sensors are included with this class.

The openni::VideoStream object

Methods to enable the mirroring of frame data and the cropping of a specific area in frames are part of this class. `openni::VideoStream` is home to methods that are responsible for customizing each frame of data.

The openni::CoordinateConverter class

If you want to convert the position and value of a depth pixel into the real-world position, distance, or color of that pixel, you need to start using the `openni::CoordinateConverter` class. This class is a standalone class that contains static methods for these sorts of operations.

The openni::CameraSettings object

`openni::CameraSettings` can be accessed by the `openni::VideoStream` object and can only be used with a color sensor. This object lets you activate or deactivate the camera's built-in features, including auto exposure and auto white balance.

Cropping and mirroring frames right from the buffer

In this recipe, we are going to show you how we can use two features of `openni::VideoStream` that give us the ability to mirror or crop frames right from the device itself. This ability is available for all three outputs based on `openni::VideoStream`.

For saving more space, we decided to use the code from the *Reading and showing a frame from the image sensor (color/IR)* recipe of *Chapter 3, Using Low-level Data*, as a template and show you only the changes.

Getting ready

Create a project in Visual Studio 2010 and prepare it for working with OpenNI using the *Creating a project in Visual Studio 2010* recipe of *Chapter 2, OpenNI and C++*. Then, configure Visual Studio 2010 to use OpenGL with the *Configuring Visual Studio 2010 to use OpenGL* recipe of *Chapter 3, Using Low-level Data*.

After that, please copy the code from the *Reading and showing a frame from the image sensor (color/IR)* recipe of *Chapter 3, Using Low-level Data*, to this project.

How to do it...

1. Add the following lines at the top of your source code (just below the `Device device;` line):

```
#include<Math.h>
bool isInCropping = false;
bool isMouseDown = false;
int mouseDownX = 0;
int mouseDownY = 0;

void gl_MouseCallback(int button, int state, int x, int y)
{
  if (button == GLUT_LEFT_BUTTON)
  {
    if (state == GLUT_DOWN && !isMouseDown)
    {
      isMouseDown = true;
      mouseDownX = x;
      mouseDownY = y;
    }
    else if (state == GLUT_UP && isMouseDown)
    {
      isMouseDown = false;

      if (isInCropping)
      {
        printf("Cropping is still active, "
          "press R to reset it first.\r\n");
        return;
      }

      GLint m_viewport[4];
      glGetIntegerv( GL_VIEWPORT, m_viewport );

      int sizeX = ((float)window_w / m_viewport[2])
        * abs(x - mouseDownX);
      int sizeY = ((float)window_h / m_viewport[3])
        * abs(y - mouseDownY);
      int offsetX = ((float)window_w / m_viewport[2])
        * min(x, mouseDownX);
```

```
    int offsetY = ((float)window_h / m_viewport[3])
      * min(y, mouseDownY);

    sizeX = floor((float)sizeX / 4) * 4;
    sizeY = floor((float)sizeY / 4) * 4;
    offsetX = floor((float)offsetX / 4) * 4;
    offsetY = floor((float)offsetY / 4) * 4;

    if (sizeX >= 128 && sizeY >= 128)
    {
      printf("\r\nRequest cropping from %d,%d "
        "with size of %dx%d pixel: \r\n",
        offsetX, offsetY,
        sizeX, sizeY);

      Status status;
      status = selectedSensor.setCropping(
        offsetX, offsetY,
        sizeX,
        sizeY);
      if (status != STATUS_OK)
      {
        printf("Failed. %s\r\n",
            OpenNI::getExtendedError());
      }
      else
      {
        printf("Done. Press R to reset.\r\n");
        memset(gl_texture,0,
          window_w * window_h *
          sizeof(OniRGB888Pixel));
        isInCropping = true;
      }
    }
  }
 }
}
```

2. Then locate the following lines of code:

```
void gl_KeyboardCallback(unsigned char key, int x, int y)
{
```

3. Replace any code inside the body of this function with the following code snippet:

```
if (key == 27) // ESC Key
{
  selectedSensor.destroy();
  device.close();
  OpenNI::shutdown();
  exit(0);
}
else if (key == 'C' || key == 'c')
{
  if (device.isValid())
  {
    printf("\r\n-->Setting active sensor to COLOR\r\n");
    SetActiveSensor(SENSOR_COLOR, &device);
    isInCropping = false;
  }
}
else if (key == 'I' || key == 'i')
{
  if (device.isValid())
  {
    printf("\r\n-->Setting active sensor to IR\r\n");
    SetActiveSensor(SENSOR_IR, &device);
    isInCropping = false;
  }
}
else if (key == 'R' || key == 'r')
{
  // Reset Cropping
  if (selectedSensor.isValid())
  {
    Status status;
    status = selectedSensor.setCropping(0, 0,
      selectedSensor.getVideoMode().getResolutionX(),
      selectedSensor.getVideoMode().getResolutionY());
    if (status == STATUS_OK)
      isInCropping = false;
  }
}
else if (key == 'M' || key == 'm')
{
```

```
      // Toggle Mirroring
      if (selectedSensor.isValid())
        selectedSensor.setMirroringEnabled(
        !selectedSensor.getMirroringEnabled());
  }
```

4. Then locate the following lines of code:

```
int _tmain(int argc, _TCHAR* argv[])
{
```

5. Replace any code inside the body of this function with the following code snippet:

```
Status status = STATUS_OK;
printf("Scanning machine for devices and loading "
    "modules/drivers ...\r\n");

status = OpenNI::initialize();
if (!HandleStatus(status)) return 1;
printf("Completed.\r\n");

printf("Opening first device ...\r\n");
status = device.open(ANY_DEVICE);
if (!HandleStatus(status)) return 1;
printf("%s Opened, Completed.\r\n",
  device.getDeviceInfo().getName());

printf("Initializing OpenGL ...\r\n");
gl_texture = (OniRGB888Pixel*)malloc(
  window_w * window_h * sizeof(OniRGB888Pixel));
glutInit(&argc, (char**)argv);
glutInitDisplayMode(GLUT_RGB | GLUT_DOUBLE | GLUT_DEPTH);
glutInitWindowSize(window_w, window_h);
glutCreateWindow ("OpenGL | OpenNI 2.x CookBook Sample");
glutKeyboardFunc(gl_KeyboardCallback);
glutMouseFunc(gl_MouseCallback);
glutDisplayFunc(gl_DisplayCallback);
glutIdleFunc(gl_IdleCallback);
glDisable(GL_DEPTH_TEST);
glEnable(GL_TEXTURE_2D);
printf("Starting OpenGL rendering process ...\r\n");
SetActiveSensor(SENSOR_COLOR, &device);
printf("Press C for color and I for IR.\r\n");
printf("Use mouse to crop output and "
    "press R to reset cropping.\r\n");
printf("By pressing M key you can toggle mirroring.\r\n");
glutMainLoop();

return 0;
```

How it works...

In the first step we defined other variables that we need and then we defined a new function called `gl_MouseCallback()` to handle all the mouse events occurring in the OpenGL window. Let's take a look at the following code snippet:

```
bool isInCropping = false;
bool isMouseDown = false;
int mouseDownX = 0;
int mouseDownY = 0;
```

Here, we are going to use `isInCropping` to keep the current state of cropping because, unfortunately, there is no way to get it from OpenNI yet. We also define another variable named `isMouseDown` to keep the state of mouse's left button. `mouseDownX` and `mouseDownY` are also used to save the position of the mouse when clicked.

Let's talk about the `gl_MouseCallback()` function. Here, we first need to be sure that an event is related to the left mouse button because we have got nothing to do with the other buttons. To do so, we need to use a simple `if` condition for the `button` argument:

```
if (button == GLUT_LEFT_BUTTON)
{
```

We need to handle key-down and key-up in completely different ways, so we need to use another `if` condition for the `state` argument:

```
if (state == GLUT_DOWN && !isMouseDown)
{
```

If the mouse's key is down, but wasn't so before, we need to first save its state (according to the fact that it is currently down) in our `isMouseDown` variable and then save its current position using `mouseDownX` and `mouseDownY`:

```
isMouseDown = true;
mouseDownX = x;
mouseDownY = y;
```

But if it is currently up but was down before:

```
else if (state == GLUT_UP && isMouseDown)
```

We need to update its state (it is not down any more) in our `isMouseDown` variable again and then make sure that we are not already in the cropping mode because we don't want to crop a cropped preview again:

```
isMouseDown = false;

if (isInCropping)
{
```

```
        printf("Cropping is still active, "
          "press R to reset it first.\r\n");
        return;
}
```

If we are in the cropping mode, we can ignore this event and end this function; if not, we must continue with calculating the selected size and location.

Please note that we have the position of the mouse from the last time its button was in the down state, because we had saved it before in the `mouseDownX` and `mouseDownY` variables. The current position of the mouse is also available in the `x` and `y` parameters, but these values are relative to the current size of the OpenGL window (and it is resizable when the stretching mode is on). So first we need to calculate the window size to texture size ratio in order to convert this number to an absolute number of pixels in the frame data. To do this, we need to have the current sizes of the OpenGL window and the size of our texture. We have the size of our texture from the `window_w` and `window_h` variables, but we are not sure about the current size of the OpenGL window; so we need to use the following code:

```
GLint m_viewport[4];
glGetIntegerv( GL_VIEWPORT, m_viewport );
```

`glGetIntegerv()` is one of OpenGL's functions that returns the value of any property you ask for. In the previous code, we want the value of `GL_VIEWPORT`, which is an array of four integers showing the position and size of the OpenGL rendering area relative to the window.

Using this value along with the position of the mouse, we can calculate the location and size of the selected area:

```
int sizeX = ((float)window_w / m_viewport[2])
  * abs(x - mouseDownX);
int sizeY = ((float)window_h / m_viewport[3])
  * abs(y - mouseDownY);
int offsetX = ((float)window_w / m_viewport[2])
  * min(x, mouseDownX);
int offsetY = ((float)window_h / m_viewport[3])
  * min(y, mouseDownY);
```

There are two other important things to note here.First, the Asus Xtion and PrimeSense sensors refuse to accept any value not divisible by 4, so we need to make sure that both the location and size of the selected area are divisible by 4:

```
sizeX = floor((float)sizeX / 4) * 4;
sizeY = floor((float)sizeY / 4) * 4;
offsetX = floor((float)offsetX / 4) * 4;
offsetY = floor((float)offsetY / 4) * 4;
```

Second, the Asus Xtion and PrimeSense sensors are not going to accept a cropping request if the size of the selected area is smaller than 128 x 128 pixels. So, we continue our code only if the selected size is bigger than 128 x 128 pixels:

```
if (sizeX >= 128 && sizeY >= 128)
{
```

 It seems that both the previously mentioned limitations are because of the identical design and SOC (chip) of the devices.

Now we are ready to ask OpenNI to apply cropping to the selected area:

```
Status status;
status = selectedSensor.setCropping(
   offsetX, offsetY,
   sizeX,
   sizeY);
```

Although we did what we can to make the requested size and location valid, OpenNI may still reject our request. So, we had better think of a way to check whether our requested task was accepted or not.

`VideoStream::setCropping()` is the method we use to apply cropping here. This method accepts four arguments, of which the first two are for the position of the desired area and last two are the size of it.

```
if (status != STATUS_OK)
{
  printf("Failed. %s\r\n",
      OpenNI::getExtendedError());
}
else
{
  printf("Done. Press R to reset.\r\n");
  memset(gl_texture,0,
    window_w * window_h *
    sizeof(OniRGB888Pixel));
  isInCropping = true;
}
```

If the return value of `VideoStream::setCropping()` was not `STATUS_OK`, our request would fail and we would have to write a failed message to the console. But if it was, it means our request got completed successfully and now we can set `isInCropping` to `true` and clean the texture buffer using the `memset()` function.

Step three is about changes in `gl_KeyboardCallback()`; we added two new handling codes for the *M* and *R* keys.

First, we need to reset cropping if the *R* or *r* key has been pressed. We can do this by requesting for the cropping of the whole resolution from the `0, 0` start point. But before requesting for this, we need to make sure that the selected `openni::VideoStream` class is valid:

```
else if (key == 'R' || key == 'r')
{
  // Reset Cropping
  if (selectedSensor.isValid())
  {
    Status status;
    status = selectedSensor.setCropping(0, 0,
      selectedSensor.getVideoMode().getResolutionX(),
      selectedSensor.getVideoMode().getResolutionY());
    if (status == STATUS_OK)
      isInCropping = false;
  }
}
```

Second, we add a new functionality to our application to toggle the mirroring of frames when the *M* or *m* key is pressed. We can do this by calling the `openni::VideoStream::setMirrorin gEnabled()` method to set the state of mirroring and `openni::VideoStream::getMirror ingEnabled()` to get the current state of mirroring. We need both the methods to toggle it:

```
else if (key == 'M' || key == 'm')
{
  // Toggle Mirroring
  if (selectedSensor.isValid())
    selectedSensor.setMirroringEnabled(
    !selectedSensor.getMirroringEnabled());
}
```

In the fifth step, we are going to make some minor changes in the `main` function. If you compare this new function with the old one, you can clearly see three new lines there. Two are only for printing some information about keyboard and mouse functionalities (*M*, *R* and mouse) in this example:

```
printf("Use mouse to crop output and "
    "press R to reset cropping.\r\n");
printf("By pressing M key you can toggle mirroring.\r\n");
```

But there is an important line here about introducing `gl_MouseCallback()` as a mouse event handler to OpenGL:

```
glutMouseFunc(gl_MouseCallback);
```

The following screenshot shows the output of our application:

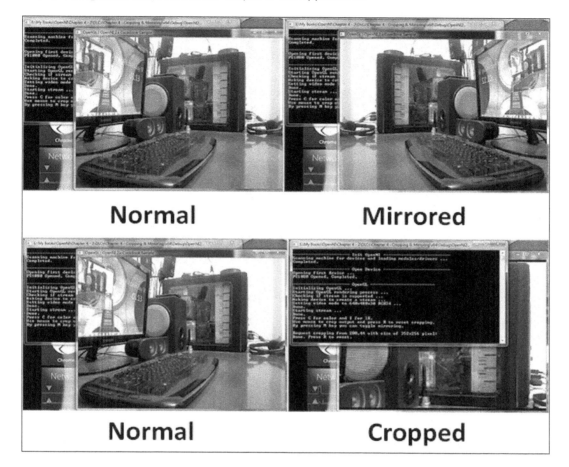

See also

▸ The *Accessing video streams (Depth/IR/RGB) and configuring them* recipe in *Chapter 2, OpenNI and C++*

▸ The *Reading and showing a frame from the image sensor (color/IR)* recipe in *Chapter 3, Using Low-level Data*

Syncing image and depth sensors to read new frames from both streams at the same time

A device, by default, captures and sends frames from each sensor independently. This means there is no guarantee that both sensors capture a snapshot of the environment at the same time, but there may be a lot of cases where you want to reduce the delay between capturing two frames from two different sensors. For example, if you want to use both image and depth streams to retrieve the color of an object recognized by the depth stream from the color stream you need to read the data from both the streams; this means one stream could have a different capture time from the other. But using frame syncing that is available for image and depth streams, you can at least decrease this difference in capture time to the lowest possible value.

In this recipe, we are going to show you how you can enable frame syncing and how much this option can reduce the difference between capture times.

Getting ready

Create a project in Visual Studio 2010 and prepare it for working with OpenNI using the *Creating a project in Visual Studio 2010* recipe of *Chapter 2, Open NI and C++*.

How to do it...

1. Add the following lines at the top of your source code (just below the #include lines):

```
#include <conio.h>
char ReadLastCharOfLine()
{
  int newChar = 0;
  int lastChar;
  fflush(stdout);
  do
  {
    lastChar = newChar;
    newChar = getchar();
  }
  while ((newChar != '\n')
    && (newChar != EOF));
  return (char)lastChar;
}
```

```
bool HandleStatus(Status status)
{
  if (status == STATUS_OK)
    return true;
  printf("ERROR: #%d, %s", status,
    OpenNI::getExtendedError());
  ReadLastCharOfLine();
  return false;
}
```

2. Then locate the following lines of code:

```
int _tmain(int argc, _TCHAR* argv[])
{
```

3. Write the following code snippet below the preceding lines of code:

```
Status status = STATUS_OK;
printf("Scanning machine for devices and loading "
    "modules/drivers ...\r\n");

status = OpenNI::initialize();
if (!HandleStatus(status)) return 1;
printf("Completed.\r\n");

printf("Opening first device ...\r\n");
Device device;
status = device.open(ANY_DEVICE);
if (!HandleStatus(status)) return 1;
printf("%s Opened, Completed.\r\n",
  device.getDeviceInfo().getName());

printf("Checking if stream is supported ...\r\n");
if (!device.hasSensor(SENSOR_DEPTH))
{
  printf("Stream not supported by this device.\r\n");
  return 1;
}
VideoStream depthSensor;
printf("Asking device to create a depth stream...\r\n");
status = depthSensor.create(device, SENSOR_DEPTH);
if (!HandleStatus(status)) return 1;

printf("Starting stream ...\r\n");
status = depthSensor.start();
```

```
if (!HandleStatus(status)) return 1;
printf("Done.\r\n");

printf("Checking if stream is supported ...\r\n");
if (!device.hasSensor(SENSOR_COLOR))
{
  printf("Stream not supported by this device.\r\n");
  return 1;
}
VideoStream colorSensor;
printf("Asking device to create a color stream...\r\n");
status = colorSensor.create(device, SENSOR_COLOR);
if (!HandleStatus(status)) return 1;

printf("Starting stream ...\r\n");
status = colorSensor.start();
if (!HandleStatus(status)) return 1;
printf("Done.\r\n");

printf("Press ESC to exit, "
    "any other key to toggle Frame Sync");
bool sync = false;
int avgDiff = 0;
int framesRead = 0;
bool canceled = false;
while (!canceled)
{
  if (kbhit())
  {
    while (kbhit())
      if (getch() == 27)
        canceled = true;
    sync = !sync;
    status = device.setDepthColorSyncEnabled(sync);
    if (!HandleStatus(status)) return 1;
    avgDiff = 0;
    framesRead = 0;
    printf("Sync is %s\r\n", ((sync) ?
      "Activated" : "Deactivated"));
  }
  VideoFrameRef newFrame;
  status = depthSensor.readFrame(&newFrame);
  if (status == STATUS_OK &&
```

```
        newFrame.isValid())
    {
      int diff = 0;
      printf("Depth Ready at %d\r\n",
        newFrame.getTimestamp());
      diff = newFrame.getTimestamp();
      status = colorSensor.readFrame(&newFrame);
      if (status == STATUS_OK &&
        newFrame.isValid())
      {
        diff = abs(
          (int)newFrame.getTimestamp() - diff);
        avgDiff = (
          (avgDiff * framesRead) + diff) /
          (framesRead + 1);
        framesRead++;
        printf("Color Ready at %d, "
            "Diff: %d, Avg Diff: %d\r\n",
          newFrame.getTimestamp(),
          diff, avgDiff);

      }
    }
    Sleep(100);
  }
  depthSensor.destroy();
  colorSensor.destroy();
  OpenNI::shutdown();
  return 0;
```

How it works...

The first step contains almost all the usual things we have in our projects, such as defining a function for handling errors and another one for handling user inputs. The only new line of code we can see here is the first line about adding the `conio.h` file to our project. This file gives us access to some of the console interface functions, such as `kbhit()` and `getch()`, that we are going to use in this recipe. This header file is mainly used by applications from the MS-DOS era and is currently not available in Linux or other modern operating systems except Windows.

```
#include <conio.h>
```

Get more information about the `conio.h` file at the following link:

`http://en.wikipedia.org/wiki/Conio.h`

As this example is not very usable alone, I don't expect anyone to try to port it into Linux; yet, a good alternative to this file in the Linux environment can be found at the following link:

`http://sourceforge.net/projects/linux-conioh/`

Our main code starts in step 3. In this step, as always, we are going to initialize OpenNI, open a device, and create a depth and image `openni::VideoSensor` class. We are not going to describe these sections again; you can read *Chapter 2, OpenNI and C++*, for more information.

After that, we defined four variables and entered into a `while` loop as we want to keep reading data from `openni::VideoStream` classes. We need to define a variable sync called `sync` to keep its value locally so we can toggle it later. Then as we want to show the average difference between the capture times of two frames, we need to keep the number of frames we read in one variable (named `framesRead` here) and the average of differences in another variable (named `avgDiff` here). Also, we need another variable to check whether the operation was canceled and whether the loop ended:

```
bool sync = false;
int avgDiff = 0;
int framesRead = 0;
bool canceled = false;
while (!canceled)
{
```

Then our main loop begins with checking whether any key was pressed and whether the pressed key was the *Esc* key:

```
if (kbhit())
{
  while (kbhit())
    if (getch() == 27)
      canceled = true;
```

If it was indeed the *Esc* key, we change the `canceled` variable value to `true`. We use another `while` loop here because the key buffer may contain multiple keys and we need to empty it before continuing.

If any key is pressed (no matter what key is pressed), we will toggle the sync mode using `openni::Device::setDepthColorSyncEnabled()` and then set the `avgDiff` and `framesRead` variables to 0 to reset older calculations. Also, we print a message to the console for the user to see the current state of frame syncing:

```
sync = !sync;
status = device.setDepthColorSyncEnabled(sync);
if (!HandleStatus(status)) return 1;
avgDiff = 0;
framesRead = 0;
printf("Sync is %s\r\n", ((sync) ?
   "Activated" : "Deactivated"));
```

After checking for the pressed keys, we must pay attention to our frame reading operation, which is the primary part of our code. First, we read a frame from the depth sensor using the `openni::VideoStream::readFrame()` method, and if it is correct, try to save its capture time in a variable named `diff` and continue to read other frames, this time from the color sensor:

```
VideoFrameRef newFrame;
status = depthSensor.readFrame(&newFrame);
if (status == STATUS_OK &&
  newFrame.isValid())
{
  int diff = 0;
  printf("Depth Ready at %d\r\n",
    newFrame.getTimestamp());
  diff = newFrame.getTimestamp();
  status = colorSensor.readFrame(&newFrame);
  if (status == STATUS_OK &&
    newFrame.isValid())
  {
```

Then, we calculate the difference between the capture time of the color frame and depth frame and update the `avgDiff` variable. Also, we increase the value of `framesRead` by 1:

```
diff = abs(
  (int)newFrame.getTimestamp() - diff);
avgDiff = (
  (avgDiff * framesRead) + diff) /
  (framesRead + 1);
framesRead++;
```

Now that we have all the information, we can print it on the console to show it to the user:

```
printf("Color Ready at %d, "
    "Diff: %d, Avg Diff: %d\r\n",
    newFrame.getTimestamp(),
    diff, avgDiff);
```

Before continuing this loop, we should wait for 100 milliseconds to make sure that the printed data on the console is readable by the user:

```
Sleep(100);
```

This process will continue until the user presses the *Esc* key. Then the program will release all the resources used by `depthSensor`, `colorSensor` and OpenNI itself; then it will terminate.

The following screenshot shows the end result of the previous code. As you can see, there is a huge difference (almost ten times less) when depth and color frame syncing is enabled.

```
Color Ready at 57222869, Diff: 8703, Avg Diff: 5281
Depth Ready at 57314560
Color Ready at 57323417, Diff: 8857, Avg Diff: 5334
Depth Ready at 57414953
Color Ready at 57423965, Diff: 9012, Avg Diff: 5388
Depth Ready at 57515347
Color Ready at 57524513, Diff: 9166, Avg Diff: 5442
Depth Ready at 57615740
Color Ready at 57625061, Diff: 9321, Avg Diff: 5497
Depth Ready at 57716134
Color Ready at 57725609, Diff: 9475, Avg Diff: 5553
```

Frame Sync: Disable

```
Color Ready at 34096829, Diff: 123, Avg Diff: 595
Depth Ready at 34197004
Color Ready at 34197377, Diff: 373, Avg Diff: 593
Depth Ready at 34297302
Color Ready at 34297925, Diff: 623, Avg Diff: 593
Depth Ready at 34397600
Color Ready at 34398473, Diff: 873, Avg Diff: 594
Depth Ready at 34497899
Color Ready at 34499021, Diff: 1122, Avg Diff: 596
Depth Ready at 34598260
Color Ready at 34599569, Diff: 1309, Avg Diff: 599
```

Frame Sync: Enable

See also

▸ The *Reading and showing a frame from the image sensor (color/IR)* recipe in *Chapter 3, Using Low-level Data*

▸ The *Reading and showing a frame from the depth sensor* recipe in *Chapter 3, Using Low-level Data*

▸ The *Overlaying the depth frame over the image frame* recipe

Overlaying the depth frame over the image frame

The depth and color streams are from two different sensors; because of the difference in their positions in the device, they see objects from two different angles. This makes it hard to figure out which two pixels in these two streams are related to each other in the physical world. Fortunately, this problem is solved by OpenNI using one of its built-in methods. Using this feature, a programmer can expect each pixel of depth to be in the same position as its color pair. This feature is very useful for different types of projects, including, but not limited to, generating a color point cloud.

Here, we try to show you how to overlay the depth data over the color data using this feature of OpenNI.

Getting ready

Create a project in Visual Studio 2010 and prepare it for working with OpenNI using the *Creating a project in Visual Studio 2010* recipe of *Chapter 2, OpenNI and C++*. Then configure Visual Studio 2010 to use OpenGL with the *Configuring Visual Studio 2010 to use OpenGL* recipe of *Chapter 3, Using Low-level Data*.

How to do it...

1. Add the following lines at the top of your source code (just below the `#include` lines):

```
#include <math.h>
int window_w = 640;
int window_h = 480;
OniRGB888Pixel* gl_texture;
VideoStream depthSensor;
VideoStream colorSensor;
Device device;
```

2. Copy the `ReadLastCharOfLine()` and `HandleStatus()` functions here from the last recipe.

3. Add the following lines of code after the definition of `HandleStatus()` function that we just copied:

```
void gl_KeyboardCallback(unsigned char key, int x, int y)
{
  if (key == 27) // ESC Key
  {
    depthSensor.destroy();
    colorSensor.destroy();
```

```
          device.close();
          OpenNI::shutdown();
          exit(0);
        }
      else if (key == 'R' || key == 'r')
      {
        if (device.isValid())
          if (device.getImageRegistrationMode() ==
              IMAGE_REGISTRATION_DEPTH_TO_COLOR)
            device.setImageRegistrationMode(
              IMAGE_REGISTRATION_OFF);
          else
            device.setImageRegistrationMode(
              IMAGE_REGISTRATION_DEPTH_TO_COLOR);
      }
    }


void gl_IdleCallback()
{
  glutPostRedisplay();
}

void gl_DisplayCallback()
{
  if (depthSensor.isValid())
  {
    Status status = STATUS_OK;
    VideoStream* streamPointer = &depthSensor;
    int streamReadyIndex;
    status = OpenNI::waitForAnyStream(&streamPointer, 1,
      &streamReadyIndex, 500);
    if (status == STATUS_OK && streamReadyIndex == 0)
    {
      VideoFrameRef depthFrame;
      status = depthSensor.readFrame(&depthFrame);
      VideoFrameRef colorFrame;
      if (status == STATUS_OK)
        status = colorSensor.readFrame(&colorFrame);
      if (status == STATUS_OK && depthFrame.isValid() &&
        colorFrame.isValid() &&
        depthFrame.getHeight() ==
                colorFrame.getHeight()
        && depthFrame.getWidth() ==
                colorFrame.getWidth())
```

```
{
  // Clear the OpenGL buffers
  glClear (
    GL_COLOR_BUFFER_BIT | GL_DEPTH_BUFFER_BIT);

  // Setup the OpenGL viewpoint
  glMatrixMode(GL_PROJECTION);
  glPushMatrix();
  glLoadIdentity();
  glOrtho(0, window_w, window_h, 0, -1.0, 1.0);

  // UPDATING TEXTURE (DEPTH & RGB888 TO RGB888)

  unsigned short maxDepth =
    depthSensor.getMinPixelValue();
  for  (int y = 0; y < depthFrame.getHeight(); ++y)
  {
    DepthPixel* depthCell = (DepthPixel*)(
      (char*)depthFrame.getData() +
      (y * depthFrame.getStrideInBytes())
      );
    for  (int x = 0; x < depthFrame.getWidth();
      ++x, ++depthCell)
    {
      if (maxDepth < *depthCell)
      {
        maxDepth = *depthCell;
      }
    }
  }

  double resizeFactor = min(
    (window_w/(double)depthFrame.getWidth()),
    (window_h/(double)depthFrame.getHeight()));
  unsigned int texture_x =
  (unsigned int)(window_w -
    (resizeFactor * depthFrame.getWidth())) /2;
  unsigned int texture_y =
  (unsigned int)(window_h -
    (resizeFactor * depthFrame.getHeight())) /2;

  for  (unsigned int y = 0;
    y < (window_h - 2 * texture_y); ++y)
  {
```

```
        OniRGB888Pixel* texturePixel = gl_texture +
          (y + texture_y) * window_w) +
          texture_x;
      for  (unsigned int x = 0;
        x < (window_w - 2 * texture_x);
        ++x, ++texturePixel)
      {
        DepthPixel* depthPixel =
          (DepthPixel*)(
            (char*)depthFrame.getData() +
            ((int)(y / resizeFactor) *
              depthFrame.getStrideInBytes())
          ) + (int)(x / resizeFactor);
        RGB888Pixel* colorPixel =
          (RGB888Pixel*)(
              (char*)colorFrame.getData() +
            ((int)(y / resizeFactor) *
              colorFrame.getStrideInBytes())
          ) + (int)(x / resizeFactor);
        if (*depthPixel != 0)
        {
          float depthValue =
            1 - ((float)*depthPixel/maxDepth);
            texturePixel->b = ceil((double)
              (colorPixel->b * depthValue));
            texturePixel->g = ceil((double)
              (colorPixel->g * depthValue));
            texturePixel->r = ceil((double)
              (colorPixel->r * depthValue));
        }
        else
        {
          texturePixel->b = 0;
          texturePixel->g = 0;
          texturePixel->r = 0;
        }
      }
    }

    // Create the OpenGL texture map
    glTexParameteri(GL_TEXTURE_2D,
      0x8191, GL_TRUE);
    glTexImage2D(GL_TEXTURE_2D, 0, GL_RGB,
      window_w, window_h,    0, GL_RGB,
```

```
        GL_UNSIGNED_BYTE, gl_texture);

    glBegin(GL_QUADS);
    glTexCoord2f(0.0f, 0.0f);
    glVertex3f(0.0f, 0.0f, 0.0f);
    glTexCoord2f(0.0f, 1.0f);
    glVertex3f(0.0f, (float)window_h, 0.0f);
    glTexCoord2f(1.0f, 1.0f);
    glVertex3f((float)window_w,
        (float)window_h, 0.0f);
    glTexCoord2f(1.0f, 0.0f);
    glVertex3f((float)window_w, 0.0f, 0.0f);
    glEnd();

    glutSwapBuffers();
      }
    }
   }
}
```

4. Then locate the following lines of code:

```
int _tmain(int argc, _TCHAR* argv[])
{
```

5. Write the following code snippet below the preceding lines of code:

```
Status status = STATUS_OK;
printf("Scanning machine for devices and loading "
    "modules/drivers ...\r\n");

status = OpenNI::initialize();
if (!HandleStatus(status)) return 1;
printf("Completed.\r\n");

printf("Opening first device ...\r\n");
status = device.open(ANY_DEVICE);
if (!HandleStatus(status)) return 1;
printf("%s Opened, Completed.\r\n",
  device.getDeviceInfo().getName());

printf("Checking if stream is supported ...\r\n");
if (!device.hasSensor(SENSOR_DEPTH))
{
  printf("Stream not supported by this device.\r\n");
  return 1;
```

```
    }

    printf("Asking device to create a depth stream...\r\n");
    status = depthSensor.create(device, SENSOR_DEPTH);
    if (!HandleStatus(status)) return 1;

    VideoMode vmod;
    vmod.setFps(30);
    vmod.setPixelFormat(PIXEL_FORMAT_DEPTH_1_MM);
    vmod.setResolution(640, 480);
    status = depthSensor.setVideoMode(vmod);
    if (!HandleStatus(status)) return 1;
    printf("Done.\r\n");

    printf("Starting stream ...\r\n");
    status = depthSensor.start();
    if (!HandleStatus(status)) return 1;
    printf("Done.\r\n");

    printf("Checking if stream is supported ...\r\n");
    if (!device.hasSensor(SENSOR_COLOR))
    {
      printf("Stream not supported by this device.\r\n");
      return 1;
    }

    printf("Asking device to create a color stream...\r\n");
    status = colorSensor.create(device, SENSOR_COLOR);
    if (!HandleStatus(status)) return 1;

    printf("Setting video mode to 640x480x30 RGB888..\r\n");
    vmod.setFps(30);
    vmod.setPixelFormat(PIXEL_FORMAT_RGB888);
    vmod.setResolution(640, 480);
    status = colorSensor.setVideoMode(vmod);
    if (!HandleStatus(status)) return 1;
    printf("Done.\r\n");

    printf("Starting stream ...\r\n");
    status = colorSensor.start();
    if (!HandleStatus(status)) return 1;
    printf("Done.\r\n");

    printf("Enabling Depth-Image frames sync\r\n");
```

```
status = device.setDepthColorSyncEnabled(true);
if (!HandleStatus(status)) return 1;

printf("Enabling Depth to Image mapping\r\n");
status = device.setImageRegistrationMode(
        IMAGE_REGISTRATION_DEPTH_TO_COLOR);
if (!HandleStatus(status)) return 1;

printf("Initializing OpenGL ...\r\n");
gl_texture = (OniRGB888Pixel*)malloc(
   window_w * window_h * sizeof(OniRGB888Pixel));
glutInit(&argc, (char**)argv);
glutInitDisplayMode(
   GLUT_RGB | GLUT_DOUBLE | GLUT_DEPTH);
glutInitWindowSize(window_w, window_h);
glutCreateWindow (
   "OpenGL | OpenNI 2.x CookBook Sample");
glutKeyboardFunc(gl_KeyboardCallback);
glutDisplayFunc(gl_DisplayCallback);
glutIdleFunc(gl_IdleCallback);
glDisable(GL_DEPTH_TEST);
glEnable(GL_TEXTURE_2D);
printf("Starting OpenGL rendering process ...\r\n");
printf("Press R to toggle "
   "depth to color registration.\r\n");
glutMainLoop();
```

How it works...

Just as with the other recipes of *Chapter 3*, *Using Low-level Data*, that use OpenGL, this chapter too has a number of known functions and variables, such as window_w and window_h, to keep the size of the texture and the default size of the window, along with gl_texture to keep the data of the generated texture and device to let us access the device object from OpenNI. But instead of one variable of type openni::VideoStream, we have two here, one for the depth stream and another for the color stream, because we want to use them both.

Apart from the variables, the ReadLastCharOfLine(), HandleStatus(), gl_KeyboardCallback(), gl_IdleCallback(), and gl_DisplayCallback() functions are also available, just as in the previous recipes, with almost the same code. The only major difference in the body of these functions can be seen in the gl_KeyboardCallback() and gl_DisplayCallback() functions.

Starting with `gl_KeyboardCallback()`, we can clearly see that, except checking for the *Esc* key, we have another condition for the *R* or *r* key too, which is the primary code of this recipe:

```
if (device.isValid())
  if (device.getImageRegistrationMode() ==
      IMAGE_REGISTRATION_DEPTH_TO_COLOR)
    device.setImageRegistrationMode(
      IMAGE_REGISTRATION_OFF);
  else
    device.setImageRegistrationMode(
      IMAGE_REGISTRATION_DEPTH_TO_COLOR);
```

In the previous code, we first check if the `device` object is valid and, if so, we try to get the current status of the image registration mode by calling the `openni::Device::getImageRegistrationMode()` method. The return value of this method is of the type `openni::ImageRegistrationMode`; it indicates the current active image registration mode that now this `enum` has only two options: `IMAGE_REGISTRATION_DEPTH_TO_COLOR` and `IMAGE_REGISTRATION_OFF`. Then we check if the current active mode is **depth to color**, and if so, we set it to off by calling `openni::Device::setImageRegistrationMode()` with `IMAGE_REGISTRATION_OFF` as an argument. But if it isn't so, we set the depth to color mode to active. In this way, we can toggle the active mode each time the user presses the *R* or *r* key.

Then we have the `gl_DisplayCallback()` function. In this function, we merged code from both the *Reading and showing a frame from the image sensor (color/IR)* and *Reading and showing a frame from the depth sensor* recipes of *Chapter 3, Using Low-level Data*.

First we check if both `depthSensor` and `colorSensor` are valid. Then we wait for a frame in the depth stream to become available and read it. Just after that, we do the same for the color stream through the following code snippet:

```
if (depthSensor.isValid() && colorSensor.isValid())
{
  Status status = STATUS_OK;
  VideoStream* streamPointer = &depthSensor;
  int streamReadyIndex;
  status = OpenNI::waitForAnyStream(&streamPointer, 1,
    &streamReadyIndex, 500);
  if (status == STATUS_OK && streamReadyIndex == 0)
  {
    VideoFrameRef depthFrame;
    status = depthSensor.readFrame(&depthFrame);
    VideoFrameRef colorFrame;
    if (status == STATUS_OK)
      status = colorSensor.readFrame(&colorFrame);
```

If everything is correct, especially if the width and height of the depth and color frames are the same (because we don't want to calculate the resize factor twice), we can continue as follows:

```
if (status == STATUS_OK &&
  depthFrame.isValid() &&
  colorFrame.isValid() &&
  depthFrame.getHeight() == colorFrame.getHeight()
  && depthFrame.getWidth() == colorFrame.getWidth())
{
```

Then, just as we did in the recipes of *Chapter 3, Using Low-level Data*, we need to clean OpenGL buffer and set its viewpoint and camera location here as well.

After this, we calculate the maximum available depth's value.

Then we need to calculate the resize factor and padding of our texture. You can guess from the similarities in the process explained in the recipes to *Chapter 3, Using Low-level Data*, that the next thing to do is to loop through all the pixels in the texture buffer and convert and copy the data from the frame to it. This is true, but this time we want to create each pixel based on two pixels from two different sources. So, we need to find a way to merge them in such a way that it can show you how the registration mode feature is useful. So, we decided to make the color pixels darker depending on their distance in the physical world:

```
for  (unsigned int y = 0;
  y < (window_h - 2 * texture_y); ++y)
{
  OniRGB888Pixel* texturePixel = gl_texture +
    ((y + texture_y) * window_w) + texture_x;
  for  (unsigned int x = 0;
    x < (window_w - 2 * texture_x);
    ++x, ++texturePixel)
  {
    DepthPixel* depthPixel =
      (DepthPixel*)(
        (char*)depthFrame.getData() +
        ((int)(y / resizeFactor) *
          depthFrame.getStrideInBytes())
      ) + (int)(x / resizeFactor);
    RGB888Pixel* colorPixel =
      (RGB888Pixel*)(
        (char*)colorFrame.getData() +
        ((int)(y / resizeFactor) *
          colorFrame.getStrideInBytes())
      ) + (int)(x / resizeFactor);
    if (*depthPixel != 0)
    {
```

```
        float depthValue =
          1 - ((float)*depthPixel / maxDepth);
          texturePixel->b = ceil((double)
            (colorPixel->b * depthValue));
          texturePixel->g = ceil((double)
            (colorPixel->g * depthValue));
          texturePixel->r = ceil((double)
            (colorPixel->r * depthValue));
      }
      else
      {
        texturePixel->b = 0;
        texturePixel->g = 0;
        texturePixel->r = 0;
      }
    }
  }
```

As you can see, we have `texturePixel` as a pixel from our texture buffer and `depthPixel` and `colorPixel` as related pixels from the depth and color frames. We need to merge the data from `depthPixel` and `colorPixel` and save it in `texturePixel`. But first, we need to make sure `depthPixel` is not 0 because, if so, the pixel is in shadow and we can leave this pixel black. But if there is a valid value for this pixel, check how near this pixel is to the device relative to the depth of the nearest pixel (`maxDepth` as we calculated before), multiply it to each color of `colorPixel`, and save the result in `texturePixel`. With this code, we have nearby objects with the same color that they are in `colorPixel`, and as they get farther away, they become darker.

Shadow: Places that have no depth data. These places (pixels) are those where laser projector fails to reach or where IR CMOS fails to capture..

```
    if (*depthPixel != 0)
    {
      float depthValue =
        1 - ((float)*depthPixel / maxDepth);
        texturePixel->b = ceil((double)
          (colorPixel->b * depthValue));
        texturePixel->g = ceil((double)
          (colorPixel->g * depthValue));
        texturePixel->r = ceil((double)
          (colorPixel->r * depthValue));
    }
    else
    {
      texturePixel->b = 0;
      texturePixel->g = 0;
      texturePixel->r = 0;
    }
```

Apart from these two loops, we have nothing new in this function and everything is like the earlier recipes. You can read more in the *Initializing and preparing OpenGL* recipe of *Chapter 3, Using Low-level Data*.

Step 5 is about the `main` function. The only differences that you can see here when compared to the earlier recipes are the new lines that we added right after defining and starting the color and depth's `openni::Videostream` object to enable the frame sync feature:

```
printf("Enabling Depth-Image frames sync\r\n");
status = device.setDepthColorSyncEnabled(true);
if (!HandleStatus(status)) return 1;
```

Then we enable depth to color registration:

```
printf("Enabling Depth to Image mapping\r\n");
status = device.setImageRegistrationMode(
        IMAGE_REGISTRATION_DEPTH_TO_COLOR);
if (!HandleStatus(status)) return 1;
```

And of course, a `printf()` function call is done to print information about how to work with this app for the user.

Let's take a look at how this app works. Note that the left-hand side picture has both depth and image data exactly in the same place, unlike the right-hand side picture that has significant displacement.

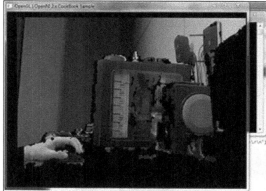 

Depth to Color Registration   **No Registration**

See also

▶ The *Reading and showing a frame from the image sensor (color/IR)* recipe in *Chapter 3, Using Low-level Data*

▶ The *Reading and showing a frame from the depth sensor* recipe in *Chapter 3, Using Low-level Data*

▶ The *Syncing image and depth sensors to read new frames from both streams at the same time* recipe

Converting the depth unit to millimetre

Until now, we have used the data of the depth stream relatively without knowing its real-world units; in this recipe, however, we are going to show you how it is possible to convert depth data into millimetre units. This could be used for generating point cloud, calculating distance, and so on.

First we try to find the depth value of the center pixel in the depth frame and then use the openni::CoordinateConverter class to convert this value into a real-world millimetre unit.

Getting ready

Create a project in Visual Studio 2010 and prepare it for working with OpenNI using the *Creating a project in Visual Studio 2010* recipe of *Chapter 2, OpenNI and C++*.

How to do it...

1. Add the following lines at the top of your source code (just below the #include lines):

```
#include <conio.h>
```

2. Copy the ReadLastCharOfLine() and HandleStatus() functions here from the last recipe.

3. Then locate the following lines of code:

```
int _tmain(int argc, _TCHAR* argv[])
{
```

4. Write the following code snippet below the preceding lines of code:

```
Status status = STATUS_OK;
printf("Scanning machine for devices and loading "
    "modules/drivers ...\r\n");
```

```
status = OpenNI::initialize();
if (!HandleStatus(status)) return 1;
printf("Completed.\r\n");

printf("Opening first device ...\r\n");
Device device;
status = device.open(ANY_DEVICE);
if (!HandleStatus(status)) return 1;
printf("%s Opened, Completed.\r\n",
  device.getDeviceInfo().getName());

printf("Checking if stream is supported ...\r\n");
if (!device.hasSensor(SENSOR_DEPTH))
{
  printf("Stream not supported by this device.\r\n");
  return 1;
}
VideoStream depthSensor;
printf("Asking device to create a depth stream...\r\n");
status = depthSensor.create(device, SENSOR_DEPTH);
if (!HandleStatus(status)) return 1;

printf("Starting stream ...\r\n");
status = depthSensor.start();
if (!HandleStatus(status)) return 1;
printf("Done.\r\n");

printf("Press any key to exit ...\r\n");
while (true)
{
  if (kbhit())
    break;
  VideoFrameRef newFrame;
  status = depthSensor.readFrame(&newFrame);
  if (status == STATUS_OK && newFrame.isValid())
  {
    DepthPixel* centerPixel =
      (DepthPixel*)((char*)newFrame.getData() +
      (newFrame.getHeight()   *
        newFrame.getStrideInBytes() / 2))
      + (newFrame.getWidth() / 2);
    float wX, wY ,wZ;
    status = CoordinateConverter::convertDepthToWorld(
      depthSensor,
```

```
            (float)(newFrame.getWidth() / 2),
            (float)(newFrame.getHeight() / 2),
            (float)(*centerPixel),
            &wX, &wY, &wZ);
        if (!HandleStatus(status)) return 1;
        printf("Center Pixel's distance is %gmm "
          "located at %gmmx%gmm\r\n",
          wZ, wX, wY);
    }
    Sleep(100);
  }
  depthSensor.destroy();
  OpenNI::shutdown();
  return 0;
```

How it works...

In the second step, we again defined the `ReadLastCharOfLine()` and `HandleStatus()` functions, as we did in all the earlier recipes, to handle user inputs and OpenNI errors. Also, we used `conio.h` as we had in the first step.

Our main code starts in step 4 where we begin with initializing OpenNI, opening the first acceptable device, creating an `openni::VideoStream` for the depth sensor, and starting it.

Now we need to read data and, as always, a `while` loop is a good idea for starting this operation. The first line of our `while` loop will check if any key is pressed. If so, we will exit the loop:

```
while (true)
{
  if (kbhit())
    break;
```

After that, we have code for reading a new frame from the depth sensor by calling `openni::V ideoStream::readFrame()` and creating a pointer to the frame's center pixel value:

```
VideoFrameRef newFrame;
status = depthSensor.readFrame(&newFrame);
if (status == STATUS_OK && newFrame.isValid())
{
  DepthPixel* centerPixel =
    (DepthPixel*)((char*)newFrame.getData() +
    (newFrame.getHeight()   *
      newFrame.getStrideInBytes() / 2))
    + (newFrame.getWidth() / 2);
```

As you can see, for calculating the position of this pixel in the buffer, we used `openni::VideoFrameRef::getHeight() / 2` and `openni::VideoFrameRef::getWidth() / 2`. Also, we used `openni::VideoFrameRef::getStrideInBytes()` for getting the number of bytes per row of pixels.

Now that we have the location and value of our preferred pixel, we can convert its data into a millimetre unit using the `openni::CoordinateConverter::convertDepthToWorld()` method. This method accepts a number of arguments, including the depth `openni::VideoStream`, the position of the pixel, the value of the pixel, and the two pointers to be filled by the calculated values. The return value of this method is of the type `openni::Status` and shows whether the operation ended successfully:

```
float wX, wY ,wZ;
status = CoordinateConverter::convertDepthToWorld(
  depthSensor,
  (float)(newFrame.getWidth() / 2),
  (float)(newFrame.getHeight() / 2),
  (float)(*centerPixel),
  &wX, &wY, &wZ);
if (!HandleStatus(status)) return 1;
printf("Center Pixel's distance is %gmm "
  "located at %gmmx%gmm\r\n",
  wZ, wX, wY);
```

We already mentioned that the position of the center pixel is `openni::VideoFrameRef::getHeight() / 2` and `openni::VideoFrameRef::getWidth() / 2` and that the data of this pixel is stored in the `centerPixel` variable. We also defined three float variables named `wX`, `wY`, and `wZ` for storing the position of the requested pixel in the real-world environment. Please note that the values of `wX` and `wY` are relative to the center of the screen and so, in our example, they are both always `0`.

The value of `wZ` is equal to `*centerPixel` when the pixel format is `PIXEL_FORMAT_DEPTH_1_MM` because the value of `centerPixel` is actually in millimetres itself. But it is highly recommended to use this method whenever any other pixel format is used.

In the end, we wait for 100 milliseconds and then start from the top of the loop again.

```
Sleep(100);
```

But if any key is pressed and the loop ends, we need to release all the resources before ending the process's execution:

```
depthSensor.destroy();
OpenNI::shutdown();
```

The following screenshot shows the output of this application:

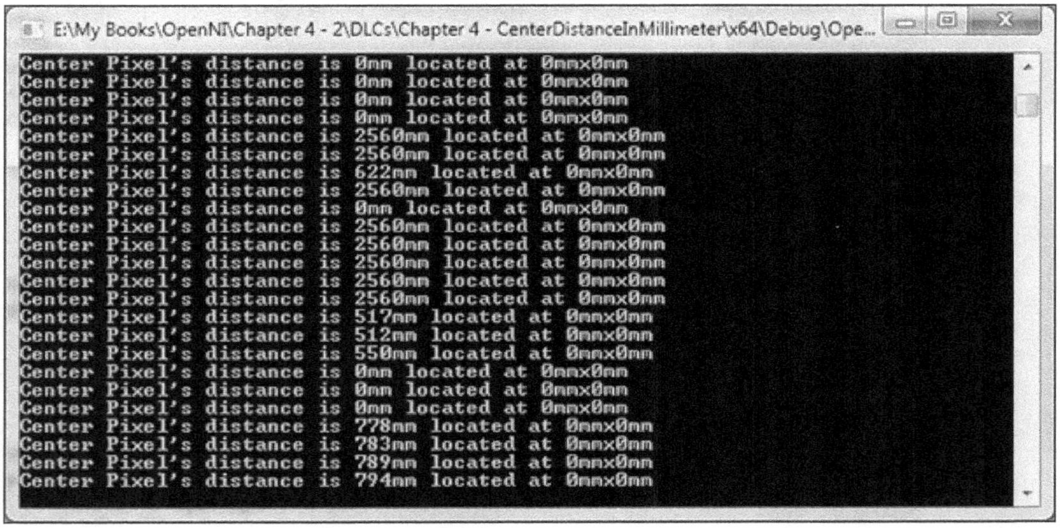

There's more...

It is possible to reverse the converting operation and convert the depth pixels to millimetre using the `openni::CoordinateConverter::convertWorldToDepth()` method. This method accepts almost the same arguments as its sibling but in a different order. An example follows:

```
float dX, dY ,dZ;
status = CoordinateConverter::convertWorldToDepth(
  depthSensor,
  wX, wY, wZ,
  &dX, &dY, &dZ);
if (!HandleStatus(status)) return 1;
```

See also

▶ The *Reading and showing a frame from the depth sensor* recipe in *Chapter 3, Using Low-level Data*

Chapter 4

Retrieving the color of the nearest point without depth over color registration

Let's say we want to retrieve the color of a pixel from its depth position but don't want to register the whole depth frame to the color frame. In this case, we can use the `openni::CoordinateConverter` class to get the position of the related depth pixel in the color frame; then, using the returned coordinates, we can get the color of this pixel. In this recipe, we try to find the nearest pixel in the depth frame and then show the color of this pixel from the color frame.

Getting ready

Create a project in Visual Studio 2010 and prepare it for working with OpenNI using the *Creating a project in Visual Studio 2010* recipe of *Chapter 2, OpenNI and C++*.

How to do it...

1. Add the following line at the top of your source code (just below the `#include` lines):

    ```
    #include <conio.h>
    ```

2. Copy the `ReadLastCharOfLine()` and `HandleStatus()` functions here from the last recipe.

3. Then locate the following lines of code:

    ```
    int _tmain(int argc, _TCHAR* argv[])
    {
    ```

4. Write the following code snippet below the preceding lines of code:

    ```
    Status status = STATUS_OK;
    printf("Scanning machine for devices and loading "
        "modules/drivers ...\r\n");

    status = OpenNI::initialize();
    if (!HandleStatus(status)) return 1;
    printf("Completed.\r\n");

    printf("Opening first device ...\r\n");
    Device device;
    status = device.open(ANY_DEVICE);
    if (!HandleStatus(status)) return 1;
    printf("%s Opened, Completed.\r\n",
      device.getDeviceInfo().getName());
    ```

205

```
printf("Checking if stream is supported ...\r\n");
if (!device.hasSensor(SENSOR_DEPTH))
{
  printf("Stream not supported by this device.\r\n");
  return 1;
}
VideoStream depthSensor;
printf("Asking device to create a depth stream...\r\n");
status = depthSensor.create(device, SENSOR_DEPTH);
if (!HandleStatus(status)) return 1;

printf("Setting video mode to 640x480x30 Depth...\r\n");
VideoMode vmod;
vmod.setFps(30);
vmod.setPixelFormat(PIXEL_FORMAT_DEPTH_1_MM);
vmod.setResolution(640, 480);
status = depthSensor.setVideoMode(vmod);
if (!HandleStatus(status)) return 1;
printf("Done.\r\n");

printf("Starting stream ...\r\n");
status = depthSensor.start();
if (!HandleStatus(status)) return 1;
printf("Done.\r\n");

printf("Checking if stream is supported ...\r\n");
if (!device.hasSensor(SENSOR_COLOR))
{
  printf("Stream not supported by this device.\r\n");
  return 1;
}
VideoStream colorSensor;
printf("Asking device to create a color stream...\r\n");
status = colorSensor.create(device, SENSOR_COLOR);
if (!HandleStatus(status)) return 1;

printf("Setting video mode to 640x480x30 RGB ...\r\n");
vmod.setFps(30);
vmod.setPixelFormat(PIXEL_FORMAT_RGB888);
vmod.setResolution(640, 480);
status = colorSensor.setVideoMode(vmod);
if (!HandleStatus(status)) return 1;
printf("Done.\r\n");
```

```
printf("Starting stream ...\r\n");
status = colorSensor.start();
if (!HandleStatus(status)) return 1;
printf("Done.\r\n");

printf("Enabling Frame Sync ...\r\n");
status = device.setDepthColorSyncEnabled(true);
if (!HandleStatus(status)) return 1;
printf("Press any key to exit ...\r\n");
while (true)
{
  if (kbhit())
    break;
  VideoFrameRef depthFrame, colorFrame;
  status = depthSensor.readFrame(&depthFrame);
  if (status == STATUS_OK && depthFrame.isValid())
  {
    DepthPixel* nearDepthPixel;
    int nearDepthX, nearDepthY;
    unsigned short maxDepth =
      depthSensor.getMinPixelValue();
    for (int y = 0; y < depthFrame.getHeight(); ++y)
    {
      DepthPixel* depthCell = (DepthPixel*)(
        (char*)depthFrame.getData() +
        (y * depthFrame.getStrideInBytes())
        );
      for (int x = 0; x < depthFrame.getWidth();
        ++x, ++depthCell)
        if (maxDepth < *depthCell)
        {
          maxDepth = *depthCell;
          nearDepthPixel = depthCell;
          nearDepthX = x;
          nearDepthY = y;
        }
    }

    status = colorSensor.readFrame(&colorFrame);
    if (status == STATUS_OK && colorFrame.isValid())
    {
      int cX, cY;
      status =
      CoordinateConverter::convertDepthToColor(
```

```
               depthSensor,
               colorSensor,
               (float)(nearDepthX),
               (float)(nearDepthY),
               (float)(*nearDepthPixel),
               &cX, &cY);
          if (!HandleStatus(status)) return 1;
          RGB888Pixel* nearColorPixel = (RGB888Pixel*)(
            (char*)colorFrame.getData() +
            (cY  * colorFrame.getStrideInBytes())) +
            (cX);
          printf("Nearest Pixel's color is %d,%d,%d\r\n",
            nearColorPixel->r,
            nearColorPixel->g,
            nearColorPixel->b);
        }
      }
      Sleep(100);
    }
    depthSensor.destroy();
    OpenNI::shutdown();
    return 0;
```

How it works...

In the second step, we again defined the `ReadLastCharOfLine()` and `HandleStatus()` functions, as we did in all the earlier recipes, to handle user inputs and OpenNI errors. Also, we used `conio.h` as we had done in the first step.

Our main code starts in step 4 where we begin with first initializing OpenNI, then opening the first acceptable device, then creating an `openni::VideoStream` for the depth sensor and another for the color sensor, and finally starting them both.

Just before starting the process of reading the data, we enabled frame syncing to make sure that there is the smallest possible difference between the two `openni::VideoStream` classes.

```
status = device.setDepthColorSyncEnabled(true);
if (!HandleStatus(status)) return 1;
```

Then we have a `while` loop again, and the first thing that we do in its body is check if any key is pressed to exit this loop:

```
while (true)
{
  if (kbhit())
    break;
```

The next step is to read a depth frame from the depth stream. If the new frame is valid, we try to find the nearest pixel to device in it:

```
status = depthSensor.readFrame(&depthFrame);
if (status == STATUS_OK && depthFrame.isValid())
{
  DepthPixel* nearDepthPixel;
  int nearDepthX, nearDepthY;
  unsigned short maxDepth =
    depthSensor.getMinPixelValue();
  for  (int y = 0; y < depthFrame.getHeight(); ++y)
  {
    DepthPixel* depthCell = (DepthPixel*)(
      (char*)depthFrame.getData() +
      (y * depthFrame.getStrideInBytes())
      );
    for  (int x = 0; x < depthFrame.getWidth();
      ++x, ++depthCell)
      if (maxDepth < *depthCell)
      {
        maxDepth = *depthCell;
        nearDepthPixel = depthCell;
        nearDepthX = x;
        nearDepthY = y;
      }
  }
```

As you can see, we looped through all the pixels of the depth frame using two `for` loops, and extracted the position and value of the nearest pixel. `nearDepthX` and `nearDepthY` represent the position of this pixel and `nearDepthPixel` contains its value.

As we need to have a color frame for use later, it is time to read it:

```
status = colorSensor.readFrame(&colorFrame);
if (status == STATUS_OK && colorFrame.isValid())
{
```

Now we have everything, the position and value of the nearest depth pixel as well as both the color and depth frames. So, we can call `openni::CoordinateConverter::convertDepthToColor()` to find out which pixel from the color frame is related to our nearest depth pixel. This method accepts two `openni::VideoStream` as the first parameters and the position and value of the depth pixel as the next parameters. The last two parameters are pointers to place of related color pixel that will be filled during the execution of this method:

```
int cX, cY;
status = CoordinateConverter::convertDepthToColor(
```

```
              depthSensor,
              colorSensor,
              (float)(nearDepthX),
              (float)(nearDepthY),
              (float)(*nearDepthPixel),
              &cX, &cY);
      if (!HandleStatus(status)) return 1;
```

So now we have the position of our pixel in the color frame and can display its color values to the user:

```
      RGB888Pixel* nearColorPixel = (RGB888Pixel*)(
        (char*)colorFrame.getData() +
        (cY  * colorFrame.getStrideInBytes())) + (cX);
      printf("Nearest Pixel's color is %d,%d,%d\r\n",
        nearColorPixel->r,
        nearColorPixel->g,
        nearColorPixel->b);
```

Before the end of the `while` loop, we have a 100-millisecond freeze and then go for the next frames:

```
      Sleep(100);
```

And as always, before ending the application, we need to release the resources.

See also

▶ The *Reading and showing a frame from the depth sensor* recipe in *Chapter 3, Using Low-level Data*

▶ The *Overlaying the depth frame over the image frame* recipe

▶ The *Converting the depth unit to millimetre* recipe

Enabling/disabling auto exposure and auto white balance

Image sensor has built-in auto exposure and auto white balance. In this recipe, we are going to show you how we can change the image sensor's settings to change the active state of these features.

Getting ready

Create a project in Visual Studio 2010 and prepare it for working with OpenNI using the *Creating a project in Visual Studio 2010* recipe of *Chapter 2, OpenNI and C++*.

Then, copy the code from the *Reading and showing a frame from the image sensor (color/IR)* recipe of *Chapter 3, Using Low-level Data*, to this project.

How to do it...

1. Locate the following lines of code:

    ```
    void gl_KeyboardCallback(unsigned char key, int x, int y)
    {
    ```

2. Replace any code inside this function with the following code snippet:

    ```
    if (key == 27) // ESC Key
    {
      selectedSensor.destroy();
      device.close();
      OpenNI::shutdown();
      exit(0);
    }
    else if (key == 'C' || key == 'c')
    {
      if (device.isValid())
      {
        printf("\r\n-->Setting active sensor to COLOR\r\n");
        SetActiveSensor(SENSOR_COLOR, &device);
      }
    }
    else if (key == 'I' || key == 'i')
    {
      if (device.isValid())
      {
        printf("\r\n-->Setting active sensor to IR\r\n");
        SetActiveSensor(SENSOR_IR, &device);
      }
    }
    else if (key == 'E' || key == 'e') // E or e key
    {
      if (selectedSensor.isValid() &&
        selectedSensor.getSensorInfo().getSensorType() ==
          SENSOR_COLOR)
      {
    ```

```
        CameraSettings cs =
          *(selectedSensor.getCameraSettings());
        cs.setAutoExposureEnabled(
          !cs.getAutoExposureEnabled());
        printf("Auto Exposure %s\r\n",
          (cs.getAutoExposureEnabled() ?
          "Activated" : "Deactivated"));
      }
    }
    else if (key == 'W' || key == 'w') // W or w key
    {
      if (selectedSensor.isValid() &&
        selectedSensor.getSensorInfo().getSensorType() ==
          SENSOR_COLOR)
      {
        CameraSettings cs =
          *(selectedSensor.getCameraSettings());
        cs.setAutoWhiteBalanceEnabled(
          !cs.getAutoWhiteBalanceEnabled());
        printf("Auto White Balance %s\r\n",
          (cs.getAutoWhiteBalanceEnabled() ?
          "Activated" : "Deactivated"));
      }
    }
```

3. Then locate the following lines of code:

```
int _tmain(int argc, _TCHAR* argv[])
{
```

4. Add the preceding lines of code at the end of this function:

```
printf("Press E to toggle exposure or W to toggle white balance");
```

How it works...

As you can see, there are no big changes in this recipe when compared to the *Reading and showing a frame from the image sensor (color/IR)* recipe of *Chapter 3, Using Low-level Data*, which we used as the base for this project. The only function that needs to be changed is `gl_KeyboardCallback()` that is responsible for the keyboard's key press events.

We alter this function to add two more functionalities to it: one is for toggling the camera's auto exposure when the *E* or *e* key is pressed and the other is for toggling the camera's auto white balance when the *W* or *w* key is pressed.

The first part of enabling and disabling the camera's auto exposure starts with a condition to see if `selectedSensor` is valid, and if it is a color stream (because this feature is only available for color sensors). If both the conditions were correct, we need to get the current status of the camera's auto exposure and then set it to a negative value. But both of these operations cannot be done directly with the `openni::VideoStream` object. We need to have `openni::CameraSettings` of our `openni::VideoStream` to retrieve and change this feature. This can be done with the `openni::VideoStream.getCameraSettings()` method:

```
CameraSettings cs =
  *(selectedSensor.getCameraSettings());
```

Now that we have access to `openni::CameraSettings`, we can toggle this feature using the `openni::CameraSettings::getAutoExposureEnabled()` and `openni::Camera Settings::setAutoExposureEnabled()` methods:

```
cs.setAutoWhiteBalanceEnabled(
  !cs.getAutoWhiteBalanceEnabled());
```

Then we print the new state of the camera's auto exposure feature:

```
printf("Auto Exposure %s\r\n",
  (cs.getAutoExposureEnabled() ?
  "Activated" : "Deactivated"));
```

We do almost the same thing for toggling the auto white balance feature too, checking if everything is valid and the selected sensor is the color sensor, and retrieving `openni::CameraSettings` of our `openni::VideoStream`. Then by using the `openni::CameraSettings::getAutoWhiteBalanceEnabled()` and `openni::CameraSetti ngs::setAutoWhiteBalanceEnabled()` methods, we get and change the active state of this feature:

```
if (selectedSensor.isValid() &&
  selectedSensor.getSensorInfo().getSensorType() ==
    SENSOR_COLOR)
{
  CameraSettings cs =
    *(selectedSensor.getCameraSettings());
  cs.setAutoWhiteBalanceEnabled(
    !cs.getAutoWhiteBalanceEnabled());
  printf("Auto White Balance %s\r\n",
    (cs.getAutoWhiteBalanceEnabled() ?
    "Activated" : "Deactivated"));
}
```

Some screenshots to compare the difference between the enabled and disabled states of these two camera settings are as follows:

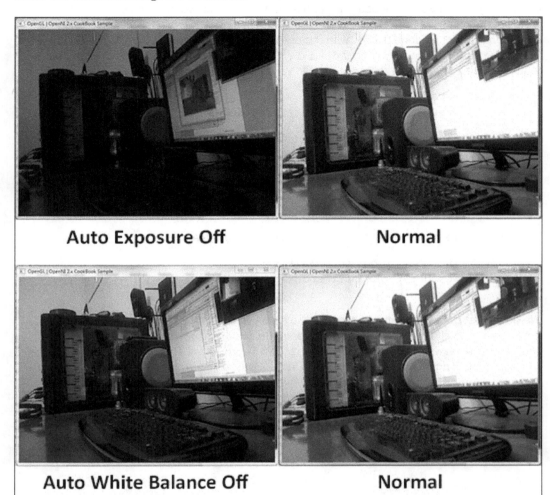

There's more...

Starting with OpenNI 2.2, it is possible to set **Gain** and **Exposure** values manually. A list of related methods to do so is as follows:

- ▶ `openni::CameraSettings::getExposure()`: This method returns the current value of Exposure in `int`.
- ▶ `openni::CameraSettings::setExposure()`: This method sets a new value for Exposure. It accepts an argument of the type `int` and returns an `openni::Status` indicating the success of the operation.
- ▶ `openni::CameraSettings::getGain()`: This method returns the current value of Gain in `int`.
- ▶ `openni::CameraSettings::setGain()`: This method sets a new value for Gain. It accepts an argument of the type `int` and returns an `openni::Status` indicating the success of the operation.

See also

- ▶ The *Reading and showing a frame from the image Sensor (color / IR)* recipe in *Chapter 3, Using Low-level Data*

5
NiTE and User Tracking

In this chapter, we will cover the following recipes:

- ▸ Getting a list of all the active users
- ▸ Identifying and coloring users' pixels in depth map
- ▸ Reading users' bounding boxes and center of mass
- ▸ Event-based reading of users' data

Introduction

Until now we talked about OpenNI and learned how to use it for accessing devices and their raw outputs. But from this chapter onwards, we will cover NiTE, which is a middleware based on OpenNI and more focused on natural interactions. NiTE is a product of the same team as OpenNI and acts as middleware above the OpenNI framework with the purpose of providing more advanced outputs as a basic natural interaction interface for developers.

In this chapter, we will show you how to use the `nite::UserTracker` class to get the list of all active users in the scene and get their location and size in OpenNI's depth stream, along with the centre of visual mass of each user.

The nite::NiTE object

`nite::NiTE`, just as with `openni::OpenNI`, is a static class and a starting point when working with NiTE.

`nite::NiTE` contains three methods: `nite::NiTE::initialize()`, `nite::NiTE::shutdown()`, and `nite::NiTE::getVersion()`. We are not sure what `nite::NiTE::initialize()` actually does because NiTE is a closed source project; however, one of its jobs is to call `openni::OpenNI::initialize()` so that developers don't need to initialize OpenNI and NiTE separately. We can also assume that `nite::NiTE::shutdown()` is used to free allocated memory and call `openni::OpenNI::shutdown()` at the end.

Except for the preceding methods, we don't have any use for the `nite::NiTE` object.

The nite::UserTracker object

One of the important classes in NiTE is `nite::UserTracker`. This class is responsible for getting any information relative to users and their bodies. `nite::UserTracker` works like `openni::VideoStream` and has similar methods. However, it is actually not a sensor or a direct output of any physical unit. `nite::UserTracker` gives us what NiTE recognized from a depth stream of OpenNI. In this chapter, we are going to use only one of the methods of this class; more methods of this class will be covered in the next chapter:

▶ `nite::UserTracker::readFrame()`: This method will wait for a new frame to become available and return the related `nite::UserTrackerFrameRef` object or return the latest unread frame

The nite::UserTrackerFrameRef object

`nite::UserTrackerFrameRef` is the object containing any available data about the current users. This class is used along with `nite::UserTracker` to give us a user-based view of a scene captured by the depth sensor. To get access to the latest produced `nite::UserTrackerFrameRef` object, you need to call the `nite::UserTracker::readFrame()` method.

The nite::UserMap object

The `nite::UserMap` class is actually a bitmap data container or, in other words, a big array that has width x height x 2 bytes of data and is of the same size as the depth frame. But unlike the depth frame, there is no data about depth in these uint16 pixels of `nite::UserMap`. The values in `nite::UserMap` are the ID of a user to whom the pixel belongs, or the number zero if that pixel belongs to no user.

The `nite::UserMap` class has the following four methods:

▶ `nite::UserMap::getWidth()`: The returned value is an `int` value showing the width of `nite::UserMap`. This value is the same as the underlying depth frame's width.

▶ `nite::UserMap::getHeight()`: The returned value is an `int` value showing the height of `nite::UserMap`. This value is the same as the underlying depth frame's height.

▶ `nite::UserMap::getPixels()`: This returns a pointer to the first pixel of data.

▶ `nite::UserMap::getStride()`: The returned value is in type `int` and shows the number of bytes you need to add to the first pixel of a row to get the first pixel of the next row. Actually, it is the width of a row in bytes.

Each `nite::UserTrackerFrameRef` object contains a `nite::UserMap` object that can be retrieved using the `nite::UserTrackerFrameRef::getUserMap()` method.

The nite::UserData object

`nite::UserData` is a class representing a user. In another words, `nite::UserTrackerFrameRef` gives you a `nite::UserData` object for each user it has recognized.

`nite::UserData` has a number of methods; we are going to use some in this chapter. These are as follows:

▶ `nite::UserData::getCenterOfMass()`: This method returns a `nite::Point3f` value that shows the center of visual mass (also known as COM and center of gravity) of a user. A `nite::Point3f` value is a structure of three `float` fields that are used to show a point in a 3D space.

▶ `nite::UserData::getBoundingBox()`: The return type in this method is the `nite::BoundingBox` object that contains two `nite::Point3f` fields, one for minimum coordinates and one for maximum coordinates. These two values can be used for calculating the 3D position and size of a user.

▶ `nite::UserData::getId()`: This method returns an integer showing a unique ID for this user. This ID is only guaranteed to be unique at the current time and may be used later again for someone else.

▶ `nite::UserData::isLost()`: This method returns a `bool` type value that can be used to indicate whether this user was not visible enough, that NiTE decided to drop him in the next frame of data.

▶ `nite::UserData::isNew()`: This method returns a `bool` type value that indicates whether this is the first appearance of a user.

▶ `nite::UserData::isVisible()`: This method returns a `bool` type value that gives us the visibility state of a user. A user can be invisible but yet not lost.

You can get access to a list (array) of all the `nite::UserData` objects by calling the `nite::UserTrackerFrameRef::getUsers()` method.

Getting a list of all the active users

In this recipe, we are going to cover one of the most basic features of NiTE—recognizing users in the scene based on the depth sensor's data.

Our main goal in this recipe is to present the `nite::UserTracker` and `nite::UserTrackerFrameRef` objects and to show you a basic way to retrieve and use them.

Getting ready

Create a project in Visual Studio and prepare it for working with OpenNI and NiTE using the *Create a project in Visual Studio 2010* recipe in *Chapter 2, OpenNI and C++*.

How to do it...

1. Add the following line to the top of your source code (just below the `#include` lines):

    ```
    #include<conio.h>
    ```

2. Add the `ReadLastCharOfLine()` and `HandleStatus()` functions from previous recipes next to the preceding line.

3. Add the following lines next to the definition of the `ReadLastCharOfLine()` and `HandleStatus()` functions:

    ```
    bool HandleStatus(nite::Status status)
    {
        return HandleStatus((openni::Status)status);
    }
    ```

4. Then locate this line:

    ```
    int _tmain(int argc, _TCHAR* argv[])
    {
    ```

5. Then add the following lines inside the preceding function:

    ```
    Status status = STATUS_OK;
    printf("Scanning machine for devices and loading "
        "modules/drivers ...\r\n");

    status = openni::OpenNI::initialize();
    if (!HandleStatus(status)) return 1;
    printf("Completed.\r\n");

    printf("Opening first device ...\r\n");
    openni::Device device;
    status = device.open(openni::ANY_DEVICE);
    if (!HandleStatus(status)) return 1;
    printf("%s Opened, Completed.\r\n",
        device.getDeviceInfo().getName());

    nite::Status niStatus = nite::STATUS_OK;
    niStatus = nite::NiTE::initialize();
    if (!HandleStatus(niStatus)) return 1;
    printf("Done\r\n");

    printf("Creating user tracker ...\r\n");
    ```

```
nite::UserTracker uTracker;
niStatus = uTracker.create(&device);
if (!HandleStatus(niStatus)) return 1;
printf("Reading data from user tracker ...\r\n");
while(!kbhit())
{
  nite::UserTrackerFrameRef newFrame;
  niStatus = uTracker.readFrame(&newFrame);
  if (!HandleStatus(niStatus) ||
    !newFrame.isValid()) return 1;
  system("cls");
  const nite::Array<nite::UserData>& users =
    newFrame.getUsers();
  for (int i = 0; i < users.getSize(); ++i)
  {
    printf("User #%d %s \r\n",
      users[i].getId(),
      (users[i].isVisible()) ? "is Visible" :
      "is not Visible");
  }
}

nite::NiTE::shutdown();
openni::OpenNI::shutdown();
return 0;
```

How it works...

We have five steps in this recipe. In the second step, we defined our functions for checking the returned `openni::Status` value (named `HandleStatus()`) and to read the key inputs (named `ReadLastCharOfLine()`). But this time we have another function too. This new function shares the same name as our old `HandleStatus()` function but with the `nite::Status` argument instead of `openni::Status`. In this new function, we convert our `nite::Status` variable to `openni::Status` and pass it to the main function. Conversion is theoretically possible because they are enum values and internally integer. Other than this, we want to check if everything is working fine in our main function. For doing so, we need to compare `nite::Status` with `nite::STATUS_OK` and `openni::Status` with `openni::STATUS_OK`. Because both `openni::STATUS_OK` and `nite::STATUS_OK` are equal to 0, it's logically possible to write a single function to handle them both. We are going to use this function in other recipes from now on.

```
bool HandleStatus(nite::Status status)
{
  return HandleStatus((openni::Status)status);
}
```

In the next step, we initialized OpenNI, opened the first device (as usual and just like other recipes), and then we initialized NiTE:

```
nite::Status niStatus = nite::STATUS_OK;
niStatus = nite::NiTE::initialize();
if (!HandleStatus(niStatus)) return 1;
```

You don't need to call `openni::OpenNI::initialize()`, or define an `openni::Device` variable and open the first device to use NiTE and `nite::UserTracker`. Calling `nite::NiTE::initialize()` will automatically call `openni::OpenNI::initialize()` and create a `nite::UserTracker` object using `nite::UserTracker::create()` without any argument, thereby, automatically opening the first device. But we thought it is better to do it manually for the first time to show you that you can do it this way too; if you want to select one of the devices when there is more than one device, you actually need to do it this way.

Creating a `nite::UserTracker` object for our device is the next step. Refer to the following code:

```
nite::UserTracker uTracker;
niStatus = uTracker.create(&device);
if (!HandleStatus(niStatus)) return 1;
```

Then we will put our application into a `while` loop until a user presses any key. In this `while` loop, we are going to read data (known as frames) from `nite::UserTracker` and show visible and nonvisible recognized users:

```
while(!_kbhit())
{
  nite::UserTrackerFrameRef newFrame;
  niStatus = uTracker.readFrame(&newFrame);
  if (!HandleStatus(niStatus) ||
    !newFrame.isValid()) return 1;
  system("cls");
  const nite::Array<nite::UserData>& users =
    newFrame.getUsers();
  for (int i = 0; i < users.getSize(); ++i)
  {
    printf("User #%d %s \r\n",
      users[i].getId(),
      (users[i].isVisible()) ? "is Visible" :
      "is not Visible");
  }
}
```

As you can see in the preceding code, we used `nite::UserTrackerFrameRef` to read data from `nite::UserTracker` and then used `nite::UserTrackerFrameRef::getUsers()` to get an array containing all the recognized users.

Then using a simple `for` loop, we printed some information about each user, including their ID and visibility status to the console.

Note that the returned value type of `nite::UserTrackerFrameRef::getUsers()` is an array of `nite::UserData` objects. Then we used two methods of `nite::UserData`, `nite::UserData::getId()` and `nite::UserData::isVisible()` to get the ID and visibility state of each user.

That's all; following is the output of our application:

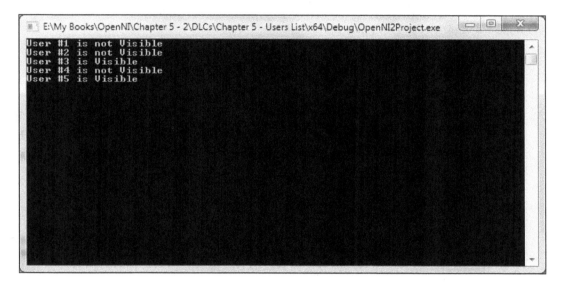

See also

- The *Identifying and coloring users' pixels in a depth map* recipe
- The *Reading users' bounding boxes and center of mass* recipe
- *Finding the related user ID for each hand ID* in *Chapter 6, NiTE and Hand Tracking*

Identifying and coloring users' pixels in depth map

In this recipe, we are going to show you how to use `nite::UserMap` to get the user ID for each pixel in the depth stream. By using this information, we can change the color of pixels belonging to one user.

Getting ready

Create a project in Visual Studio and prepare it for working with OpenNI and NiTE using the *Create a project in Visual Studio 2010* recipe in *Chapter 2, OpenNI and C++*. Then configure Visual Studio to use OpenGL using the *Configuring Visual Studio 2010 to use OpenGL* recipe in *Chapter 4, More about Low Level Outputs*.

How to do it...

1. Add these lines to the top of your source code (just below `#include` lines). Here we have defined variables to be used with OpenGL along with a `nite::UserTracker` variable that is going to hold a list of users and any other information about users in all the functions.

```
int window_w = 640;
int window_h = 480;
OniRGB888Pixel* gl_texture;
nite::UserTracker uTracker;
```

2. Add the `ReadLastCharOfLine()` function from previous recipes next to the preceding lines that are used to read a user's input.

3. Add the following lines next to the definition of the `ReadLastCharOfLine()` function. This function is responsible for checking whether the passed `nite::Status` value indicates any failure or not:

```
bool HandleStatus(nite::Status status)
{
  if (status == nite::STATUS_OK)
    return true;
  printf("ERROR: #%d, %s", status,
    OpenNI::getExtendedError());
  ReadLastCharOfLine();
  return false;
}
```

4. Then we need to add some of the usual OpenGL's functions:
   `gl_KeyboardCallback()`, which is the OpenGL keyboard callback and is
   responsible for any key press in the OpenGL window. Currently, its purpose is to check
   whether the *Esc* key is pressed to close the application. And `gl_IdleCallback()`,
   which tells OpenGL to render the scene again when the screen becomes idle. Copy
   the following code next to the definition of the `HandleStatus()` function:

```
void gl_KeyboardCallback(unsigned char key, int x, int y)
{
  if (key == 27) // ESC Key
  {
    uTracker.destroy();
    nite::NiTE::shutdown();
    exit(0);
  }
}
void gl_IdleCallback()
{
  glutPostRedisplay();
}
```

5. The primary part of our code is in the `gl_DisplayCallback()` function that you
   need to define after the `gl_IdleCallback()` function. Add the following lines to
   the source code to do so:

```
void gl_DisplayCallback()
{
  if (uTracker.isValid())
  {
    nite::Status niStatus = nite::STATUS_OK;
    nite::UserTrackerFrameRef usersFrame;
    niStatus = uTracker.readFrame(&usersFrame);
    if (niStatus == nite::STATUS_OK &&
      usersFrame.isValid())
    {
      // Clear the OpenGL buffers
      glClear (
        GL_COLOR_BUFFER_BIT | GL_DEPTH_BUFFER_BIT);

      // Setup the OpenGL viewpoint
      glMatrixMode(GL_PROJECTION);
      glPushMatrix();
      glLoadIdentity();
      glOrtho(0, window_w, window_h, 0, -1.0, 1.0);

      // UPDATING TEXTURE (DEPTH 1MM TO RGB888)
```

```
VideoFrameRef depthFrame =
    usersFrame.getDepthFrame();

int depthHistogram[65536];
int numberOfPoints = 0;
memset(depthHistogram, 0,
  sizeof(depthHistogram));
for   (int y = 0;
    y < depthFrame.getHeight(); ++y)
{
  DepthPixel* depthCell = (DepthPixel*)(
    (char*)depthFrame.getData() +
    (y * depthFrame.getStrideInBytes())
    );
  for   (int x = 0; x < depthFrame.getWidth();
      ++x, ++depthCell)
  {
    if (*depthCell != 0)
    {
      depthHistogram[*depthCell]++;
      numberOfPoints++;
    }
  }
}

for (int nIndex=1;
nIndex < sizeof(depthHistogram) / sizeof(int);
nIndex++)
{
  depthHistogram[nIndex] +=
    depthHistogram[nIndex-1];
}

int colors[] = {16777215,
  14565387, 32255, 7996159, 16530175, 8373026,
  14590399, 7062435, 13951499, 55807};
double resizeFactor = min(
  (window_w / (double)depthFrame.getWidth()),
  (window_h / (double)depthFrame.getHeight()));
unsigned int texture_x = (unsigned int)(window_w -
  (resizeFactor * depthFrame.getWidth())) / 2;
unsigned int texture_y = (unsigned int)(window_h -
  (resizeFactor * depthFrame.getHeight())) / 2;
```

```
nite::UserMap usersMap = usersFrame.getUserMap();

for  (unsigned int y = 0;
  y < (window_h - 2 * texture_y); ++y)
{
  OniRGB888Pixel* texturePixel = gl_texture +
    ((y + texture_y) * window_w) + texture_x;
  for  (unsigned int x = 0;
    x < (window_w - 2 * texture_x);
    ++x, ++texturePixel)
  {
    DepthPixel* depthPixel =
      (DepthPixel*)(
        (char*)depthFrame.getData() +
        ((int)(y / resizeFactor) *
          depthFrame.getStrideInBytes())
      ) +    (int)(x / resizeFactor);
    nite::UserId* userPixel =
      (nite::UserId*)(
        (char*)usersMap.getPixels() +
        ((int)(y / resizeFactor) *
          usersMap.getStride())
      ) +    (int)(x / resizeFactor);
    if (*depthPixel != 0)
    {
      float depthValue =
        (1 - ((float)depthHistogram[*depthPixel]
        / numberOfPoints));
      int userColor =
        colors[(int)*userPixel % 10];
      texturePixel->b =
        ((userColor / 65536) % 256) * depthValue;
      texturePixel->g =
        ((userColor / 256) % 256) * depthValue;
      texturePixel->r =
        ((userColor / 1) % 256) * depthValue;
    }
    else
    {
      texturePixel->b = 0;
      texturePixel->g = 0;
      texturePixel->r = 0;
    }
  }
```

```
        }

        // Create the OpenGL texture map
        glTexParameteri(GL_TEXTURE_2D,
           0x8191, GL_TRUE); // 0x8191 = GL_GENERATE_MIPMAP
        glTexImage2D(GL_TEXTURE_2D, 0, GL_RGB,
           window_w, window_h,        0, GL_RGB,
           GL_UNSIGNED_BYTE, gl_texture);

        glBegin(GL_QUADS);
        glTexCoord2f(0.0f, 0.0f);
        glVertex3f(0.0f, 0.0f, 0.0f);
        glTexCoord2f(0.0f, 1.0f);
        glVertex3f(0.0f, (float)window_h, 0.0f);
        glTexCoord2f(1.0f, 1.0f);
        glVertex3f((float)window_w,
           (float)window_h, 0.0f);
        glTexCoord2f(1.0f, 0.0f);
        glVertex3f((float)window_w, 0.0f, 0.0f);
        glEnd();

        glutSwapBuffers();
      }
    }
  }
```

6. Then locate the following line:

```
int _tmain(int argc, _TCHAR* argv[])
{
```

7. Replace the code inside this function with the following code:

```
nite::Status niStatus = nite::STATUS_OK;
printf("Initializing NiTE ...\r\n");
niStatus = nite::NiTE::initialize();

printf("Creating a user tracker object ...\r\n");
niStatus = uTracker.create();
if (!HandleStatus(niStatus)) return 1;
printf("Done.\r\n");

printf("Initializing OpenGL ...\r\n");
gl_texture = (OniRGB888Pixel*)malloc(
  window_w * window_h * sizeof(OniRGB888Pixel));
glutInit(&argc, (char**)argv);
glutInitDisplayMode(GLUT_RGB | GLUT_DOUBLE | GLUT_DEPTH);
glutInitWindowSize(window_w, window_h);
glutCreateWindow ("OpenGL | OpenNI 2.x CookBook Sample");
glutKeyboardFunc(gl_KeyboardCallback);
glutDisplayFunc(gl_DisplayCallback);
```

```
glutIdleFunc(gl_IdleCallback);
glDisable(GL_DEPTH_TEST);
glEnable(GL_TEXTURE_2D);
printf("Starting OpenGL rendering process ...\r\n");
glutMainLoop();

return 0;
```

How it works...

All functions are well-known if you have read the previous recipes. We just want to speak more about our primary function in this part, which is `gl_DisplayCallback()`.

If you look at this function, you can clearly see that we don't have the `depthSensor` variable as with the previous recipes any more. We now only have a variable named `uTracker`. So first of all in this function, we checked if our `uTracker` variable is valid and then we tried to read a frame from it. Then we checked if the returned `nite::UserTrackerFrameRef` value is valid and the reading operation has completed successfully:

```
if (uTracker.isValid())
{
  nite::Status niStatus = nite::STATUS_OK;
  nite::UserTrackerFrameRef usersFrame;
  niStatus = uTracker.readFrame(&usersFrame);
  if (niStatus == nite::STATUS_OK && usersFrame.isValid())
  {
```

Then we cleared the OpenGL buffer and positioned the camera as with all older recipes when we used OpenGL. After this, we are going to calculate a histogram of the depth map. But for doing so, we need to have access to the depth frame. Fortunately, `nite::UserTrackerFra meRef::getDepthFrame()` gives us access to the related depth frame:

```
VideoFrameRef depthFrame =
        usersFrame.getDepthFrame();
```

> Note that `nite::UserTracker` tries to recognize users in screen using depth stream data, so each `nite::UserTrackerFrameRef` object is created from a depth `openni::VideoFrameRef` value. From this fact, we can expect to have access to the underlying depth frame when working with a user tracker frame.

We are not going to talk more about the histogram calculation process as we have already discussed enough in the previous recipes. So let's just skip it.

The next part is expected to be our famous double loop over all the pixels of the depth frame and converting and copying them to the texture. But before doing it, we need to define some variables. One is the `colors` array that we are going to use later to show each user in a unique color. We defined an array of 10 colors starting with white (that means no user) and continuing with nine colors in decimal value. From left to right: white, red, light blue, Curacao, pink, light green, light pink, light sea green, yellow, and cyan.

```
int colors[] = {16777215,
    14565387, 32255, 7996159, 16530175, 8373026,
    14590399, 7062435, 13951499, 55807};
```

Then we need to request our `nite::UserMap` object. This object lets us know which pixel belongs to which user. So we defined a variable of type `nite::UserMap` named `usersMap` and then filled it using `nite::UserTrackerFrameRef::getUserMap()`:

```
nite::UserMap usersMap = usersFrame.getUserMap();
```

After this we are going to use two `for` loops to loop over the width and height of the depth frame's data as always. But this time the code in the inner loop is different (that is, the converting and copying part). Let's take a look at the code before talking about it:

```
DepthPixel* depthPixel =
    (DepthPixel*)(
        (char*)depthFrame.getData() +
        ((int)(y / resizeFactor) *
            depthFrame.getStrideInBytes())
    ) + (int)(x / resizeFactor);
nite::UserId* userPixel =
    (nite::UserId*)(
        (char*)usersMap.getPixels() +
        ((int)(y / resizeFactor) *
            usersMap.getStride())
    ) + (int)(x / resizeFactor);
if (*depthPixel != 0)
{
    float depthValue =
        (1 - ((float)depthHistogram[*depthPixel]
        / numberOfPoints));
    int userColor =
        colors[(int)*userPixel % 10];
    texturePixel->b =
        ((userColor / 65536) % 256) * depthValue;
    texturePixel->g =
        ((userColor / 256) % 256) * depthValue;
    texturePixel->r =
        (userColor / 1) % 256) * depthValue;
```

```
    }
    else
    {
      texturePixel->b = 0;
      texturePixel->g = 0;
      texturePixel->r = 0;
    }
```

As you can see, unlike always, here we have a `userPixel` variable of type
`nite::UserId` after our usual `openni::DepthPixel` variable. As you may remember,
our `openni::DepthPixel` variable named `depthPixel` is responsible for reading data
from the depth frame. Now our new `userPixel` variable contains the related used ID for
that pixel. We used the `nite::UserMap` object to extract this value:

```
nite::UserId* userPixel =
  (nite::UserId*)(
    (char*)usersMap.getPixels() +
    ((int)(y / resizeFactor) *
      usersMap.getStride())
  ) + (int)(x / resizeFactor);
```

It is just like reading from a bitmap. This is because `nite::UserMap` is actually a bitmap
with a 16-bit-per-pixel format, storing a user's ID instead of color.

Then in the following lines, we checked whether `depthPixel` is 0, meaning if it is a shadow
pixel; if it isn't, we tried to use histogram data to equalize the depth value. Just after that,
we selected a color depending on the user ID from the `colors` array and wrote that color
to the texture:

```
float depthValue =
  (1 - ((float)depthHistogram[*depthPixel]
  / numberOfPoints));
int userColor =
  colors[(int)*userPixel % 10];
texturePixel->b =
  ((userColor / 65536) % 256) * depthValue;
texturePixel->g =
  ((userColor / 256) % 256) * depthValue;
texturePixel->r =
  ((userColor / 1) % 256) * depthValue;
```

After these lines, there are some other OpenGL stuffs, but we have talked about them in
previous recipes.

In the next step, which is the beginning of our program, we have the initializing process. As you can see, there is no more `openni::OpenNI::initialize()` calling here. We just used `nite::NiTE::initialize()`, which does the calling for us. And also we didn't select a device this time; we just used `nite::UserTracker::create()` to automatically open the first device:

```
nite::Status niStatus = nite::STATUS_OK;
printf("Initializing NiTE ...\r\n");
niStatus = nite::NiTE::initialize();

printf("Creating a user tracker object ...\r\n");
niStatus = uTracker.create();
if (!HandleStatus(niStatus)) return 1;
printf("Done.\r\n");
```

The other lines are about how to configure and prepare OpenGL, starting the rendering process that also includes reading from the `nite::UserTracker`.

Here is the output of our application. You can see the second user in blue color. The first user is currently out of view, but he was visible in the color red.

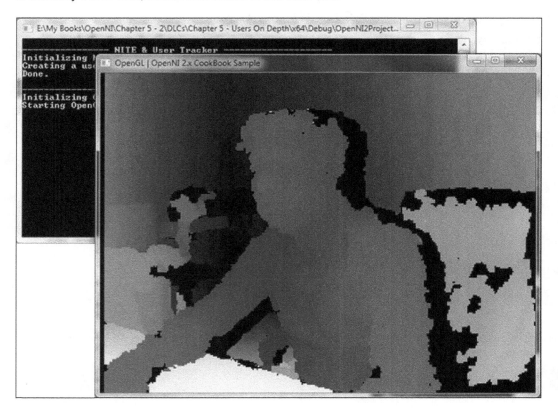

▸ *Reading and showing a frame from the Depth Sensor* in *Chapter 3, Using Low-level Data*

▸ The *Getting a list of all the active users* recipe

▸ *Finding the related user ID for each hand ID* in *Chapter 6, NiTE and Hand Tracking*

Reading users' bounding boxes and center of mass

In this recipe, we are going to expand on the preceding recipe by showing the bounding box and the center of visual mass (COM) of a user. The bounding box of a user shows the size and location of a user in screen and, for any user, the center of the visual mass is the center of distribution of the pixels.

More precisely, its x position is equal to the average of all the users' pixels x position, and its y position is equal to the average of all the users' pixels y position.

Almost the same is true about its z position, which is equal to the average of all the depth values of users' pixels.

Getting ready

Create a project in Visual Studio and prepare it for working with OpenNI and NiTE using the *Create a project in Visual Studio 2010* recipe in *Chapter 2, OpenNI and C++,* and then configure Visual Studio to use OpenGL using the *Configuring Visual Studio 2010 to use OpenGL* recipe in the previous chapter.

Then copy the code from the *Identifying and coloring users' pixels in the depth map* recipe from this chapter to this project.

How to do it...

1. Locate the ensuing line in the `gl_DisplayCallback()` function:

   ```
   glEnd();
   ```

2. And add the following code next to it:

   ```
   glBegin(GL_POINTS);
   glColor3f( 1.f, 0.f, 0.f );
      const nite::Array<nite::UserData>& users =
   usersFrame.getUsers();
      for (int i = 0; i < users.getSize(); ++i)
   ```

```
  {
    float posX, posY;
    niStatus =
      uTracker.convertJointCoordinatesToDepth(
      users[i].getCenterOfMass().x,
      users[i].getCenterOfMass().y,
      users[i].getCenterOfMass().z,
      &posX, &posY);
    if (HandleStatus(niStatus)){
      glVertex2f(
        (posX * resizeFactor) + texture_x,
        (posY * resizeFactor) + texture_y);
    }
  }
  glEnd();
  for (int i = 0; i < users.getSize(); ++i)
  {
    nite::BoundingBox userbb =
    users[i].getBoundingBox();
    float minPosX = (userbb.min.x * resizeFactor) +
      texture_x;
    float maxPosX = (userbb.max.x * resizeFactor) +
      texture_x;
    float minPosY = (userbb.min.y * resizeFactor) +
      texture_y;
    float maxPosY = (userbb.max.y * resizeFactor) +
      texture_y;
    glBegin(GL_LINE_LOOP);
      glVertex2f(minPosX, minPosY);
      glVertex2f(maxPosX, minPosY);
      glVertex2f(maxPosX, maxPosY);
      glVertex2f(minPosX, maxPosY);
    glEnd();
  }
  glColor3f( 1.f, 1.f, 1.f );
```

3. Then locate the ensuing line in the `_tmain()` function:
```
glutMainLoop();
```

4. And add the following line above the preceding line:
```
glPointSize(10.0);
```

How it works...

In the second step, we added some lines of code to show COM of all the users in screen. This operation happens after adding the texture to the OpenGL output (we added it after `glEnd()`).

As we want to draw a point for the users' COM position, we need to call `glBegin(GL_POINTS)` before doing anything. And then the process is to simply loop though all the users and convert their COM position to the depth pixel's position, and then draw a point in that position using OpenGL:

```
glBegin(GL_POINTS);
glColor3f( 1.f, 0.f, 0.f );
for (int i = 0; i < users.getSize(); ++i)
{
  float posX, posY;
  niStatus =
    uTracker.convertJointCoordinatesToDepth(
    users[i].getCenterOfMass().x,
    users[i].getCenterOfMass().y,
    users[i].getCenterOfMass().z,
    &posX, &posY);
    if (HandleStatus(niStatus)){
    glVertex2f(
      (posX * resizeFactor) + texture_x,
      (posY * resizeFactor) + texture_y);
  }
}
glEnd();
```

Here, we have used the `glColor3f()` function from OpenGL to change the active color to red.

`nite::UserTracker::convertJointCoordinatesToDepth()` is responsible for converting the COM position to the depth pixel's values, which is something similar to what the `openni::CoordinateConverter::convertWorldToDepth()` method does. If the returned value of this function is `nite::STATUS_OK`, the conversion process is completed without any problem, and we are able to use the `posX` and `posY` variables as the position of COM related to the depth frame. The next step is to use `glVertex2f()` from OpenGL to draw a point there:

```
niStatus =
  uTracker.convertJointCoordinatesToDepth(
  users[i].getCenterOfMass().x,
  users[i].getCenterOfMass().y,
  users[i].getCenterOfMass().z,
  &posX, &posY);
```

Note that these two values (coordinates of COM point) are relative to the depth frame, and we need to calculate their position relative to the OpenGL window and its texture size:

```
glVertex2f (
    (posX * resizeFactor) + texture_x,
    (posY * resizeFactor) + texture_y);
```

Now that we have placed all the COM points, we can start drawing rectangles for the users' bounding boxes. Of course, we do this after calling the `glEnd()` function to show that we are not interested in drawing points any more:

```
glEnd();
for (int i = 0; i < users.getSize(); ++i)
{
```

Lopping over all users and extracting their bounding boxes' start and end points, and then converting these numbers relative to our OpenGL window and its texture size, is what we are doing here:

```
nite::BoundingBox userbb =
users[i].getBoundingBox();
float minPosX = (userbb.min.x * resizeFactor) +
    texture_x;
float maxPosX = (userbb.max.x * resizeFactor) +
    texture_x;
float minPosY = (userbb.min.y * resizeFactor) +
    texture_y;
float maxPosY = (userbb.max.y * resizeFactor) +
    texture_y;
```

Then we asked OpenGL to let us draw some closed lines and also requested four points for our rectangle:

```
glBegin(GL_LINE_LOOP);
    glVertex2f(minPosX, minPosY);
    glVertex2f(maxPosX, minPosY);
    glVertex2f(maxPosX, maxPosY);
    glVertex2f(minPosX, maxPosY);
glEnd();
```

As you can see, we didn't convert these coordinates using `nite::UserTrac ker::convertJointCoordinatesToDepth()`. We don't know if it was a mistake in development or a feature but returned values for users' bounding boxes are already converted to the depth frame coordinates.

And the last line is where we changed the active color to white again:

```
glColor3f( 1.f, 1.f, 1.f );
```

This is all we did in the first two steps.

In the next two steps, we only added one line of code:

```
glPointSize(10.0);
```

This line of code tells OpenGL to draw each point with a width and height having 10 pixels. Note that points in OpenGL are filled rectangles.

Here is the output of our application:

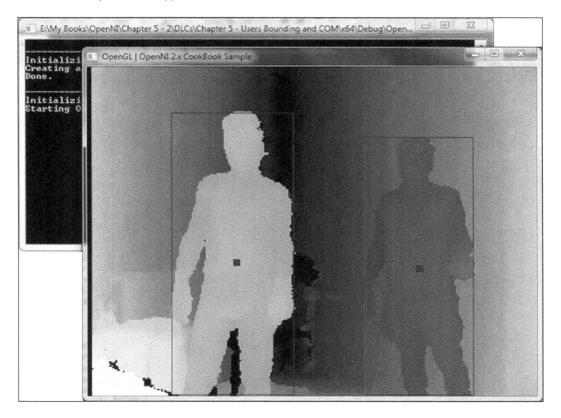

There's more...

Here we learn about `nite::UserTracker::convertJointCoordinatesToDepth()`, which is capable of converting any coordinates returned by the `nite::UserTracker` methods (or its child classes' methods) to coordinate the related pixel in the depth frame. Apart from this method, there is another method named `nite::UserTracker::convertDepthCoordinatesToJoint()` that does the same thing but in a reverse direction. Both of them accept five parameters and fill the last two parameters with calculated coordinates from the first three parameters.

See also

- ▸ *Reading and showing a frame from the depth sensor* in *Chapter 3, Using Low-level Data*
- ▸ The *Identifying and coloring users' pixels in a depth map* recipe
- ▸ *Get a user's skeleton joints and display their position in the depth map* in *Chapter 7, NiTE and Skeleton Tracking*

Event-based reading of users' data

You don't need to call `nite::UserTracker::readFrame()` and wait for it to return each time you want to read a frame of data from `nite::UserTracker`. This is because NiTE developers give us this ability to define a callback (also known as event listener) when a new frame becomes available, just as `openni::VideoStream` does. In this recipe, we are going to cover this feature and rewrite the first recipe of this chapter, this time based on events.

Getting ready

Create a project in Visual Studio and prepare it for working with OpenNI and NiTE using the *Create a project in Visual Studio 2010* recipe in *Chapter 2, OpenNI and C++*.

How to do it...

1. Add the `ReadLastCharOfLine()` function from previous recipes to the top of your source code (just below `#include` lines).
2. Then add the `HandleStatus()` function from the previous recipe, right after the `ReadLastCharOfLine()` function.

3. Add these lines after the definition of the `HandleStatus()` function:

```
struct uTrackerNewFrameListener :
  public nite::UserTracker::NewFrameListener
{
    void onNewFrame(nite::UserTracker& utracker)
    {
    nite::Status status = nite::STATUS_OK;
    nite::UserTrackerFrameRef newFrame;
    status = utracker.readFrame(&newFrame);
    if (!HandleStatus(status) ||
      !newFrame.isValid()) return;
    system("cls");
    const nite::Array<nite::UserData>& users =
      newFrame.getUsers();
    for (int i = 0; i < users.getSize(); ++i)
    {
      printf("User #%d %s \r\n",
        users[i].getId(),
          (users[i].isVisible()) ? "is Visible" :
                        is not Visible");
    }
    }
};
```

4. Then locate the following line:

```
int _tmain(int argc, _TCHAR* argv[])
{
```

5. Write the following code inside this function:

```
    nite::Status status = nite::STATUS_OK;
    printf("Initializing NiTE ...\r\n");
    status = nite::NiTE::initialize();
    if (!HandleStatus(status)) return 1;
    printf("Done\r\n");

    printf("Creating user tracker ...\r\n");
    nite::UserTracker utracker;
    status = utracker.create();
    if (!HandleStatus(status)) return 1;
    uTrackerNewFrameListener listener;
    utracker.addNewFrameListener(&listener);
```

```
printf("Reading data from user tracker ...\r\n");

ReadLastCharOfLine();

utracker.destroy();
nite::NiTE::shutdown();
return 0;
```

How it works...

As you can see in the first step, we again have the `ReadLastCharOfLine()` and `HandleStatus()` functions. But just after these two famous functions, in the third step, we have the definition of a structure named `uTrackerNewFrameListener`.

We created this structure by inheriting the `nite::UserTracker::NewFrameListener` class and overriding its `onNewFrame()` method. In this method, we wrote our desired code that we want to be executed when a new `nite::UserTrackerFrameRef` object becomes available to be read. If you check the first recipe of this chapter, it's doing exactly the same thing you can see in the output (the code in the `while` loop), but now we moved them here.

In the second line, we read the newly available frame and then check whether this new frame is valid:

```
nite::UserTrackerFrameRef newFrame;
status = utracker.readFrame(&newFrame);
if (!HandleStatus(status) ||
  !newFrame.isValid()) return;
```

If it's valid, we clear the screen using the `cls` system command and then retrieve all the recognized users in the current frame:

```
system("cls");
const nite::Array<nite::UserData>& users =
  newFrame.getUsers();
```

Then we loop through over all of the users and print their ID and visibility state to the console:

```
printf("User #%d %s \r\n",
  users[i].getId(),
  (users[i].isVisible()) ? "is Visible" :
              "is not Visible");
```

In the fourth step, we initialize NiTE and create our `nite::UserTracker` object. Everything is as usual in the first 11 lines.

```
nite::Status status = nite::STATUS_OK;
printf("Initializing NiTE ...\r\n");
status = nite::NiTE::initialize();
if (!HandleStatus(status)) return 1;
printf("Done\r\n");

printf("Creating user tracker ...\r\n");
nite::UserTracker utracker;
status = utracker.create();
if (!HandleStatus(status)) return 1;
```

Then, as we want to listen to the `nite::UserTracker` events, we introduce our newly defined structure (or class) to NiTE:

```
uTrackerNewFrameListener listener;
utracker.addNewFrameListener(&listener);
```

These two lines will do the entire job. Then we somehow need to make the main thread busy or our application may exit without doing anything. To do so, we used the `ReadLastCharOfLine()` function, which waits until the user presses a key. And after pressing a key, which means that the user is not interested in our app any more, we can destroy our `nite::UserTracker` object and shut `nite::NiTE` down:

```
ReadLastCharOfLine();

utracker.destroy();
nite::NiTE::shutdown();
return 0;
```

The output of this application is similar to the output of the first recipe:

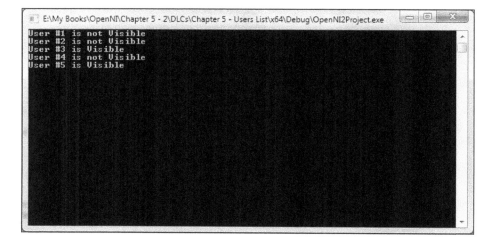

See also

▸ *Event based reading of data* in *Chapter 3, Using Low-level Data*

▸ *Event-based reading of hands' data* in *Chapter 6, NiTE and Hand Tracking*

6
NiTE and Hand Tracking

In this chapter, we will cover:

- ▶ Recognizing predefined hand gestures
- ▶ Tracking hands
- ▶ Finding the related user ID for each hand ID
- ▶ Event-based reading of hands' data
- ▶ The working sample for controlling the mouse by hand

Introduction

In this chapter, we are going to cover every topic related to hand tracking in NiTE, from finding hand gestures to tracking hand movements and finding which hand belongs to which user.

Unfortunately, the new version of NITE does not have some commands, such as the hand swipe, from the old API.

The nite::HandTracker object

Just as with `nite::UserTracker`, which is responsible for giving us information about users, `nite::HandTracker` is responsible for giving us information about hand tracking and hand's gestures on the scene. The two main functionalities of `nite::HandTracker` are recognizing hand gestures and tracking hands. Let's take a look at the important methods of this class:

- ▶ `nite:HandTracker::startGestureDetection()`: This method starts the process of searching for a specific hand gesture in the scene. It accepts only a single argument from the `nite::GestureType` enum type. This `enum` type has three predefined members that are the only supported gestures by `nite::HandTracker`. It is impossible to expand this functionality.

- ❑ `nite::GESTURE_WAVE`: This value represents the wave gesture.

- ❑ `nite::GESTURE_CLICK`: This value represents the click gesture. This is the new name of the old push gesture.

- ❑ `nite::GESTURE_HAND_RAISE`: This value represents the hand raise gesture.

▶ `nite::HandTracker::startHandTracking()`: This method will start tracking a point that is recognized as a hand. Arguments of this method are a `nite::Point3f` value that indicates the position of the hand and you need to provide it as an argument to this method, and a `nite::HandId` value that will be filled with the ID of the hand from the method itself. The return value of this method is in the type `nite::Status` and indicates the success of the method.

▶ `nite::HandTracker::stopGestureDetection()`: By using this method, you can suspend the search for a specific gesture.

▶ `nite::HandTracker::stopHandTracking()`: This method can be used to abort the event of the tracking of a hand.

▶ `nite::HandTracker::convertHandCoordinatesToDepth()`: Just as with `nite::UserTracker::convertJointCoordinatesToDepth()`, this method lets you convert the position of the hand returned by NiTE to the number of pixels in the depth stream frame.

▶ `nite::HandTracker::readFrame()`: This method will wait for a new frame and update the passed `nite::HandTrackerFrameRef` variable or return the latest unread frame of data from `nite::HandTracker`. This is explained in the following section.

The nite::HandTrackerFrameRef object

`nite::HandTrackerFrameRef` represents a frame of data from `nite::HandTracker`, which contains the currently recognized gestures and hands in the scene. Here are some important methods of this class:

▶ `nite::HandTrackerFrameRef::getGestures()`: This returns an array of the recognized gestures in the current scene.

▶ `nite::HandTrackerFrameRef::getHands()`: This returns an array of the requested hands and of those that are being tracked in the current scene.

▶ `nite::HandTrackerFrameRef::getDepthFrame()`: This returns the underlying depth `openni::VideoFrameRef` that is used by `nite::HandsTracker` to create this data. This is useful if you need to access the depth frame without using an `openni::VideoStream` object and if you require extra code to read data from it.

The nite::HandData object

`nite::HandData` represents a real-life hand. This class contains some information about the position and status of an under-tracking hand. Let's take a look at its important methods:

- ▶ `nite::HandData::getId()`: The return value is in the type `nite::HandId`; this is actually a `uint16` variable and contains a unique ID for the hand.

- ▶ `nite::HandData::getPosition()`: The return value of this method is in the type `nite::Point3f` and contains the current position of the hand.

- ▶ `nite::HandData::isLost()`: The return value is a `bool` value, indicating that this hand was invisible enough that NiTE decided to remove it from the next frame of data.

- ▶ `nite::HandData::isNew()`: This method returns a `bool` value that indicates if this is the first frame of data that we have for this hand.

- ▶ `nite::HandData::isTouchingFov()`: This method also returns a `bool` value that indicates if the hand is currently touching the edge of the field of view of a device.

- ▶ `nite::HandData::isTracking()`: This is another method with a `bool` return value. It indicates if the hand is visible and is under tracking.

We need to use the `nite::HandTrackerFrameRef::getHands()` method to retrieve a list of active hands.

The nite::GestureData object

`nite::GestureData` is very similar to `nite::HandData` with the only difference that this class is simpler than `nite::HandData` and contains less data. `nite::GestureData` is the representation of a real-world gesture:

- ▶ `nite::GestureData::getCurrentPosition()`: This returns a `nite::Point3f` value that shows the position of where this gesture occurs. It can be used to start the tracking of a hand.

- ▶ `nite::GestureData::getType()`: This returns a `nite::GestureType` enum value that shows the type of recognized gesture.

- ▶ `nite::GestureData::isComplete()`: This method gives you a `bool` value that can be used to indicate if this gesture completed successfully or if it is still in progress. From our observation, this is always `true` if the gesture is in the list of recognized gestures.

- ▶ `nite::GestureData::isInProgress()`: This is another method with a `bool` return value. It indicates if the gesture has not yet completed and if it is still in progress. But we never saw this with the `true` value in our experiments.

Compared to skeleton tracking

The next chapter is about the tracking of a user's body and its skeleton joints. This means that in the next chapter, we will be able to track a user's hand joints and simulate a similar result. Now a question may pop up in your mind: what are the advantages of using `HandTracker` when we can use `UserTracker` too? Here is the answer:

► Unlike `UserTracker` that can only track a user when he/she is in a standing position, `HandTracker` is able to track hands independent of the user's body.

► `HandTracker` doesn't need to see users' full bodies whereas `UserTracker` can only detect users with their bodies completely in the field of view. This also means that `UserTracker` can't recognize a user at a distance of less than 2 metres whereas `HandTracker` can recognize a user at such as distance.

► The result of `HandTracker` is more accurate compared to `UserTracker` as it doesn't need to track the full body.

Recognizing predefined hand gestures

In this recipe, we are going to request a search for all the three predefined hand gestures and wait for new data. These predefined hand gestures are the **Hand Raise Gesture**, **Click Gesture**, and **Wave Gesture**. Check whether any of these three hand gestures are recognized in the scene and write this info to the console.

Getting ready

Create a project in Visual Studio and prepare it for working with OpenNI and NiTE using the *Create a project in Visual Studio 2010* recipe in *Chapter 2, OpenNI and C++*.

How to do it...

1. Add these lines to the top of your source code (just below the `#include` lines):

```
#include<conio.h>
char ReadLastCharOfLine()
{
  int newChar = 0;
  int lastChar;
  fflush(stdout);
  do
  {
    lastChar = newChar;
    newChar = getchar();
  }
```

```
    while ((newChar != '\n')
      && (newChar != EOF));
    return (char)lastChar;
}

bool HandleStatus(nite::Status status)
{
    if (status == nite::STATUS_OK)
      return true;
    printf("ERROR: #%d, %s", status,
      openni::OpenNI::getExtendedError());
    ReadLastCharOfLine();
    return false;
}
```

2. Then locate the following line:

```
int _tmain(int argc, _TCHAR* argv[])
{
```

3. Replace any code inside the preceding function with the following code:

```
    nite::Status status = nite::STATUS_OK;
    status = nite::NiTE::initialize();
    if (!HandleStatus(status)) return 1;

    printf("Creating hand tracker ...\r\n");
    nite::HandTracker hTracker;
    status = hTracker.create();
    if (!HandleStatus(status)) return 1;
    printf("Searching for Wave, Hand Raise and "
      "Click gestures ...\r\n");
    hTracker.startGestureDetection(nite::GESTURE_WAVE);
    hTracker.startGestureDetection(nite::GESTURE_HAND_RAISE);
    hTracker.startGestureDetection(nite::GESTURE_CLICK);
    printf("Reading data from hand tracker ...\r\n");

    while(!_kbhit())
    {
      nite::HandTrackerFrameRef newFrame;
      status = hTracker.readFrame(&newFrame);
      if (!HandleStatus(status) ||
        !newFrame.isValid()) return 1;
      const nite::Array<nite::GestureData>& gestures =
        newFrame.getGestures();
      for (int i = 0; i < gestures.getSize(); ++i)
```

```
        {
          printf("%s Gesture Detected @ %g,%g,%g - %s \r\n",
            (gestures[i].getType() ==
            nite::GESTURE_CLICK) ? "Click" :
            ((gestures[i].getType() ==
            nite::GESTURE_HAND_RAISE) ? "Hand Raise" :
            "Wave"),
            gestures[i].getCurrentPosition().x,
            gestures[i].getCurrentPosition().y,
            gestures[i].getCurrentPosition().z,
            (gestures[i].isInProgress()) ? "In Progress" :
            ((gestures[i].isComplete()) ? "Completed" :
            "Initializing"));
        }
      }

      nite::NiTE::shutdown();
      return 0;
```

How it works...

As always, we have our famous `ReadLastCharOfLine()` and `HandleStatus()` functions in step one. They don't need any explanation.

In step two, again similar to almost all of the recipes in the previous chapter, we initialize `nite::NiTE`. Then we define and create a `nite::HandTracker` object that will also automatically open the first device:

```
nite::HandTracker hTracker;
status = hTracker.create();
```

Before reading data from our `nite::HandTracker` object, we should request a search for our desired hand gestures. We request a search for all of the three available gestures here:

```
hTracker.startGestureDetection(nite::GESTURE_WAVE);
hTracker.startGestureDetection(nite::GESTURE_HAND_RAISE);
hTracker.startGestureDetection(nite::GESTURE_CLICK);
```

Then we need to read the data; for doing this, we use a `while` loop until the user presses a key. Moreover, in this loop we define a `nite::HandTrackerFrameRef` variable, and then using `nite::HandTracker::readFrame()`, we read a new frame of data. This call will wait for new data to become available. If not any:

```
nite::HandTrackerFrameRef newFrame;
status = hTracker.readFrame(&newFrame);
```

The next step is to get a list of all the recognized gestures by defining an array of `nite::GestureData` and calling the `nite::HandTrackerFrameRef::getGestures()` method:

```
const nite::Array<nite::GestureData>& gestures =
  newFrame.getGestures();
```

Then, loop through this list and show some information about each gesture to the user:

```
printf("%s Gesture Detected @ %g,%g,%g - %s \r\n",
  (gestures[i].getType() ==
  nite::GESTURE_CLICK) ? "Click" :
  ((gestures[i].getType() ==
  nite::GESTURE_HAND_RAISE) ? "Hand Raise" :
  "Wave"),
  gestures[i].getCurrentPosition().x,
  gestures[i].getCurrentPosition().y,
  gestures[i].getCurrentPosition().z,
  (gestures[i].isInProgress()) ? "In Progress" :
  ((gestures[i].isComplete()) ? "Completed" :
  "Initializing"));
```

In the preceding lines of code, we printed the type of gesture, the position of the gesture, and the state of the gesture to the console.

This is an infinite loop waiting for the user's intervention. So when a user issues a key press, we exit the `while` loop and free all of the allocated memory before exiting the program:

```
nite::NiTE::shutdown();
return 0;
```

The output of our application is as follows:

```
■ E:\My Books\OpenNI\Chapter 6 - 2\DLCs\Chapter 6 - Hand Gusture\x64\Debug\OpenNI2Project.e...

--------------- Init NiTE and Hand Tracker ---------------
Done
Creating hand tracker ...
Searching for Wave, Hand Raise and Click gestures ...
Reading data from hand tracker ...
Hand Raise Gesture Detected @ 443.329,160.993,1120.22 - Completed
Hand Raise Gesture Detected @ 442.873,320.73,1260.58 - Completed
Hand Raise Gesture Detected @ 438.782,377.921,1293.31 - Completed
Hand Raise Gesture Detected @ 444.39,388.602,1319.2 - Completed
Hand Raise Gesture Detected @ 449.712,397.423,1342.26 - Completed
Hand Raise Gesture Detected @ 457.649,409.798,1365.59 - Completed
Hand Raise Gesture Detected @ 458.009,416.824,1385.88 - Completed
Hand Raise Gesture Detected @ 461.947,417.217,1401.58 - Completed
Hand Raise Gesture Detected @ 196.312,246.99,1235.93 - Completed
Wave Gesture Detected @ 307.747,260.856,1484.6 - Completed
Hand Raise Gesture Detected @ 252.643,249.921,1459.23 - Completed
Hand Raise Gesture Detected @ 231.52,157.661,1432.84 - Completed
Hand Raise Gesture Detected @ 131.82,279.179,943.981 - Completed
Hand Raise Gesture Detected @ 127.902,275.499,964.342 - Completed
Hand Raise Gesture Detected @ 127.97,273.478,1011.82 - Completed
Hand Raise Gesture Detected @ 141.909,270.826,1077.14 - Completed
Hand Raise Gesture Detected @ 151.581,259.815,1159.99 - Completed
Click Gesture Detected @ 190.001,199.793,1319.61 - Completed
```

See also

▶ The *Tracking hands* recipe

▶ The *Event-based reading of hands' data* recipe

▶ The *User pose detecting* recipe in *Chapter 7, NiTE and Skeleton Tracking*

Tracking hands

In this recipe, we are going to expand on the previous recipe and add hand tracking after recognizing a gesture. Moreover, we will also show the location of a hand in the screen overlying the depth frame data.

Getting ready

Create a project in Visual Studio and prepare it for working with OpenNI and NiTE using the *Create a project in Visual Studio 2010* recipe in *Chapter 2, OpenNI and C++*, and then configure Visual Studio to use OpenGL using the *Configuring Visual Studio 2010 to use OpenGL* recipe in *Chapter 3, Using Low-level Data*.

How to do it...

1. Define the `window_w`, `window_h`, and `gl_texture` variables on top of your source code, below the `#include` lines, just as with the other examples we wrote using OpenGL and GLUT.

2. Add the following code right below them:

```
nite::HandTracker hTracker;
```

3. Copy `ReadLastCharOfLine()` and `HandleStatus()` from the first recipe of this chapter and paste it here. Also, copy `gl_IdleCallback()` from the *Initialize and prepare OpenGL* recipe in *Chapter 3, Using Low-level Data*.

4. Then add the following lines of code:

```
void gl_KeyboardCallback(unsigned char key, int x, int y)
{
  if (key == 27) // ESC Key
  {
    hTracker.destroy();
    nite::NiTE::shutdown();
    exit(0);
  }
}
```

5. Also, add your primary function to render the scene right after that:

```
void gl_DisplayCallback()
{
  if (hTracker.isValid())
  {
    nite::Status status = nite::STATUS_OK;
    nite::HandTrackerFrameRef handsFrame;
    status = hTracker.readFrame(&handsFrame);
    if (status == nite::STATUS_OK && handsFrame.isValid())
    {
      const nite::Array<nite::GestureData>& gestures =
          handsFrame.getGestures();
      for (int i = 0; i < gestures.getSize(); ++i){
        if (gestures[i].isComplete()){
          nite::HandId handId;
          hTracker.startHandTracking(
            gestures[i].getCurrentPosition(), &handId);
        }
      }

      // Clear the OpenGL buffers
```

```
glClear (
  GL_COLOR_BUFFER_BIT | GL_DEPTH_BUFFER_BIT);

// Setup the OpenGL viewpoint
glMatrixMode(GL_PROJECTION);
glPushMatrix();
glLoadIdentity();
glOrtho(0, window_w, window_h, 0, -1.0, 1.0);

// UPDATING TEXTURE (DEPTH 1MM TO RGB888)
VideoFrameRef depthFrame =
  handsFrame.getDepthFrame();
int depthHistogram[65536];
int numberOfPoints = 0;
memset(depthHistogram, 0,
  sizeof(depthHistogram));
for  (int y = 0;
    y < depthFrame.getHeight(); ++y)
{
  DepthPixel* depthCell = (DepthPixel*)(
    (char*)depthFrame.getData() +
    (y * depthFrame.getStrideInBytes())
    );
  for  (int x = 0; x < depthFrame.getWidth();
      ++x, ++depthCell)
  {
    if (*depthCell != 0)
    {
      depthHistogram[*depthCell]++;
      numberOfPoints++;
    }
  }
}

for (int nIndex=1;
nIndex < sizeof(depthHistogram) / sizeof(int);
nIndex++)
{
  depthHistogram[nIndex] +=
    depthHistogram[nIndex-1];
}

double resizeFactor = min(
  (window_w / (double)depthFrame.getWidth()),
```

```
      (window_h / (double)depthFrame.getHeight()));
unsigned int texture_x = (unsigned int)(window_w -
  (resizeFactor * depthFrame.getWidth())) / 2;
unsigned int texture_y = (unsigned int)(window_h -
  (resizeFactor * depthFrame.getHeight())) / 2;

for   (unsigned int y = 0;
  y < (window_h - 2 * texture_y); ++y)
{
  OniRGB888Pixel* texturePixel = gl_texture +
    ((y + texture_y) * window_w) + texture_x;
  for   (unsigned int x = 0;
    x < (window_w - 2 * texture_x);
    ++x, ++texturePixel)
  {
    DepthPixel* depthPixel =
      (DepthPixel*)(
        (char*)depthFrame.getData() +
        ((int)(y / resizeFactor) *
          depthFrame.getStrideInBytes())
      ) +      (int)(x / resizeFactor);
    if (*depthPixel != 0)
    {
      float depthValue =
       ((float)depthHistogram[*depthPixel] /
         numberOfPoints) * 255;
      texturePixel->b = 255 - depthValue;
      texturePixel->g = 255 - depthValue;
      texturePixel->r = 255 - depthValue;
    }
    else
    {
      texturePixel->b = 0;
      texturePixel->g = 0;
      texturePixel->r = 0;
    }
  }
}

// Create the OpenGL texture map
glTexParameteri(GL_TEXTURE_2D,
  0x8191, GL_TRUE); // 0x8191 = GL_GENERATE_MIPMAP
glTexImage2D(GL_TEXTURE_2D, 0, GL_RGB,
  window_w, window_h,      0, GL_RGB,
```

```
            GL_UNSIGNED_BYTE, gl_texture);

    glBegin(GL_QUADS);
    glTexCoord2f(0.0f, 0.0f);
    glVertex3f(0.0f, 0.0f, 0.0f);
    glTexCoord2f(0.0f, 1.0f);
    glVertex3f(0.0f, (float)window_h, 0.0f);
    glTexCoord2f(1.0f, 1.0f);
    glVertex3f((float)window_w,
       (float)window_h, 0.0f);
    glTexCoord2f(1.0f, 0.0f);
    glVertex3f((float)window_w, 0.0f, 0.0f);
    glEnd();

    glBegin( GL_POINTS );
    glColor3f( 1.f, 0.f, 0.f );
    const nite::Array<nite::HandData>& hands =
      handsFrame.getHands();
    for (int i = 0; i < hands.getSize(); ++i){
      if (hands[i].isTracking()){
        float posX, posY;
        status =
          hTracker.convertHandCoordinatesToDepth(
          hands[i].getPosition().x,
          hands[i].getPosition().y,
          hands[i].getPosition().z,
          &posX, &posY);
        if (HandleStatus(status)){
          glVertex2f(
            (posX * resizeFactor) + texture_x,
            (posY * resizeFactor) + texture_y);
        }
      }
    }
    glEnd();
    glColor3f( 1.f, 1.f, 1.f );

    glutSwapBuffers();
    }
  }
}
```

6. Then, locate the following line:

```
int _tmain(int argc, _TCHAR* argv[])
{
```

7. Add the following function inside the preceding line:

```
nite::Status status = nite::STATUS_OK;
printf("Initializing NiTE ...\r\n");
status = nite::NiTE::initialize();
if (!HandleStatus(status)) return 1;

printf("Creating a hand tracker object ...\r\n");
status = hTracker.create();
if (!HandleStatus(status)) return 1;
printf("Done.\r\n");
printf("Searching for wave gesture ...\r\n");
status =
uTracker.startGestureDetection(nite::GESTURE_WAVE);
if (!HandleStatus(status)) return 1;

printf("Initializing OpenGL ...\r\n");
gl_texture = (OniRGB888Pixel*)malloc(
  window_w * window_h * sizeof(OniRGB888Pixel));
glutInit(&argc, (char**)argv);
glutInitDisplayMode(GLUT_RGB | GLUT_DOUBLE | GLUT_DEPTH);
glutInitWindowSize(window_w, window_h);
glutCreateWindow ("OpenGL | OpenNI 2.x CookBook Sample");
glPointSize(10.0);
glutKeyboardFunc(gl_KeyboardCallback);
glutDisplayFunc(gl_DisplayCallback);
glutIdleFunc(gl_IdleCallback);
glDisable(GL_DEPTH_TEST);
glEnable(GL_TEXTURE_2D);
printf("Starting OpenGL rendering process ...\r\n");
glutMainLoop();

return 0;
```

How it works...

In the second step, we defined our `nite::HandTracker` variable named `hTracker` to make it accessible from any function in our application. In the third step, we have our famous `ReadLastCharOfLine()` and `HandleStatus()` functions, which we don't think need any extra explanation.

Then, similar to the older recipes where we worked with GLUT and OpenGL, we have the `gl_KeyboardCallback()` function, which is responsible for key presses from the user, in the same step.

In the following step, we define the `gl_IdleCallback()` function that will ask OpenGL to render the scene again. In this step, we will view the most important part of our app—the `gl_DisplayCallback()` function. This function is responsible for assembling a scene. We are familiar with the first two functions and their code, so here we are only going to talk about `gl_DisplayCallback()`.

In the initial lines of `gl_DisplayCallback()`, we have to check the `nite::HandTracker` variable's availability. If it is available, we define and read a frame of data from `nite::HandTracker`. Then we check whether the process of reading a frame ended successfully and also check whether the returned frame is a valid object.

```
if (hTracker.isValid())
{
  nite::Status status = nite::STATUS_OK;
  nite::HandTrackerFrameRef handsFrame;
  status = hTracker.readFrame(&handsFrame);
  if (status == nite::STATUS_OK && handsFrame.isValid())
  {
```

For tracking a hand, we first need to locate it; one of the ways to do it is to ask the user to do a hand gesture. We then use the position of the hand gesture to start tracking the hand. So currently, we need to read all of the recognized gestures in the scene and request for them to be tracked:

```
const nite::Array<nite::GestureData>& gestures =
    handsFrame.getGestures();
for (int i = 0; i < gestures.getSize(); ++i){
  if (gestures[i].isComplete()){
    nite::HandId handId;
    hTracker.startHandTracking(
      gestures[i].getCurrentPosition(), &handId);
  }
}
```

As you can see, we called `nite::HandTrackerFrameRef::getGesture()` to get a list of all the active gestures and then looped through all of the gestures in the array. If a gesture is in a complete state, we will request the tracking of a hand at the position of the gesture using `nite::HandTracker::startHandTracking()` and `nite::GestureData::getCurrentPosition()`.

After this, we have our other usual lines of code about clearing the OpenGL buffer, creating a texture from depth data, and so on. You can skip up till this line:

```
glEnd();
```

The preceding line indicates that the placing of the texture is complete. Then, we request adding some points with the color red to the buffer:

```
glBegin( GL_POINTS );
glColor3f( 1.f, 0.f, 0.f );
```

Then we used `nite::HandTrackerFrameRef::getHands()` to get an array of the hands under tracking and looped through this array to get a hand's position using the `nite::HandData::getPosition()` method. But as this position is not acceptable enough to be used for displaying on screen, we need to convert it and calculate the correct position relative to the depth frame resolution. The returned value is in millimetres when using Kinect, Asus Xtion, or PrimeSense's sensors, and we need to convert it into pixels. This can be done using the `nite::HandTracker::convertHandCoordinatesToDepth()` method. After this function has been called, `posX` and `posY` will contain the correct position of the hand relative to the depth frame. But as we need to display them in OpenGL, which is not necessary in the same resolution of the depth frame, we need to calculate this number again relative to the OpenGL window. Then, using the `glVertex2f()` function from OpenGL and the correct position of the hand, we can ask OpenGL to draw a point there. Refer to the following code:

```
const nite::Array<nite::HandData>& hands =
  handsFrame.getHands();
for (int i = 0; i < hands.getSize(); ++i){
  if (hands[i].isTracking()){
    float posX, posY;
    status =
      hTracker.convertHandCoordinatesToDepth(
      hands[i].getPosition().x,
      hands[i].getPosition().y,
      hands[i].getPosition().z,
      &posX, &posY);
    if (HandleStatus(status)){
      glVertex2f(
        (posX * resizeFactor) + texture_x,
        (posY * resizeFactor) + texture_y);
    }
  }
}
glEnd();
glColor3f( 1.f, 1.f, 1.f );
```

As you can see in the preceding lines of code, we need to inform OpenGL about quitting the point drawing by calling `glEnd()` again and then setting the color to white, as it was before.

But in the next step, which includes our initialization function, the lines of code are very similar to the preceding recipe. We initialize NiTE and create a `nite::HandTracker` variable as always. Then, we request a search for the Wave gesture by calling the `nite::HandTracker::startGestureDetection()` method:

```
status =
uTracker.startGestureDetection(nite::GESTURE_WAVE);
if (!HandleStatus(status)) return 1;
```

The other lines of code are about initializing and configuring the OpenGL and GLUT behaviors.

The output of our application is as follows:

See also

▸ The *Recognizing predefined hand gestures* recipe

▸ The *Event-based reading of hands' data* recipe

▸ The *Get a user's skeleton joints and display their position in depth map* recipe in *Chapter 7, NiTE and Skeleton Tracking*

Finding the related user ID for each hand ID

When dealing with `nite::HandTracker` and `nite::HandData`, there is no way to find out which hand belongs to which user. Actually, there is no direct way of finding this out in NiTE at all. In this recipe, we will show you how it's possible to use `nite::UserTracker` and `nite::UserMap` along with `nite::HandTracker` and `nite::HandData` to determine the user ID of each hand.

Getting ready

Create a project in Visual Studio and prepare it for working with OpenNI and NiTE using the *Create a project in Visual Studio 2010* recipe in *Chapter 2, OpenNI and C++*.

How to do it...

1. Copy `ReadLastCharOfLine()` and `HandleStatus()` from the first recipe of this chapter to the top of your source code (just below the `#include` lines).

2. Then, locate the following line:

```
int _tmain(int argc, _TCHAR* argv[])
{
```

3. Add the following code inside the preceding line:

```
nite::Status status = nite::STATUS_OK;
status = nite::NiTE::initialize();
if (!HandleStatus(status)) return 1;

printf("Creating user tracker ...\r\n");
nite::UserTracker uTracker;
status = uTracker.create();
if (!HandleStatus(status)) return 1;

printf("Creating hand tracker ...\r\n");
nite::HandTracker hTracker;
status = hTracker.create();
```

```
if (!HandleStatus(status)) return 1;
printf("Searching for Hand Raise gestures ...\r\n");
hTracker.startGestureDetection(nite::GESTURE_HAND_RAISE);

printf("Reading data from hand/user trackers ...\r\n");

while(!_kbhit())
{
  nite::HandTrackerFrameRef handFrame;
  status = hTracker.readFrame(&handFrame);
  if (!HandleStatus(status) ||
    !handFrame.isValid()) return 1;
  nite::UserTrackerFrameRef userFrame;
  status = uTracker.readFrame(&userFrame);
  if (!HandleStatus(status) ||
    !userFrame.isValid()) return 1;
  nite::UserMap usersMap = userFrame.getUserMap();
  const nite::Array<nite::GestureData>& gestures =
    handFrame.getGestures();
  for (int i = 0; i < gestures.getSize(); ++i){
    if (gestures[i].isComplete()){
      nite::HandId handId;
      status = hTracker.startHandTracking(
        gestures[i].getCurrentPosition(), &handId);
    }
  }
  const nite::Array<nite::HandData>& hands =
    handFrame.getHands();
  for (int i = 0; i < hands.getSize(); ++i){
    if (hands[i].isTracking()){
      float posX, posY;
      status =
        hTracker.convertHandCoordinatesToDepth(
        hands[i].getPosition().x,
        hands[i].getPosition().y,
        hands[i].getPosition().z,
        &posX, &posY);
      if (status == nite::STATUS_OK)
      {
        nite::UserId* userId =
          (nite::UserId*)(
            (char*)usersMap.getPixels() +
            ((int)posY * usersMap.getStride())
          ) +       (int)posX;
```

```
            printf("User %d: Hand #%d @%g,%g,%g \r\n",
                *userId, hands[i].getId(),
                hands[i].getPosition().x,
                hands[i].getPosition().y,
                hands[i].getPosition().z);
            }
        }
      }
    }

    hTracker.destroy();
    uTracker.destroy();
    nite::NiTE::shutdown();
    return 0;
```

How it works...

Again in the first step, we have the two `ReadLastCharOfLine()` and `HandleStatus()` functions that are going to be used for handling the returned `nite::Status` value and to read keys from the user.

Our main code starts at the second step, which is about the main function (starting point) of our project. In this function, we first initialize NiTE, as always, and then define and create a `nite::HandTracker` object. But as we need to recognize each user in the scene as well as each hand, we need to define and create a `nite::UserTracker` object too.

```
    nite::UserTracker uTracker;
    status = uTracker.create();
    .
    .
    .
    nite::HandTracker hTracker;
    status = hTracker.create();
```

Then, as we need a gesture to locate hands, we need to request a search for one. In this recipe, we prefer using the `Hand Raise` gesture:

```
    hTracker.startGestureDetection(nite::GESTURE_HAND_RAISE);
```

To read data from NiTE, we need to put our application almost in an infinite loop. So we used a `while` loop to wait until the user presses a key to read the data.

In our `while` loop, we must read a frame of data from both `nite::HandTracker` and `nite::UserTracker`. This can be done using the `nite::HandTracker::readFrame()` and `nite::UserTracker::readFrame()` methods:

```
nite::HandTrackerFrameRef handFrame;
status = hTracker.readFrame(&handFrame);
if (!HandleStatus(status) ||
  !handFrame.isValid()) return 1;
nite::UserTrackerFrameRef userFrame;
status = uTracker.readFrame(&userFrame);
if (!HandleStatus(status) ||
  !userFrame.isValid()) return 1;
```

As you can clearly see, we checked whether the reading process has successfully been completed and also checked whether the returned frame is valid before doing anything.

We will use the `nite::UserMap` object associated with the returned `nite::UserTrackerFrameRef` object later, so keeping it in another variable will help in enhancing the readability of our code.

```
nite::UserMap usersMap = userFrame.getUserMap();
```

Before you start looping through the hands being tracked and find the related user IDs of each, you need to take care of each recognized gesture by `nite::HandTracker` and request hand tracking in the location of the gesture. To do this, we need to use the `nite::HandTrackerFrameRef::getGestures()` method for retrieving an array of recognized gestures and the `nite::HandTracker::startHandTracking()` method to start the tracking of a hand:

```
const nite::Array<nite::GestureData>& gestures =
  handFrame.getGestures();
for (int i = 0; i < gestures.getSize(); ++i){
  if (gestures[i].isComplete()){
    nite::HandId handId;
    status = hTracker.startHandTracking(
      gestures[i].getCurrentPosition(), &handId);
  }
}
```

Now is the time to loop through the list of hands being tracked and see which ones are retrievable using the `nite::HandTrackerFrameRef::getHands()` method:

```
const nite::Array<nite::HandData>& hands =
  handFrame.getHands();
for (int i = 0; i < hands.getSize(); ++i){
  if (hands[i].isTracking()){
```

`nite::UserMap` is like a depth frame, only with different values stored in each frame instead of the depth value. So if we want to know the value of a pixel, we first need to convert the position of the tracked hand to the position of the pixel relative to the depth frame. As we did before, this can be done using the `nite::HandTracker::convertHandCoordinates ToDepth()` method:

```
float posX, posY;
status =
  hTracker.convertHandCoordinatesToDepth(
  hands[i].getPosition().x,
  hands[i].getPosition().y,
  hands[i].getPosition
```

If the process of converting ends without a problem, we will have the correct coordinates of the hand either relative to the depth frame or relative to `nite::UserMap` in the `posX` and `posY` variables. Now we can use these variables to read the value of this pixel from `nite::UserMap`:

```
if (status == nite::STATUS_OK)
{
  nite::UserId* userId =
    (nite::UserId*)(
      (char*)usersMap.getPixels() +
      ((int)posY * usersMap.getStride())
    ) + (int)posX;
```

After these lines of code, the `userId` variable contains the address of the related value that indicates the user ID of a hand. The value of this address is either 0, which means no user or an unknown user, or a value other than 0, which is the user ID of the user. As you can see in the preceding lines of code, reading from a `nite::UserMap` object is no different than reading from an `openni::VideoFrameRef` variable.

Now after having this info, we can print it to the console:

```
printf("User %d: Hand #%d @%g,%g,%g \r\n",
  *userId, hands[i].getId(),
 hands[i].getPosition().x,
  hands[i].getPosition().y,
  hands[i].getPosition().z);
```

The output of our application is as follows:

```
 E:\My Books\OpenNI\Chapter 6 - 2\DLCs\Chapter 6 - Hand's UserId\x64\Debug\OpenNI2Project.e...
----------------------- Init NiTE -----------------------
Creating user tracker ...
Creating hand tracker ...
Searching for Wave, Hand Raise and Click gestures ...
Reading data from hand/user trackers ...
User 1: Hand #1  @538.521,262.325,1429.32
User 1: Hand #2  @512.836,304.323,1461.71
User 1: Hand #3  @488.751,327.811,1488.5
User 1: Hand #4  @468.869,334.797,1505.33
User 1: Hand #5  @456.976,328.217,1510.9
User 1: Hand #6  @449.433,322.132,1508.71
User 1: Hand #7  @445.119,287.492,1491.09
User 1: Hand #8  @446.183,335.139,1418.19
User 1: Hand #9  @441.748,352.628,1441.9
User 1: Hand #10 @439.124,368.936,1457.64
User 1: Hand #11 @441.58,376.428,1463.42
User 1: Hand #12 @447.92,379.279,1460.56
User 1: Hand #13 @456.269,376.36,1446.15
User 1: Hand #14 @468.884,364.052,1422.68
User 0: Hand #15 @484.886,337.23,1388.52
User 1: Hand #16 @-9.72288,394.581,1250.12
User 1: Hand #17 @16.8481,407.241,1261.9
User 1: Hand #18 @27.5235,405.445,1263.28
User 1: Hand #19 @19.0152,388.985,1247.29
```

See also

▶ The *Getting a list of all the active users* recipe in *Chapter 5, NiTE and User Tracking*

▶ The *Identifying and coloring users' pixels in depth map* recipe in *Chapter 5, NiTE and User Tracking*

▶ The *Event-based reading of hands' data* recipe

Event-based reading of hands' data

In the preceding recipes, we use a `while` loop to read frames of data from `nite::HandTracker`. This is not a good idea since this will block our application and even the `while` loop itself until new data becomes available. Fortunately, NiTE has given us this ability to introduce a class/struct with a method in it to be called when a new frame of data becomes available. So our application can do what we want it to do and, when new data becomes available, we can read it without busying our main application thread. In this recipe, we will show you how to use this feature.

Getting ready

Create a project in Visual Studio and prepare it for working with OpenNI and NiTE using the *Create a project in Visual Studio 2010* recipe in *Chapter 2, OpenNI and C++*.

How to do it...

1. Copy `ReadLastCharOfLine()` and `HandleStatus()` from the first recipe of this chapter to the top of your source code (just below the `#include` lines).

2. Define the `hTrackerNewFrameListener` structure (or class) right after that as follows:

```
struct hTrackerNewFrameListener :
  public nite::HandTracker::NewFrameListener
{
    void onNewFrame(nite::HandTracker& hTracker)
    {
    nite::Status status = nite::STATUS_OK;
    nite::HandTrackerFrameRef newFrame;
    status = hTracker.readFrame(&newFrame);
    if (!HandleStatus(status) ||
      !newFrame.isValid()) return;
    system("cls");
    const nite::Array<nite::GestureData>& gestures =
      newFrame.getGestures();
    for (int i = 0; i < gestures.getSize(); ++i){
      if (gestures[i].isComplete()){
        nite::HandId handId;
        status = hTracker.startHandTracking(
          gestures[i].getCurrentPosition(), &handId);
      }
    }
    const nite::Array<nite::HandData>& hands =
      newFrame.getHands();
    for (int i = 0; i < hands.getSize(); ++i){
      if (hands[i].isTracking()){
        printf("Tracking Hand #%d @ %g,%g,%g \r\n",
          hands[i].getId(),
          hands[i].getPosition().x,
          hands[i].getPosition().y,
          hands[i].getPosition().z);
      }
    }
    }
};
```

3. Then, locate the following line:

```
int _tmain(int argc, _TCHAR* argv[])
{
```

4. Add the following code inside the preceding function:

```
nite::Status status = nite::STATUS_OK;
status = nite::NiTE::initialize();
if (!HandleStatus(status)) return 1;

printf("Creating hand tracker ...\r\n");
nite::HandTracker hTracker;
status = hTracker.create();
if (!HandleStatus(status)) return 1;
hTrackerNewFrameListener listener;
hTracker.addNewFrameListener(&listener);

hTracker.startGestureDetection(nite::GESTURE_CLICK);
printf("Reading data from hand tracker ...\r\n");

ReadLastCharOfLine();

nite::NiTE::shutdown();
openni::OpenNI::shutdown();
return 0;
```

How it works...

As always, we have `ReadLastCharOfLine()` and `HandleStatus()` in the first step of this recipe. In the next step, we declare a structure named `hTrackerNewFrameListener` that has been inherited from `nite::HandTracker::NewFrameListener` as follows:

```
struct hTrackerNewFrameListener :
  public nite::HandTracker::NewFrameListener
{
```

`nite::HandTracker::NewFrameListener` itself has an empty method named `onNewFrame()` that we need to override in our child structure/class so we can capture the frame available event as follows:

```
void onNewFrame(nite::HandTracker& hTracker)
{
```

In the body of this method, we first read the newly available frame from
`nite::HandTracker` and then clear the console using a system command:

```
nite::HandTrackerFrameRef newFrame;
status = hTracker.readFrame(&newFrame);
if (!HandleStatus(status) ||
  !newFrame.isValid()) return;
system("cls");
```

Then, we retrieve a list of recognized gestures and of the requested hands that are being
tracked where a gesture happened:

```
const nite::Array<nite::GestureData>& gestures =
  newFrame.getGestures();
for (int i = 0; i < gestures.getSize(); ++i){
  if (gestures[i].isComplete()){
    nite::HandId handId;
    status = hTracker.startHandTracking(
      gestures[i].getCurrentPosition(), &handId);
  }
}
```

And at the end, we print the ID and position of each hand currently under tracking, as follows:

```
const nite::Array<nite::HandData>& hands =
  newFrame.getHands();
for (int i = 0; i < hands.getSize(); ++i){
  if (hands[i].isTracking()){
    printf("Tracking Hand #%d @ %g,%g,%g \r\n",
      hands[i].getId(),
      hands[i].getPosition().x,
      hands[i].getPosition().y,
      hands[i].getPosition().z);
  }
}
```

You can change the body of this method with what you want depending on your application's
behavior. Step two has nothing more.

In the next steps, we have the initialization process; this includes the initialization of NiTE and
the creation of the `nite::HandTracker` variable:

```
status = nite::NiTE::initialize();
.
.
.
nite::HandTracker hTracker;
status = hTracker.create();
```

Then we add our newly defined structure/class as a listener to `nite::HandTracker`, so `nite::HandTracker` can call it later when a new frame becomes available.

```
hTrackerNewFrameListener listener;
hTracker.addNewFrameListener(&listener);
```

Also, we need to have an active search for a hand gesture because we need to locate the position of the hands. So we need to call the `nite::HandTracker::startGestureDetection()` method. We used the `Click` (also known as the push) gesture here:

```
hTracker.startGestureDetection(nite::GESTURE_CLICK);
```

At the end, we wait until a user presses the *Enter* key to end the app. We do nothing more in our main thread except just waiting. Everything happens in the other thread.

```
ReadLastCharOfLine();

nite::NiTE::shutdown();
openni::OpenNI::shutdown();
return 0;
```

The output of our application is as follows:

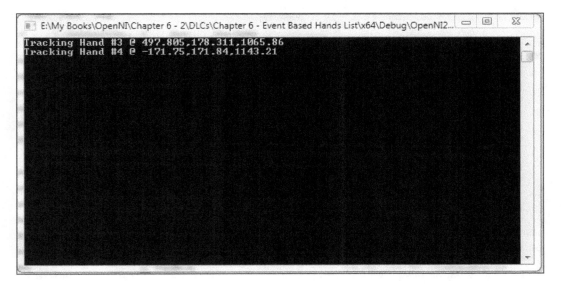

See also

▶ *Event-based reading of data* in Chapter 3, *Using Low-level Data*
▶ *Event-based reading of users' data* in Chapter 5, *NiTE and User Tracking*
▶ The *Working sample for controlling the mouse by hand* recipe

Working sample for controlling the mouse by hand

As a last recipe of this chapter, we will write a working example for using `nite::HandTracker`. In this recipe, we will show you how to control the position of the mouse cursor using the NiTE hand tracker feature and how to simulate a click event.

We are going to use the **Hand Raise** gesture for the tracking of hands and the **Click** (push) gesture for the mouse click. Also, because of the low resolution of the depth output compared to the resolution of the monitor, which results in low accuracy of the hand tracker, we decided to move the mouse depending on its distance with the starting point. This is similar to how you control your mouse with a joystick.

 This sample is Windows only because it uses the Microsoft Windows API.

Getting ready

Create a project in Visual Studio and prepare it for working with OpenNI and NiTE using the *Create a project in Visual Studio 2010* recipe in *Chapter 2, OpenNI and C++*.

How to do it...

1. Copy `ReadLastCharOfLine()` and `HandleStatus()` from the first recipe of this chapter to the top of your source code (just below the `#include` lines).

2. Then add following lines of code:

```
class MouseController :
    public nite::HandTracker::NewFrameListener
{
private:
    float startPosX, startPosY;
    int curX, curY;
    nite::HandId handId;
    RECT desktopRect;
public:
    MouseController(){
        startPosX = startPosY = -1;
        POINT curPos;
        if (GetCursorPos(&curPos)) {
            curX = curPos.x;
            curY = curPos.y;
```

```
      }else{
        curX = curY = 0;
      }
    handId = -1;
    const HWND hDesktop = GetDesktopWindow();
    GetWindowRect(hDesktop, &desktopRect);
  }
    void onNewFrame(nite::HandTracker& hTracker){
    nite::Status status = nite::STATUS_OK;
    nite::HandTrackerFrameRef newFrame;
    status = hTracker.readFrame(&newFrame);
    if (!HandleStatus(status) ||
      !newFrame.isValid()) return;
    const nite::Array<nite::GestureData>& gestures =
      newFrame.getGestures();
    for (int i = 0; i < gestures.getSize(); ++i){
      if (gestures[i].isComplete()){
        if (gestures[i].getType() == nite::GESTURE_CLICK){
          INPUT Input = {0};
          Input.type = INPUT_MOUSE;
          Input.mi.dwFlags =
            MOUSEEVENTF_LEFTDOWN | MOUSEEVENTF_LEFTUP;
          SendInput(1, &Input, sizeof(INPUT));
        }else{
          nite::HandId handId;
          status = hTracker.startHandTracking(
            gestures[i].getCurrentPosition(), &handId);
        }
      }
    }
    const nite::Array<nite::HandData>& hands =
      newFrame.getHands();
    for (int i = hands.getSize() -1 ; i >= 0 ; --i){
      if (hands[i].isTracking()){
        if (hands[i].isNew() ||
          handId != hands[i].getId()){
            status =
            hTracker.convertHandCoordinatesToDepth(
            hands[i].getPosition().x,
            hands[i].getPosition().y,
            hands[i].getPosition().z,
            &startPosX, &startPosY);
            handId = hands[i].getId();
          if (status != nite::STATUS_OK){
```

```
                startPosX = startPosY = -1;
              }
            }else if (startPosX >= 0 && startPosY >= 0){
              float posX, posY;
              status =
                hTracker.convertHandCoordinatesToDepth(
                hands[i].getPosition().x,
                hands[i].getPosition().y,
                hands[i].getPosition().z,
              &posX, &posY);
              if (status == nite::STATUS_OK){
                if (abs(int(posX - startPosX)) > 10)
                  curX += ((posX - startPosX) - 10) / 3;
                if (abs(int(posY - startPosY)) > 10)
                  curY += ((posY - startPosY) - 10) / 3;
                curX = min(curX, desktopRect.right);
                curX = max(curX, desktopRect.left);
                curY = min(curY, desktopRect.bottom);
                curY = max(curY, desktopRect.top);
                SetCursorPos(curX, curY);
              }
            }
            break;
          }
        }
      }
  };
```

3. Then locate the following line:

```
int _tmain(int argc, _TCHAR* argv[])
{
```

4. Add the following inside this function:

```
    nite::Status status = nite::STATUS_OK;
    status = nite::NiTE::initialize();
    if (!HandleStatus(status)) return 1;

    printf("Creating hand tracker ...\r\n");
    nite::HandTracker hTracker;
    status = hTracker.create();
    if (!HandleStatus(status)) return 1;
    MouseController* listener = new MouseController();
    hTracker.addNewFrameListener(listener);
```

```
hTracker.startGestureDetection(nite::GESTURE_HAND_RAISE);
hTracker.startGestureDetection(nite::GESTURE_CLICK);
printf("Reading data from hand tracker ...\r\n");

ReadLastCharOfLine();

nite::NiTE::shutdown();
openni::OpenNI::shutdown();
return 0;
```

How it works...

As with other recipes, both the `ReadLastCharOfLine()` and `HandleStatus()` functions are present here too. These functions are well known to you and don't need any explanation.

Then in the second part, just as in the previous recipe, we declared a class/struct that we are going to use for capturing the new data available event from the `nite::HandTracker` object.

But the definition of this class is a little different here. Other than the `onNewFrame()` method, we defined a number of variables and a constructor method for this class too. We also changed its name to `MouseController` to be able to make more sense of it.

```
class MouseController :
  public nite::HandTracker::NewFrameListener
{
private:
  float startPosX, startPosY;
  int curX, curY;
  nite::HandId handId;
  RECT desktopRect;
```

As you can see, our class is still a child class of `nite::HandTracker::NewFrameList ener` because we are going use it to listen to the `nite::HandTracker` events. Also, we defined six variables in our class. `startPosX` and `startPosY` are going to hold the initial position of the active hand whereas `curY` and `curX` are going to hold the position of the mouse when in motion. The `handId` variable is responsible for holding the ID of the active hand and `desktopRect hold` for holding the size of the desktop so that we can move our mouse only in this area. These variables are all private variables; this means they will not be accessible from the outside of the class. Then we have the class's constructor method that initializes some of the preceding variables. Refer to the following code:

```
public:
  MouseController(){
    startPosX = startPosY = -1;
    POINT curPos;
    if (GetCursorPos(&curPos)) {
      curX = curPos.x;
```

```
      curY = curPos.y;
    }else{
      curX = curY = 0;
    }
    handId = -1;
    const HWND hDesktop = GetDesktopWindow();
    GetWindowRect(hDesktop, &desktopRect);
  }
```

In the constructor, we set both `startPosX` and `startPosY` to `-1` and then store the current position of the mouse in the `curX` and `curY` variables. Then we set the `handId` variable to `-1` to know-mark that there is no active hand currently, and retrieve the value of `desktopRect` using two Windows API methods, `GetDesktopWindow()` and `GetWindowRect()`.

As with the previous recipe, the most important tasks are happening in the `onNewFrame()` method. This method is the one that will be called when new data becomes available in `nite::HandTracker`; after that, this method will be responsible for processing this data.

As the running of this method means that new data is available, the first thing to do in its body is to read this data. So we used the `nite::HandTracker::readFrame()` method to read the data from this object:

```
    void onNewFrame(nite::HandTracker& hTracker){
    nite::Status status = nite::STATUS_OK;
    nite::HandTrackerFrameRef newFrame;
    status = hTracker.readFrame(&newFrame);
```

When working with `nite::HandTracker`, the first thing to do after reading the data is to handle gestures if you expect any. We expect to have Hand Raise to detect new hands and click gesture to perform the mouse click:

```
    const nite::Array<nite::GestureData>& gestures =
      newFrame.getGestures();
    for (int i = 0; i < gestures.getSize(); ++i){
      if (gestures[i].isComplete()){
        if (gestures[i].getType() == nite::GESTURE_CLICK){
          INPUT Input = {0};
        Input.type = INPUT_MOUSE;
          Input.mi.dwFlags =
            MOUSEEVENTF_LEFTDOWN | MOUSEEVENTF_LEFTUP;
          SendInput(1, &Input, sizeof(INPUT));
        }else{
          nite::HandId handId;
          status = hTracker.startHandTracking(
            gestures[i].getCurrentPosition(), &handId);
        }
      }
    }
```

As you can see, we retrieved the list of all the gestures using `nite::HandTrackerFram eRef::getGestures()` and then looped through them, searching for the ones that are in the completed state. Then if they are the `nite::GESTURE_CLICK` gesture, we need to perform a mouse click. We used the `SendInput()` function from the Windows API to do it here. But if the recognized gesture wasn't of the type `nite::GESTURE_CLICK`, it must be a `nite::GESTURE_HAND_RAISE` gesture; so, we need to request for the tracking of this newly recognized hand using the `nite::HandTracker::startHandTracking()` method.

The next thing is to take care of the hands being tracked. To do so, we first need to retrieve a list of them using the `nite::HandTrackerFrameRef::getHands()` method and then loop through them. This can be done using a simple `for` loop as we used for the gestures. But as we want to read this list in a reverse order, we need to use a reverse `for` loop. The reason we need to read this list in the reverse order is that we always want the last recognized hand to control the mouse:

```
const nite::Array<nite::HandData>& hands =
  newFrame.getHands();
for (int i = hands.getSize() - 1 ; i >= 0 ; --i){
```

Then we need to make sure that the current hand is under-tracking because we don't want an invisible hand to control the mouse. The first hand being tracked is the one we want, so we will break the looping there, of course, after the processing part, which we will remove from the following code to make it clearer.

```
if (hands[i].isTracking()){
  .
  .
  .

  break;
}
```

Speaking of processing, in the preceding three lines of code (with periods) we have another condition. This condition is responsible for finding out if this hand is the same one that had control of the mouse in the last frame. If it is a new hand (either it is a newly recognized hand or it is a newly active hand), we need to save its current position in the `startPosX` and `startPosY` variables.

```
if (hands[i].isNew() ||
  handId != hands[i].getId()){
  status =
    hTracker.convertHandCoordinatesToDepth(
    hands[i].getPosition().x,
    hands[i].getPosition().y,
    hands[i].getPosition().z,
    &startPosX, &startPosY);
  handId = hands[i].getId();
  if (status != nite::STATUS_OK){
    startPosX = startPosY = -1;
  }
```

If it was the same hand, we have another condition.

Do we have the `startPosX` and `startPosY` variables already or do we not have them yet? If we have them, we can calculate the mouse's movement. But first we need to calculate the position of the hand relative to the depth frame.

```
}else if (startPosX >= 0 && startPosY >= 0){
  float posX, posY;
  status =
    hTracker.convertHandCoordinatesToDepth(
    hands[i].getPosition().x,
    hands[i].getPosition().y,
    hands[i].getPosition().z,
    &posX, &posY);
```

Once the process of conversation ends, we need to calculate the new position of the mouse depending on how the hand's position changes. But we want to define a safe area for it to be static when small changes happen. So we calculate the new position of the mouse only if it has moved by more than 10 pixels in our depth frame:

```
if (status == nite::STATUS_OK){
  if (abs(int(posX - startPosX)) > 10)
    curX += ((posX - startPosX) - 10) / 3;
  if (abs(int(posY - startPosY)) > 10)
    curY += ((posY - startPosY) - 10) / 3;
```

As you can see in the preceding code, we also divided the changes by 3 because we didn't want it to move too fast.

But before setting the position of the mouse, we need to first make sure that the new positions are in the screen view port using the `desktopRect` variable:

```
curX = min(curX, desktopRect.right);
curX = max(curX, desktopRect.left);
curY = min(curY, desktopRect.bottom);
curY = max(curY, desktopRect.top);
```

After calculating everything, we can set the new position of the mouse using `SetCursorPos()` from the Windows API:

```
SetCursorPos(curX, curY);
```

Step three and four are not markedly different from the previous recipe's last step. In this step, we have the initialization process; this includes the initialization of NiTE and the creation of the `nite::HandTracker` variable.

```
status = nite::NiTE::initialize();
.


.


.

nite::HandTracker hTracker;
status = hTracker.create();
```

Then we should add our newly defined structure/class as a listener to `nite::HandTracker` so that `nite::HandTracker` can call it later when a new frame becomes available:

```
MouseController* listener = new MouseController();
hTracker.addNewFrameListener(listener);
```

Also, we need to have an active search for a hand gesture because we need to locate the position of the hands and we also have to search for another gesture for the mouse click. So we need to call the `nite::HandTracker::startGestureDetection()` method twice for both the `Click` (also known as push) and `Hand Raise` gestures here:

```
hTracker.startGestureDetection(nite::GESTURE_HAND_RAISE);
hTracker.startGestureDetection(nite::GESTURE_CLICK);
```

At the end, we will wait until the user presses the *Enter* key to end the app. We do nothing more in our main thread except just waiting. Everything happens in another thread.

```
ReadLastCharOfLine();

nite::NiTE::shutdown();
openni::OpenNI::shutdown();
return 0;
```

See also

- ▶ The *Tracking hands* recipe
- ▶ The *Event-based reading of hands' data* recipe
- ▶ The *Simple pong game using skeleton tracking* recipe in *Chapter 7, NiTE and Skeleton Tracking*

7
NiTE and Skeleton Tracking

In this chapter, we will cover:

- ▸ Detecting a user's pose
- ▸ Getting a user's skeleton joints and displaying their position in the depth map
- ▸ Designing a simple pong game using skeleton tracking

Introduction

The most important feature of NiTE is recognizing a user's skeleton structure and giving developers the approximate position of each joint. In this chapter, we are going to cover this topic in the first two recipes. Then we will show you how to use this data to create a simple, pong-like game.

The nite::UserTracker object

We already talked about `nite::UserTracker` in *Chapter 5, NiTE and User Tracking*. In this chapter, we will introduce some of the other methods of this class that are going to be used.

A list of the most important methods of this class is as follows:

- ▸ `nite::UserTracker::startPoseDetection()`: This method starts searching for a specific pose of a specific user. If you want to search for more than one pose for a user, you can simply call this method multiple times with different arguments.
- ▸ `nite::UserTracker::startSkeletonTracking()`: This method starts the process of recognizing the position and orientation of the skeleton joints of a specific user.

▶ `nite::UserTracker::stopPoseDetection()`: This method will stop searching for a specific pose for a specific user. You need to call this method once for each pose if you added multiple poses.

▶ `nite::UserTracker::stopSkeletonTracking()`: This method will stop the processes of recognizing a user's skeleton and that of tracking him/her.

The nite::PoseData object

`nite::PoseData` is responsible for one of the user's current poses. In other words, a user can have more than one `nite::PoseData` object and each one will show the user's status about that pose.

`nite::PoseData` has a number of methods; some of them are listed as follows:

▶ `nite::PoseData::getType()`: The returned value of this method is of the `nite::PoseType` type. `nite::PoseType` is an `enum` value that contains only two members, `nite::POSE_PSI` and `nite::POSE_CROSSED_HANDS`

▶ `nite::PoseData::isEntered()`: This method's return value is a `bool` value that indicates if this is the first frame that this pose recognizes

▶ `nite::PoseData::isExited()`: This method's return value is a `bool` type that indicates if this is the first frame in which the user left the pose

▶ `nite::PoseData::isHeld()`: Just as with the preceding two methods, this method's return value is of the type `bool` and indicates whether a user is currently in this pose

The nite::Skeleton object

The `nite::Skeleton` object is responsible for giving you access to a list of all the skeleton joints (`nite::SkeletonJoint`) and lets you see the status of the user being tracked, lets you recognize the skeleton, and enables calibration. By using this object, which has only two methods, you can see if skeleton tracking is active and whether you can request more information about each joint.

▶ `nite::Skeleton::getJoint()`: This returns the `nite::SkeletonJoint` object of the selected joint. This method accepts one argument that is of the type `nite::JointType enum`.

▶ `nite::Skeleton::getState()`: The return value is of the type `nite::SkeletonState enum`; it shows the current state of a user's skeleton being tracked. The members of `nite::SkeletonState` are as follows:

  ❑ `nite::SKELETON_NONE`: There is no skeleton data available or that has been requested

  ❑ `nite::SKELETON_CALIBRATING`: This indicates that the skeleton is being prepared, but it's not ready yet

- ❑ `nite::SKELETON_TRACKED`: The skeleton is available and can be read

- ❑ `nite::SKELETON_CALIBRATION_ERROR_NOT_IN_POSE`: Usually, there is no need for a user to be in the PSI pose for calibration in the new version of NiTE; yet if it was needed, and NiTE found any reason to use this pose, but the user wasn't in the PSI pose, this is what the state of the `nite::Skeleton::getState()` method would be

- ❑ `nite::SKELETON_CALIBRATION_ERROR_HANDS`: The calibration failed to find the hands

- ❑ `nite::SKELETON_CALIBRATION_ERROR_HEAD`: The calibration failed to find head

- ❑ `nite::SKELETON_CALIBRATION_ERROR_LEGS`: The calibration failed to find legs

- ❑ `nite::SKELETON_CALIBRATION_ERROR_TORSO`: The calibration failed to find the torso

The nite::SkeletonJoint object

`nite::SkeletonJoint` gives you more information about a skeleton joint. Every recognized skeleton joint of a user has a `nite::SkeletonJoint` class to store its information. You can access each `nite::SkeletonJoint` object from the `nite::Skeleton` object. Here are some methods of this object:

- ▶ `nite::SkeletonJoint::getOrientation()`: This method gives you a `nite::Quaternion` struct that shows the current orientation of a joint. The `nite::Quaternion` structure contains four `float` fields that can be used to find out the normal vector and radius of a rotation.

> **Read more about quaternions:**
> - ▶ http://en.wikipedia.org/wiki/Gimbal_lock#The_quaternion_solution
> - ▶ http://en.wikipedia.org/wiki/Quaternions_and_spatial_rotation

- ▶ `nite::SkeletonJoint::getOrientationConfidence()`: The return value is of the `float` type and shows the confidence value of NiTE for returning the `Quaternion` orientation. This value is between 0 and 1.

- ▶ `nite::SkeletonJoint::getPosition()`: This returns a `nite::Point3f` struct value that contains three `float` fields showing the position of a joint in 3D space.

- `nite::SkeletonJoint::getPositionConfidence()`: This method's return value is of the `float` type and shows the confidence value of NiTE for returning the position point. This value is between `0` and `1`.

- `nite::SkeletonJoint::getType()`: This method's return value is of the type `nite::JointType` enum and shows the types of this joint. `nite::JointType` enum contains the following members:

    - `nite::JOINT_HEAD`

    - `nite::JOINT_NECK`

    - `nite::JOINT_LEFT_SHOULDER`

    - `nite::JOINT_RIGHT_SHOULDER`

    - `nite::JOINT_LEFT_ELBOW`

    - `nite::JOINT_RIGHT_ELBOW`

    - `nite::JOINT_LEFT_HAND`

    - `nite::JOINT_RIGHT_HAND`

    - `nite::JOINT_TORSO`

    - `nite::JOINT_LEFT_HIP`

    - `nite::JOINT_RIGHT_HIP`

    - `nite::JOINT_LEFT_KNEE`

    - `nite::JOINT_RIGHT_KNEE`

    - `nite::JOINT_LEFT_FOOT`

    - `nite::JOINT_RIGHT_FOOT`

The nite::UserData object

`nite::UserData` is a class representing a user. In another words, `nite::UserTrackerFrameRef` gives you a `nite::UserData` object for each user it has recognized.

We already introduced some of the `nite::UserData` object's methods in *Chapter 5, NiTE and User Tracking*. Here we are going to show you some other methods related to the subject of this recipe as follows:

- `nite::UserData::getPose()`: This method gives you access to the related `nite::PoseData` object of the requested pose of a user. The only argument of this method is a `nite::PoseType` enum value that lets you select your desired pose to give you more information about it.

- `nite::UserData::getSkeleton()`: This method gives you the `nite::Skeleton` object of the selected user. In the next section, we will tell you what a `nite::Skeleton` object is and expound on its important methods.

Detecting a user's pose

In this recipe, we are going to show you how to request a search for a specific pose on a user and show the status of all the users' poses.

In the current version of NiTE, there are only two predefined poses that can be tracked and recognized: the **PSI pose** that was formally used as a calibration pose and the **crossed hands** pose that is a newly introduced pose. What follows is an image of a PSI pose:

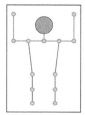

In the new version of NiTE, there is no practical need to find out if a user is in one of these two predefined poses, because there is no need to be in a PSI pose for calibration and no requirement for the crossed hands pose that we are aware of. But you can still use these poses alone or if you want to support other third-party middleware. Also, even when it seems there is no need for PSI poses for calibration, it is still an error to indicate that calibration failed because of a lack of poses. So it may be used in some rare cases.

Getting ready

Create a project in Visual Studio and prepare it for working with OpenNI and NiTE using the *Create a project in Visual Studio 2010* recipe in *Chapter 2, OpenNI and C++*.

How to do it...

1. Add these lines at the top of your source code (just below the #include lines):

```
char ReadLastCharOfLine()
{
  int newChar = 0;
  int lastChar;
  fflush(stdout);
  do
  {
    lastChar = newChar;
    newChar = getchar();
  }
  while ((newChar != '\n')
```

```
        && (newChar != EOF));
    return (char)lastChar;
}
bool HandleStatus(nite::Status status)
{
    if (status == nite::STATUS_OK)
        return true;
    printf("ERROR: #%d, %s", status,
        openni::OpenNI::getExtendedError());
    ReadLastCharOfLine();
    return false;
}
```

2. Then locate the following line:

```
int _tmain(int argc, _TCHAR* argv[])
{
```

3. Now add the following inside this function:

```
nite::Status status = nite::STATUS_OK;
status = nite::NiTE::initialize();
if (!HandleStatus(status)) return 1;
printf("Creating user tracker ...\r\n");
nite::UserTracker uTracker;
status = uTracker.create();
if (!HandleStatus(status)) return 1;
printf("Reading data from user tracker ...\r\n");
while(!_kbhit())
{
    nite::UserTrackerFrameRef newFrame;
    status = uTracker.readFrame(&newFrame);
    if (!HandleStatus(status) ||
        !newFrame.isValid()) return 1;
    system("cls");
    const nite::Array<nite::UserData>& users =
        newFrame.getUsers();
    for (int i = 0; i < users.getSize(); ++i)
    {
        if (users[i].isNew()){
            uTracker.startPoseDetection(
                users[i].getId(),
                nite::POSE_PSI);
        }
        printf("User #%d %s - %s \r\n",
            users[i].getId(),
            (users[i].isVisible()) ?
            "is Visible" : "is not Visible",
            (users[i].getPose(nite::POSE_PSI).isHeld()) ?
```

```
                "In PSI Pose"  :  "In No Pose");
        }
    }
    uTracker.destroy();
    nite::NiTE::shutdown();
    return 0;
```

How it works...

This is a fairly simple recipe. As you can see in step one, we have nothing except two of our famous functions: `ReadLastCharOfLine()` for reading input from the console and `HandleStatus()` for checking if a `nite::Status` object is indicating an error.

Also, in the initial lines of step two, we have the same lines of code as given in the previous recipes. We initialized NiTE and created a `nite::UserTracker` object. But just after that we entered a `while` loop to read data from `nite::UserTracker` until a user pressed a key in the console. In our `while` loop, we have the code for reading a frame of data; this can be seen in the second line of the following code:

```
    nite::UserTrackerFrameRef newFrame;
    status = uTracker.readFrame(&newFrame);
```

And then we cleared the console by calling a system command:

```
    system("cls");
```

Then, to get the status of each user's pose information, we read the list of all the recognized users and their properties, including their poses, by defining an array of the `nite::UserData` variable and calling the `nite::UserTrackerFrameRef::getUsers()` method:

```
    const nite::Array<nite::UserData>& users =
      newFrame.getUsers();
```

The next step is to loop through the users using another loop:

```
    for (int i = 0; i < users.getSize(); ++i)
```

Then we can show the status of each user's pose to the user via the console; however, how can we expect to recognize a pose when we didn't request a search for it? That's why we need to call the `nite::UserTracker::startPoseDetection()` method when a new user is recognized:

```
    if (users[i].isNew()){
      uTracker.startPoseDetection(
        users[i].getId(),
        nite::POSE_PSI);
    }
```

As you can see in the preceding code, we checked if this user is a newly recognized user and if so, asked for a search for the PSI pose on this user.

> From what we experienced, `nite::POSE_CROSSED_HANDS` is not recognizable before tracking begins, at least not in the current beta version. You will learn more about tracking in the next recipe.

Then we are going to show the current user's active pose to the user:

```
printf("User #%d %s - %s \r\n",
  users[i].getId(),
  (users[i].isVisible()) ?
    "is Visible" : "is not Visible",
  (users[i].getPose(nite::POSE_PSI).isHeld()) ?
    "In PSI Pose" : "In No Pose");
```

This is a little complicated because we tried to do all the things in one line. But as you can clearly see, we used the `nite::UserData::getPose()` method to retrieve the status of one of the poses of the user, and then using `nite::PoseData::isHeld()`, we found out if the user is currently in this pose.

Based on these two methods, we wrote an inline `if` to show the name of the active pose (the PSI pose in our case) and `In No Pose` if the user wasn't in the PSI pose.

The output of our application is as follows:

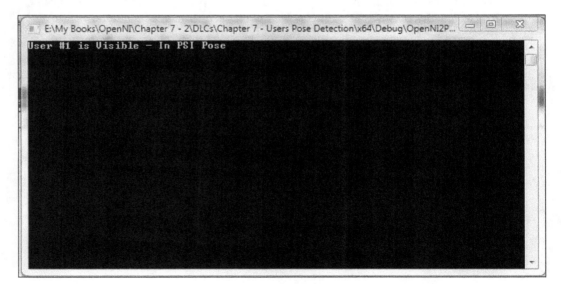

See also

- The *Recognizing predefined hand gestures* recipe in *Chapter 6, NiTE and Hand Tracking*
- The *Getting a user's skeleton joints and displaying their position in the depth map* recipe
- The *Designing a simple pong game using skeleton tracking* recipe

Getting a user's skeleton joints and displaying their position in the depth map

In this recipe, we are going to show you how to request calibration for a user's skeleton and for tracking a user's skeleton joints; we will then show these joints on a screen overlaying the depth stream.

Getting ready

Create a project in Visual Studio and prepare it for working with OpenNI and NiTE using the *Create a project in Visual Studio 2010* recipe in *Chapter 2, OpenNI and C++*; then, configure Visual Studio to use OpenGL using the *Configuring Visual Studio 2010 to use OpenGL* recipe in *Chapter 3, Using Low-level Data*.

Then copy the code from the *Identifying and coloring users' pixels in depth map* recipe of *Chapter 5, NiTE and User Tracking* to this project.

How to do it...

1. Locate the following line in the `gl_DisplayCallback()` function:

```
glEnd();
```

2. Add the following lines of code relative to the preceding line:

```
glBegin( GL_POINTS );
glColor3f( 1.f, 0.f, 0.f );
const nite::Array<nite::UserData>&users =
usersFrame.getUsers();
    for (int i = 0; i < users.getSize(); ++i)
    {
      if (users[i].isNew())
      {
        uTracker.startSkeletonTracking(
          users[i].getId());
      }
```

```
nite::Skeleton user_skel = users[i].getSkeleton();
if (user_skel.getState() ==
  nite::SKELETON_TRACKED)
{
  for (int joint_Id = 0; joint_Id < 15;
    ++joint_Id)
  {
    float posX, posY;
    niStatus =
    uTracker.convertJointCoordinatesToDepth(
      user_skel.getJoint((nite::JointType)
        joint_Id).getPosition().x,
      user_skel.getJoint((nite::JointType)
        joint_Id).getPosition().y,
      user_skel.getJoint((nite::JointType)
        joint_Id).getPosition().z,
      &posX, &posY);
    if (HandleStatus(niStatus){
      glVertex2f(
        (posX * resizeFactor) + texture_x,
        (posY * resizeFactor) + texture_y);
    }
  }
}
}
glEnd();
glColor3f( 1.f, 1.f, 1.f );
```

3. Then locate this line in the _tmain() function:

```
glutMainLoop();
```

4. Add the following line above the preceding line of code:

```
glPointSize(10.0);
```

How it works...

In the first step, after placing the texture in OpenGL, we informed OpenGL that we want to draw some points with the color red:

```
glBegin( GL_POINTS );
glColor3f( 1.f, 0.f, 0.f );
```

Then we used an already defined variable containing a list of all the users to loop through them:

```
for (int i = 0; i < users.getSize(); ++i)
{
```

Now we can request the position of each recognized skeleton joint of the user and show them to the user. But before doing so, we need to request skeleton tracking of users because skeleton information is not available by default. If we don't request this for each user, we won't have any data about their skeleton and skeleton joints. So we add a condition when a user is recognized for the first time and then request skeleton tracking for that user:

```
if (users[i].isNew())
{
  uTracker.startSkeletonTracking(
    users[i].getId());
}
```

Now is the time to check the user's skeleton state. To do so, we need to have access to the related `nite::Skeleton` object of the user, so we used the `nite::UserData::getSkeleton()` method first:

```
nite::Skeleton user_skel = users[i].getSkeleton();
```

The first step before trying to read the position of each joint is to check whether there is any data to show, whether the calibration process ended successfully, and whether the user is in the tracking state now. To do this, we need to check the return value of `nite::Skeleton::getState()`:

```
if (user_skel.getState() ==
  nite::SKELETON_TRACKED)
{
```

The return value of this method is of the type `nite::SkeletonState`, which we talked about before in the introduction of this chapter. You can read about the possible states there. But here we used `nite::SKELETON_TRACKED` because it means the calibration process has been completed successfully and the skeleton data is available for this user.

Please note that, if the user goes out of FOV, if NiTE fails to see the entire part of a user's body, or if there is any other internal problem, we shouldn't expect `nite::SKELETON_TRACKED` as the status.

The next step is to request each of the 15 joints from `nite::JointType` enum and ask for the corresponding `nite::SkeletonJoint` objects that represent them. But this means lots of coding, so we decided to place a `for` loop that is counting from 0 to 14 (these are values of the `nite::JointType` enum members) to save some space:

```
for (int joint_Id = 0; joint_Id < 15;
  ++joint_Id)
{
```

Then we can access each of these 15 joints using the `nite::Skeleton::getJoint()` method and using their positions with the `nite::SkeletonJoint::getPosition()` method. But the returned value is not in the unit that we need to display these points in the depth stream, so we need to first convert them using the `nite::UserTracker::convertJointCoordinatesToDepth()` method:

```
float posX, posY;
status =
uTracker.convertJointCoordinatesToDepth(
  user_skel.getJoint((nite::JointType)
    joint_Id).getPosition().x,
  user_skel.getJoint((nite::JointType)
    joint_Id).getPosition().y,
  user_skel.getJoint((nite::JointType)
    joint_Id).getPosition().z,
  &posX, &posY);
```

As you can see, we got access to the `nite::SkeletonJoint` object and its position by calling the following method:

```
user_skel.getJoint((nite::JointType)joint_Id).getPosition()
```

Then we calculated the coordinates relative to the depth stream's frame size. And in the next step, we checked if this conversation was completed without any error. If so, we'll ask OpenGL to draw a point there:

```
if (HandleStatus(status)){
  glVertex2f(
    (posX * resizeFactor) + texture_x,
    (posY * resizeFactor) + texture_y);
}
```

There is one thing that you can see in the preceding code, and that is the conversion of `posX` and `posY` again. We did this to find out the coordinates of the points relative to the OpenGL window.

This was the end of our code in this step. In the next two lines, we inform OpenGL that we don't have any more points to draw and inform it to again set the active color to white:

```
glEnd();
glColor3f( 1.f, 1.f, 1.f );
```

In the next steps, we only defined the size of each point and nothing more:

```
glPointSize(10.0);
```

The output of our application is as follows:

See also

- The *Reading users' bounding boxes and center of mass* recipe in *Chapter 5, NiTE and User Tracking*
- The *Tracking hands* recipe in *Chapter 6, NiTE and Hand Tracking*
- The *Detecting a user's pose* recipe
- The *Designing a simple pong game using skeleton tracking* recipe

Designing a simple pong game using skeleton tracking

We will use the output of skeleton tracking on a simple game to show you how we can use this data to make the user a bigger part of the game than he was in old times. This pong-like game is the simplest game we could think of.

Unfortunately because of the number of lines of code, we removed the *How to do it...* section, but you can download the source code of this recipe from Packt Publishing's website.

Also, in the *How it works...* section that follows, you can read information about almost every line of code.

How it works...

The gameplay is fairly simple; we have a pong-like ball that can interact with a user's skeleton. It is not a great game, but it's still a game, and it is fun enough as a mini-game from a personal perspective.

If you'll take a look at the code (the main file is `OpenNI2Project.cpp`), you can clearly see that we used two new `#include` lines. `vector` helps us to define arrays with dynamic-size behavior that we are going to use in our program to store skeleton lines, and `sstream` makes working with strings easier.

After these lines, we defined a structure named `PongBall`. This structure is going to be our main ball. While defining this structure, we used the following different fields:

- ► `PongBall::location`: This is a `POINTFLOAT` variable and contains the position of our ball
- ► `PongBall::speed`: This is an `integer` variable indicating the speed of the movement of our ball
- ► `PongBall::angle`: This is a `float` variable and shows the direction of the movement of our ball. We will keep this in radiant

Also, we have defined a method named `PongBall::init()` that fills the location and angle variables with a random number:

```
void init(int w, int h){
  srand(time(NULL));
  angle = (((float)rand() / RAND_MAX)
        * PI * 2);
  location.x = (((float)rand() / RAND_MAX)
        * (w - 40)) + 20;
  location.y = (((float)rand() / RAND_MAX)
        * (h - 40)) + 20;
}
```

We then defined a global variable from this struct named `mainBall`. We are going to use this variable as a representation of our ball in the application/game.

```
PongBall mainBall;
```

Then we defined a class named `Line` so we can use it later for storing our lines' end points. Actually, each skeleton line or screen bounding box is a line.

In this class, we defined two fields named `Line::a` and `Line::b`. These are the locations of the start points and end points of our line.

We also defined a class constructor method with four parameters (X and Y for both end points) so we can easily create instances of this class:

```
Line
    (float x1, float y1, float x2, float y2)
    : a (new POINTFLOAT), b (new POINTFLOAT)
{
  a->x = x1;
  a->y = y1;
  b->x = x2;
  b->y = y2;
}
```

As this class has two pointers (for each endpoints), we need to take care of them before destroying them to prevent a memory leak. So in the destructor of this class, we deleted both the variables:

```
~Line()
  {
  delete a;
  delete b;
  }
```

This class has only one method named `Line::getAngle()` that can be used for giving us the angle of segments between two points in a radiant using a simple mathematical calculation as follows:

```
float getAngle()
{
  return atan2(
      (float)a->y - b->y, a->x - b->x);
}
```

Then in our main code, we have `window_w` and `window_h` for storing the size of the OpenGL window as always. After that, we have the `uTracker` variable with a `nite::UserTracker` type that is our user tracker object from NiTE. We also have a variable named `lines` from the type `std::vector<Line*>`, which simply means a dynamic array for pointers of the `Line` class. We are going to use it for storing active lines in a scene.

There are two more variables named `wallScore` and `userScore` that will be used for storing a user's and walls' hits:

```
int window_w = 640;
int window_h = 480;
nite::UserTracker uTracker;
std::vector<Line*> lines;
int wallScore = 0;
int userScore = 0;
```

As with any other recipe you have read until now, we have our two famous functions here too. `ReadLastCharOfLine()`, which is a function that reads a character from the user and waits for the user to press the *Enter* key, and `HandleStatus()`, which is responsible for checking the `nite::Status` object returned by other functions/methods.

After these two functions, we have `gl_KeyboardCallback()` that is responsible for handling key presses in the OpenGL window. In this example, we are going to check only if the pressed key was the *Esc* key so we can end the program:

```
void gl_KeyboardCallback(unsigned char key, int x, int y)
{
  if (key == 27) // ESC Key
  {
    uTracker.destroy();
    nite::NiTE::shutdown();
    exit(0);
  }
}
```

`gl_IdleCallback()` is the next function that has been defined in the source code. This function will be executed when OpenGL is idle and has nothing to do. In this function, we will request the re-rendering of a scene using the `glutPostRedisplay()` function of GLUT:

```
void gl_IdleCallback()
{
  glutPostRedisplay();
}
```

After these two functions, we defined three functions to enable drawing in the OpenGL window. The first one is a function named `drawText()` that we wrote for adding text to the OpenGL output. In the first line of this function, we changed the active color to white and then asked OpenGL to set the cursor to a specific pixel. Then we wrote each character from the string to the OpenGL buffer, one by one, using the `glutBitmapCharacter()` function and with the Helvetica font set to a size of `12pt`:

```
void drawText(int x, int y, const char *string)
{
  glColor3f(255, 255, 255);
  glRasterPos2f(x, y);
  for (int i = 0; i < strlen(string); i++){
    glutBitmapCharacter(
      GLUT_BITMAP_HELVETICA_12, string[i]);
  }
}
```

The second function we defined is a function named `drawLineBetweenJoints()`. This function is going to draw a line between the two users' skeleton joints. To do this, we first converted the real-world position of these two joints to their positions on the screen using the `nite::UserTracker::convertJointCoordinatesToDepth()` method. Then we used the OpenGL functions to draw a line between these two positions. In the end, we also added this new line to the `lines` vector/array as follows:

```
void drawLineBetweenJoints(nite::Skeleton skel,
    nite::JointType a, nite::JointType b)
{
    float posX1, posY1, posX2, posY2;
    nite::Status status1 =
    uTracker.convertJointCoordinatesToDepth(
      skel.getJoint(a).getPosition().x,
      skel.getJoint(a).getPosition().y,
      skel.getJoint(a).getPosition().z,
      &posX1, &posY1);
    nite::Status status2 =
      uTracker.convertJointCoordinatesToDepth(
      skel.getJoint(b).getPosition().x,
      skel.getJoint(b).getPosition().y,
      skel.getJoint(b).getPosition().z,
      &posX2, &posY2);
    if (status1 == nite::STATUS_OK &&
    status2 == nite::STATUS_OK ){
    glBegin(GL_LINES);
    glVertex2f(posX1,posY1);
    glVertex2f(posX2,posY2);
```

```
    glEnd();
    lines.push_back(new Line(posX1, posY1, posX2, posY2));
  }
}
```

The third function is the `drawCircle()` function. We are going to use this function to show the position of the user's head. This function accepts three arguments, x and y of the center of the circle and the radius of the circle. Then we will try to find 100 points in the perimeter of this circle and draw a line joining one point to the other:

```
void drawCircle(float x, float y, float r){
  glBegin(GL_LINE_LOOP);
  for(int i = 0; i < 100; i++) {
      float angle = i*2*PI/100;
      glVertex2f(    x + (cos(angle) * r),
        y + (sin(angle) * r));
  }
  glEnd();
}
```

In our game, we also want to see if the ball is going to collide with the user's skeleton or walls. To calculate this, we defined a function named `IsSegmentsColliding()`. We also used another function named `IsBetween()` to check if a number is in the desired region or not. We are going to use this function in `IsSegmentsColliding()` later. `IsBetween()` is based on simple logic: our number must be smaller than the first bound and bigger than the second bound, or in reverse. This is because we are not sure which one is upper bound and which one is lower bound.

```
bool IsBetween (float x, float b1, float b2)
{
   return (      ((x >= (b1 - 0.1f)) &&
        (x <= (b2 + 0.1f))) ||
        ((x >= (b2 - 0.1f)) &&
        (x <= (b1 + 0.1f)))));
}
```

Please note the `0.1f` number in the preceding code. As you may know, `float` variables are not very reliable for direct comparison because they have an error margin. So, we used this number as a tolerance.

In the `IsSegmentsColliding()` function, we need to find out if two lines cross each other. These two lines are each a product of two points, so they are a sum of four points, which is the same as the number of arguments for this function. After finding out if these two lines crossed each other, we need to make sure that this point is part of the two segments (because actually they are not a line but a segment):

```
bool IsSegmentsColliding(     POINTFLOAT lineA,
               POINTFLOAT lineB,
               POINTFLOAT line2A,
               POINTFLOAT line2B)
```

The first step is to calculate the place of collision using the following two formulas to see if these two lines have any collision at all:

$$X_{col} = \frac{(\Delta X_1 \Delta X_2)(Y_{2A} - Y_{1A}) - X_{2A} \Delta Y_2 \Delta X_1 + X_{1A} \Delta Y_1 \Delta X_2}{\Delta Y_1 \Delta X_2 - \Delta Y_2 \Delta X_1}$$

$$Y_{col} = \frac{X_{col} \Delta Y + Y_A \Delta X - X_A \Delta Y}{\Delta X}$$

 Read more about these mathematical formulas on Wikipedia (http://en.wikipedia.org/wiki/Line-line_intersection).

Before using these formulas, we need to first calculate the first line's Delta X and Delta Y and then the second line's Delta X and Delta Y:

```
float deltaX1 = lineB.x - lineA.x;
float deltaX2 = line2B.x - line2A.x;
float deltaY1 = lineB.y - lineA.y;
float deltaY2 = line2B.y - line2A.y;
```

Then we must check if both the lines are vertical lines and/or if they are parallel because we can't use the preceding formula for two parallel lines or two vertical lines (that are also parallel):

```
if (abs(deltaX1) < 0.01f &&
  abs(deltaX2) < 0.01f) // Both are vertical lines
  return false;
if (abs((deltaY1 / deltaX1) -
  (deltaY2 / deltaX2)) < 0.001f) // Two parallel line
  return false;
```

In the next step, we calculate the x value of the collision point:

```
float xCol = ( (        (deltaX1 * deltaX2) *
        (line2A.y - lineA.y)) -
      (line2A.x * deltaY2 * deltaX1) +
      (lineA.x * deltaY1 * deltaX2)) /
      ((deltaY1 * deltaX2) - (deltaY2 * deltaX1));
```

Then we calculate the y value of this point. It is important to know that, to do so, we need to use the equation of one of these lines, and we can't do it with a vertical line. So the first thing to do is to check if the first line is a vertical line. If it is, we need to use the equation of the second line for calculation purposes. If it isn't, we can use the first one without a problem:

```
float yCol = 0;
if (deltaX1 < 0.01f) // L1 is a vertical line
  yCol = ((xCol * deltaY2) +
      (line2A.y * deltaX2) -
        (line2A.x * deltaY2)) / deltaX2;
else // L1 is acceptable
  yCol = ((xCol * deltaY1) +
      (lineA.y * deltaX1) -
        (lineA.x * deltaY1)) / deltaX1;
```

After these two calculations, we have the position of impact. Yet we are not sure if this position is between the two points (is part of two segments or not), so we need to use the `IsBetween()` function to check if both x and y of the points are within the range of these two segments:

```
return  IsBetween(xCol, lineA.x, lineB.x) &&
      IsBetween(yCol, lineA.y, lineB.y) &&
      IsBetween(xCol, line2A.x, line2B.x) &&
      IsBetween(yCol, line2A.y, line2B.y);
```

We also defined a function here to empty the `lines` array, named `ClearLines()`:

```
void ClearLines(){
  for(int i = 0; i < lines.size(); ++i)
    delete lines[i];
  lines.clear();
}
```

In the preceding function, we first released the memory held by the `Line` objects and then removed them from the array by clearing the vector.

The next thing we need to do is to define a function for rendering a scene. As always, we defined our `gl_DisplayCallback()` function. In this function, after requesting for a new frame from `nite::UserTracker`, we checked whether the size of the newly returned frame is the same as the older frames and whether it is the current size of the OpenGL window or not. If it is different, we will change the size of the OpenGL window and update the `window_h` and `window_w` variables:

```
status = uTracker.readFrame(&usersFrame);
if (status == nite::STATUS_OK && usersFrame.isValid())
{
  VideoFrameRef depthFrame = usersFrame.getDepthFrame();
  if  (window_w != depthFrame.getWidth() ||
    window_h != depthFrame.getHeight())
  {
    window_w = depthFrame.getWidth();
    window_h = depthFrame.getHeight();
    glutReshapeWindow(window_w, window_h);
  }
```

The next step is to clear the OpenGL buffer and set up the OpenGL viewpoint. And after that, we can search for the recognized users in the screen. But just before doing this, we need to first clear the `lines` array using the `ClearLines()` function that we defined before and then add walls to it:

```
ClearLines();
lines.push_back(new Line(0, 0, 0, window_h));
lines.push_back(new Line(0, 0, window_w, 0));
lines.push_back(new Line(0, window_h,
          window_w, window_h));
lines.push_back(new Line(window_w, 0,
          window_w, window_h));
```

Then we can request for the list of users as follows:

```
const nite::Array<nite::UserData>& users =
  usersFrame.getUsers();
```

Then, we can loop through this list and request to track a user's skeleton or draw the skeleton of users being tracked to the screen. But it is better to change the active color to something else and set the size of `lines` to 5 pixels:

```
glColor3f( 0.f, 1.f, 0.f );
glLineWidth(5.0);
```

When a new user is detected, we will request skeleton tracking and restart the game with the following code:

```
if (users[i].isNew())
{
  uTracker.startSkeletonTracking(
    users[i].getId());
  mainBall.init(window_w, window_h);
  wallScore = 0;
  userScore = 0;
}
```

The next step is to check if the user is currently being tracked. If he/she is, we will try to draw a line between the related skeleton joints to give it some visual representation as follows:

```
nite::Skeleton user_skel = users[i].getSkeleton();
if (user_skel.getState() ==
  nite::SKELETON_TRACKED)
{
  drawLineBetweenJoints(user_skel,
    nite::JOINT_LEFT_HAND, nite::JOINT_LEFT_ELBOW);
  ...
  drawLineBetweenJoints(user_skel,
    nite::JOINT_LEFT_HIP,
    nite::JOINT_LEFT_SHOULDER);
```

We also want to draw a circle in place of the user's head:

```
float posX, posY;
status =
uTracker.convertJointCoordinatesToDepth(
  user_skel.getJoint(nite::JOINT_HEAD)
    .getPosition().x,
  user_skel.getJoint(nite::JOINT_HEAD)
    .getPosition().y,
  user_skel.getJoint(nite::JOINT_HEAD)
    .getPosition().z,
  &posX, &posY);
if (status == nite::STATUS_OK){
  drawCircle(posX, posY,
    (1 - (user_skel.getJoint(nite::JOINT_HEAD)
    .getPosition().z / 5000)) * 35);
```

Then we need to take care of our ball, including moving it and checking for collision between it and the defined lines. To do so, we first need to know the next position of the ball. Calculating this position is possible with two simple mathematical functions:

```
POINTFLOAT newPosition;
newPosition.x = mainBall.speed *
    cos(mainBall.angle) + mainBall.location.x;
newPosition.y = mainBall.speed *
    sin(mainBall.angle) + mainBall.location.y;
```

Then we loop through all the registered lines in the `lines` variable and check if the next movement of the ball will cross any of them. If so, we need to change the direction of the ball's movement depending on the angle of the line itself (you can read about specular reflection on the Web):

```
for (int i = 0; i < lines.size(); ++i){
    if (IsSegmentsColliding(*(lines[i]->a),
                    *(lines[i]->b),
                    mainBall.location,
                    newPosition)){
        mainBall.angle = lines[i]->getAngle() -
                (mainBall.angle -
                lines[i]->getAngle());
```

We also increase the score of the wall or player(s) by one:

```
if (i < 4)
    wallScore += 1;
else
    userScore += 1;
```

Then we set the new location of the ball and draw it:

```
mainBall.location.x +=
    mainBall.speed * cos(mainBall.angle);
mainBall.location.y +=
    mainBall.speed * sin(mainBall.angle);
glPointSize(10);
glColor3f( 1.f, 0.f, 0.f );
glBegin( GL_POINTS );
glVertex2f(     mainBall.location.x,
        mainBall.location.y);
glEnd();
```

At the end, we print the number of hits by user(s) or by walls to the output:

```
std::ostringstream stringStream;
stringStream << "User(s)' Hits: " << userScore;
const std::string tmp = stringStream.str();
drawText( 20, 20, tmp.c_str());
stringStream.str("");
stringStream << "Walls' Hits: " << wallScore;
const std::string tmp2 = stringStream.str();
drawText( 120, 20, tmp2.c_str());
```

In our main function, we performed the same steps as always, initializing NiTE, creating a user tracker, and registering GLUT functions. The only new lines in the _tmain() function, compared with other related recipes, are these lines:

```
mainBall.init(120, 240);
mainBall.speed = 5;
```

We used these lines to initialize the position of the ball the first time. We also defined a constant speed for the ball.

The output of our game-like experience is as follows:

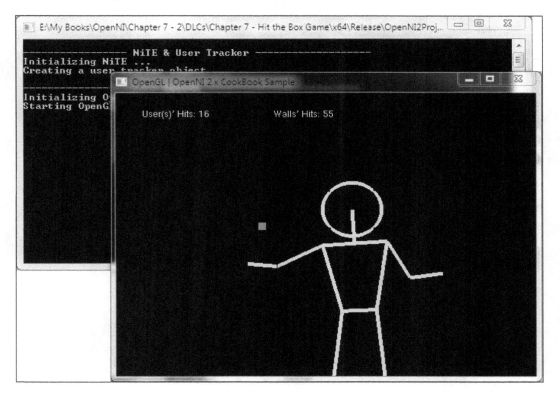

See also

▶ The *Working sample for controlling the mouse by hand* recipe in *Chapter 6, NiTE and Hand Tracking*

▶ The *Detecting a user's pose* recipe

▶ The *Getting a user's skeleton joints and displaying their position in the depth map* recipe

Index

Thank you for buying
OpenNI Cookbook

About Packt Publishing

Packt, pronounced 'packed', published its first book "*Mastering phpMyAdmin for Effective MySQL Management*" in April 2004 and subsequently continued to specialize in publishing highly focused books on specific technologies and solutions.

Our books and publications share the experiences of your fellow IT professionals in adapting and customizing today's systems, applications, and frameworks. Our solution based books give you the knowledge and power to customize the software and technologies you're using to get the job done. Packt books are more specific and less general than the IT books you have seen in the past. Our unique business model allows us to bring you more focused information, giving you more of what you need to know, and less of what you don't.

Packt is a modern, yet unique publishing company, which focuses on producing quality, cutting-edge books for communities of developers, administrators, and newbies alike. For more information, please visit our website: www.packtpub.com.

About Packt Open Source

In 2010, Packt launched two new brands, Packt Open Source and Packt Enterprise, in order to continue its focus on specialization. This book is part of the Packt Open Source brand, home to books published on software built around Open Source licences, and offering information to anybody from advanced developers to budding web designers. The Open Source brand also runs Packt's Open Source Royalty Scheme, by which Packt gives a royalty to each Open Source project about whose software a book is sold.

Writing for Packt

We welcome all inquiries from people who are interested in authoring. Book proposals should be sent to author@packtpub.com. If your book idea is still at an early stage and you would like to discuss it first before writing a formal book proposal, contact us; one of our commissioning editors will get in touch with you.

We're not just looking for published authors; if you have strong technical skills but no writing experience, our experienced editors can help you develop a writing career, or simply get some additional reward for your expertise.

open source*
community experience distilled

[PACKT]
PUBLISHING

OpenCV Computer Vision with Python

ISBN: 978-1-78216-392-3   Paperback: 122 pages

Learn to capture videos, manipulate images, and track objects with Python using the OpenCV Library

1. Set up OpenCV, its Python bindings, and optional Kinect drivers on Windows, Mac or Ubuntu

2. Create an application that tracks and manipulates faces

3. Identify face regions using normal color images and depth images

Kinect in Motion – Audio and Visual Tracking by Example

ISBN: 978-1-84969-718-7   Paperback: 112 pages

A fast-paced, practical guide including examples, clear instructions, and details for building your multimodal user interface

1. Step-by-step examples on how to master the essential features of Kinect technology

2. Fully-functioning code samples ready to expand and adjust to your need

3. Compact and handy reference on how to adopt a multimodal user interface in your application

Please check **www.PacktPub.com** for information on our titles

Kinect for Windows SDK Programming Guide

ISBN: 978-1-84969-238-0   Paperback: 392 pages

Build motion-sensing applications with Microsoft's Kinect for Windows SDK quickly and easily

1. Building application using Kinect for Windows SDK

2. Covers the Kinect for Windows SDK v1.6

3. A practical step-by-step tutorial to make learning easy for a beginner

4. A detailed discussion of all the APIs involved and the explanations of their usage in detail

Augmented Reality with Kinect

ISBN: 978-1-84969-438-4   Paperback: 120 pages

Develop your own handsfree and attractive augmented reality applications with Microsoft Kinect

1. Understand all major Kinect API features including image streaming, skeleton tracking and face tracking

2. Understand the Kinect APIs with the help of small examples

3. Develop a comparatively complete Fruit Ninja game using Kinect and augmented Reality techniques

Please check **www.PacktPub.com** for information on our titles

www.ingramcontent.com/pod-product-compliance
Lightning Source LLC
Chambersburg PA
CBHW080352060326
40689CB00019B/3987